A Cunning Kind of Play

Old friends are the best friends
& you're the best —

Warren Hilbert
8/04

A CUNNING KIND OF PLAY

The Cubs-Giants Rivalry, 1876–1932

by Warren N. Wilbert

McFarland & Company, Inc., Publishers

Jefferson, North Carolina, and London

Library of Congress Cataloguing-in-Publication Data

Wilbert, Warren N., 1927–
    A cunning kind of play : the Cubs-Giants rivalry, 1876–1932 / by
Warren N. Wilbert.
        p.   cm.
    Includes bibliographical references and index.
    ISBN 0-7864-1156-2 (softcover : 50# alkaline paper)
    1. Chicago Cubs (Baseball team)—History.   2. New York Giants
(Baseball team)—History.   I. Title: Cubs-Giants rivalry, 1876–
1932.   II. Title.
GV875.C6W57   2002
796.357'64'0977311—dc21   2002001563

British Library cataloguing data are available

Manufactured in the United States of America

Cover art: Polo Grounds and Wrigley Field ©*2002 Wood River Gallery*

McFarland & Company, Inc., Publishers
   Box 611, Jefferson, North Carolina 28640
      www.mcfarlandpub.com

To my brother Bill

ACKNOWLEDGMENTS

The baseball writing fraternity, a surprisingly diverse and dedicated group of authors with near insatiable appetites for detail and ever more information, takes special care to acknowledge those who have helped put together still another book about the national pastime. And as a matter of fact, I've come to realize, after reading extensively in a number of disciplines, that they are probably more conscientious about expressing their gratitude than most in the many fields authors explore.

Well they might, and I, among the least of these accomplished talents, also recognize that every baseball author rubs "literary elbows" with the outstanding professionals who've been there and done it before. Those who grace the list that follows will never know just how much their time, insights, and assistance have meant to me. But I hope that my public acknowledgement of their contributions to this book will in a small way express my very sincere thanks. To all of you: Thanks, and God go with you!

Alice Barva, Allen County Library, Fort Wayne, IN
George and Mary Brace, photographic services
Dennis Colgin, photographic services
Steve Gietschier, *The Sporting News*
William Hageman, *Chicago Tribune*
Ellen Macke
Jim Meier, *The Sporting News*
Diann Murphy
Pete Palmer, Total Sports
Dave Nemec, SABR
Karen Reynolds
Joyce Saltsman, Indiana-Purdue University Library, Fort Wayne, IN

Dave Smith, SABR
Blaine Thompson, Indiana-Purdue University Library, Fort Wayne, IN
Bob Tiemann, SABR
Bill Wilbert
Ginny Wilbert
John Zajc, SABR

CONTENTS

INTRODUCTION

On September 22, 1905, John McGraw's defending National League champions opened a three-game set at Chicago's West Side Park, intent on either padding their six game lead over Pittsburgh or at least maintaining a status quo in the late September standings. They accomplished neither.

Playing before standing room only crowds, beginning with a 7 to 4 win, Frank Chance's scrappy charges provided the Cubs with their eighth victory over the Giants in the season series. Chance then named rookie Ed Reulbach to face New York, and "Big Ed" responded with another win, followed by Carl Lundgren, a 1 to 0 winner over fabled Christy Mathewson. Bob Wicker, who that season beat the Giants three times, presided over the final, 10 to 5 pounding of the Giants. For Chicagoans, hyper-sensitive to New York–Chicago rivalries—whether architecture, baseball teams or zoos were involved—the series sweep of the hated Giants was like Christmas come early. There was no less joy in Gotham when a series sweep went to the Giants, or when they knocked the Cubs out of first place to take command of the pennant race.

The series was one of those typical New York–Chicago confrontations. Tough, rowdy, unrelenting ballplayers playing heady baseball went at each other in no-holds-barred warfare right on down to the very last out and every last pitch every time they took the field. Every game brought with it an impending Armageddon when these implacable foes crossed swords. Put simply, the Cubs and the Giants were baseball's most bitter rivals, and that rivalry produced an unprecedented string of National League pennants stretching from the 1870s to the 1930s, when the two teams regularly dominated the Senior Circuit.

During the formative years of Organized Baseball they stood like goliaths, and during those crucial early years for professional baseball, many of their games had pennant implications. Under the tempestuous perfectionist McGraw, the Giants recovered from their "Chicago Disaster" and moved on to Pittsburgh to put the Pirates out of contention for the 1905 flag, winning it themselves, and then moving on to whip Connie Mack's Athletics in World Series play. But the first game of the Chicago series exemplified the high-voltage emotion and intensity that surfaced whenever the Cubs played. This is the way the *New York Times* opened its coverage of the September 22 ballgame:

> After nearly two hours of wrangling at the umpire and each other, during which Umpire Emslie chased three players to the clubhouse to preserve order, the Chicagos came off victorious in the opening game of their final series with New York today by a score of 7 to 4. An immense Friday crowd was present, expecting to see a real ball game, but they saw an exhibition of rowdyism which had its climax in a slight mix-up between Manager McGraw and a spectator in the street when the players were leaving the grounds. This last was stopped by police interference, and would have provoked serious results if the crowd outside had not been in good humor over the victory.

Baseball warfare and the animosities it produced between players and fans (and indeed between the two largest American metropolitan hubs themselves) aside, there was something else that was equally intriguing about this incandescent rivalry, and that was the sheer brilliance of the players, their play, and the annual stakes that goaded them to excellence afield. That excellence reached dizzying heights during the deadball era, when Mathewson and Chance and McGinnity and Brown and Evers and McGraw and all the rest of those famous warriors pulled on their uniforms for an afternoon of all-out warfare. And a closer check of the years that followed reveals that during the 1920s and '30s the Giants and Cubs fielded teams that were just as determined and just as talented, though in different ways. Nor were they any less combative, especially when they met at the Polo Grounds or at Wrigleyville.

There was a special magic, a special luster, however, that attached itself to those deadball era games, when magnificent pitching, "inside baseball" and cerebral strategies ruled the day. And that was accomplished despite moistened and scuffed baseballs, cumbersome equipment, sewn leather hand coverings hardly recognizable anymore as fielding gloves, and inadequately manicured playing fields.

The 1905 New York championship, capped by Mathewson's stunning World Series trifecta of shutout wizardry, was one of no fewer than 30 won either by the Giants or the Cubs between 1876, when the Cubs, née White

Stockings, won the first National League flag, and 1940, when their lengthy era of transcendency came to an end. It's worth noting that 30 out of 65 pennant possibilities represents an astonishing 46.2 percent of the number of titles available. Further, the domination of the National League by these two prestigious franchises extended to nine 1–2 finishes and eight more 2–3 place finishes during that time. Small wonder, then, that Giants and Cubs fans greeted each new season with great expectations, and were, on the other hand, reduced to grousing when their heroes stumbled, finishing out of the money.

During the National League's first half century it was, furthermore, reasonable to expect that one ball club or another would run off a sizeable winning streak that might well distance it from the pack, put the club back into contention, or, at very least, enable it to recover from a shaky start. Such was the case in 1916 when the Giants got off to a miserable start, losing nine of their first ten, eight in a row, and then winning 17 straight—all on the road. But hold on. Later in that very same season of 1916, the McGrawmen tore apart everything in sight to run up 26 successive wins, all at the Polo Grounds. The two streaks accounted for half their wins that season. But, irony of ironies, those 26 consecutive wins left them in the same place they started—fourth place. John McGraw's only consolation was the confirmation of a rebuilding job during the season that was right on target. He hit the bull's-eye the very next year with his 1917 ball club, still another pennant winner.

There were a number of other Cub and Giant streaks worth noting. The 1885 White Stockings pieced together an 18-gamer; Chicago's 1906 and 1932 championship teams each won 14 straight; New York's 1912 and 1913 teams each won 14 in a row; and in 1928 the Cubs ran off another 13 straight to move all the way from seventh place into the league lead, though they wound up in third place that season. All of these, and more, are accounted for as the story of these teams' run for pennant gold over three score and ten years unfolds.

Note, dear reader, that those 70 years, between 1870 and 1940, represent just about one half of professional baseball's history. And during that time the two teams were not just occasionally good enough to win it all. At the height of their supremacy, between 1904 and 1913, only once (in 1909) did a team other than the Giants or Cubs manage to wrest first place laurels from them. That team, the Pirates of Phillippe, Clarke, Leach, and above all, the legendary Wagner, had to win 110 games to get the job done to win out over the second and third place teams who were, as you might have guessed, the Cubs (winners of 106) and the Giants. When all's said and done, that's beyond remarkable.

To the nub of the story, then. This book takes a fast-paced look at the national pastime as it moved "from boyhood to manhood," propelled by an ever improving ambience, supremely gifted ball players, and the competitive fires that spurred intra and interleague rivalries. It was during that very time that the Cubs and Giants were baseball's *crème de la crème*. And they're the ones that will command our attention.

I

BEGINNINGS

In March of 1871, not much more than a decade removed from the first pay-for-play matches, the newly formed National Association of Professional Base Ball Players pulled some of their more intrepid forces together into a ten team league. The teams in this pioneering venture, today recognized as baseball's first professional major league, were located in a number of baseball hotbeds stretching from the Atlantic Ocean to the American heartland, where Rockford, Illinois, a tiny dot on the map northwest of Chicago, became the loosely tied federation's westernmost outpost. Several of the clubs had already fielded professional teams, New York's Mutuals, formed originally in 1857, and Chicago's White Stockings among them.

New York's professional ball club, the Mutuals, with roots extending back into the Alexander Cartwright years and the fabled Knickerbockers, was but one of many teams in the New York–Brooklyn area that had previously paid its ball players to play exclusively under their particular team's banner. It should be noted, furthermore, that these two neighbors played in what is recognized today as the first baseball exhibition at which admission was charged. At 50 cents a head several thousand patrons paid their way into Long Island's Fashion Race Course to see picked teams, that is to say, all-stars, from New York and Brooklyn to do battle in a "match," as it was then called, that the New York team won on July 17, 1858 by the score of 22 to 15. It seems the picked New Yorkers had come from a long line of sturdy baseball stock. Playing center field for the New York nine that day was, incidentally, 21-year old Harry Wright, a brilliant, knowledgeable young baseball player who would, some years later, come back to haunt New Yorkers with championship teams based in Cincinnati and Boston.

Not to be outdone by the New Yorkers, Chicago rallied forces of its own, sensing still another opportunity to engage America's number one metropolis in a competitive scenario that would pit two of America's cosmopolitan centers against one another. By 1870 Chicago's 298,977 population had almost trebled its 1860 figure, in itself an astounding development, and had become a muscular mid–American hub of commercial and civic enterprise, ready to take on all comers, whether captains of industry, artists and writers, titans in the social whirl, or sportsmen. Particularly that latter: sportsmen. The era of the national pastime was indeed underway. To field the nation's best on baseball greenery was fast becoming a consuming passion. Knock-down, drag-out competition between the New Yorks and the Chicagos, even as early as 1870, took on huge stakes in us-and-them one-upmanship when the two teed it up for an afternoon's engagement. No less than bragging rights for the title of America's number one city were at stake. Well, now. That was bound to rouse a primal urge or two.

Both cities had, in fact, fielded professionals prior to joining the National Association in 1871. Both had already been involved with Cincinnati's amazing Red Stockings in 1870. And it's well worth remembering that it was the Brooklyn Atlantics that halted the awesome Cincinnati winning streak on June 14, 1870, with an 8–7 extra-inning decision that brought an end to the Red Stockings' incredible 84-game streak. New York area ball players were a formidable, proud lot, unaccustomed to second place status. Cincinnati's dethronement as the nation's number one baseball team was, therefore, appropriately taken care of by New Yorkers, albeit from Brooklyn.

Later in 1870 after the Red Stockings' streak had been broken, Chicago's newly organized White Stockings went to Cincinnati to take on Harry Wright's fabled charges, beating them 10 to 6 on September 7 in a ballgame that embarrassed the good burghers of the Queen City. The game was reported in the *Chicago Tribune* in gushing and gloating tones. Nor was the outcome of that game lost on New York's press, not even some 40 years later, when the *New York Sun,* in a review column of baseball memories that included a paragraph on the White Stockings–Cincinnati game, reported:

> Disappointment and chagrin marked the visage of every man, woman and child in Cincinnati who had the interest of the team at heart, and gloom like a pall spread over the town. The people of Redland could not realize that their great team had been beaten after going nearly two years without losing a game. Then, to add insult to injury, along came Chicago's 'White Elephant' (ed: note the New York slant on Chicago's conquest)...and gave the Reds another beating. Whether or not the feeling of weariness that was manifested throughout Redland had seized the players has never been stated, but it is a fact that they lost games frequently after their first defeat, and as the

Reds had not been a great financial sucess, the enthusiasm in Redland petered out as the season waned. [*New York Sun*, October 15, 1911.]

To drive home a point, the White Stockings took the measure of those magnificent Wrightmen in their red stockings again a month later, this time in Chicago, by a 16–13 count, once again driving Chicagoans into a tizzy over their baseball heroes. That the Chicagos had accomplished something the New Yorks hadn't was not lost on Chicago's elated faithful.

What New York's Mutuals hadn't accomplished, of course, was to take the measure of the Red Stockings during their "mother of all winning streaks." During the 1869 and 1870 seasons the Mutuals met Cincinnati five times, twice in 1869 and twice in 1870 while the streak was still intact, and for a fifth encounter near the end of the 1870 campaign. Each time they came up empty, a most distressing development that, if nothing else, stiffened their resolve for the seasons ahead.

Before the elation of Chicago's successive conquests in 1870, they, too, had to overcome the dejection that accompanied their devastating annihilation in a June 30 game, when they absorbed a 56–19 licking at the hands of baseball's Wright brothers and their Cincinnati teammates. Things were set straight in due time, however, when a "new and improved" White Stockings club, armed at every position with paid pros, returned the favor in the September and October meetings. Buoyed by their late season success, Chicagoans looked forward with great enthusiasm to another season, unaware that the day of professional baseball leagues was about to dawn. When it came, surprisingly, just a few months later, Chicagoans jumped at the opportunity, and saw to it that their White Stockings were in the right place at the right time, which was in March of 1871 at Collier's Rooms, one of New York's many cafe-tavern-rooming establishments. There, with representatives of nine other teams from Washington D.C, which sent officials from two of the nation's capital city's baseball clubs, the Olympics and the Nationals, along with Boston, Philadelphia, Cleveland, Rockford, Illinois, upstate New York's Troy, Fort Wayne, Indiana, and the host city's Mutuals, they helped to put together the foundation pieces of the first American professional sports league.

Before getting into the National Association and especially the National League phase of the rancorous rivalry between the New York and Chicago teams, however, we might be well served to trace this raging and unruly relationship back to its very first encounters. That takes us back to the summer of 1870.

By the time New York's Mutuals and the Chicago White Stockings played their first game on July 6, 1870, at New York's Union Grounds, the

The 1870 New York Mutuals. *Standing:* Nelson, 3b; Martin, rf; Swandell, 2b; Eggler, cf. *Seated:* E. Mills, 1b; Hatfield, ss; C. Mills, c; Wolters, p; Patterson, lf.

Mutuals had met professional teams eleven times, winning six, tying twice and losing three times. Chicago's fledgling pros had won four straight against professional teams before losing to the Brooklyn Atlantics on July 4, to end a streak of 31 conquests dating back to the 1870 season opener on April 21 against a Chicago amateur club. Of course, both clubs had arranged extensive schedules, playing all comers, and running up decisive winning numbers over the course of the season (New York: 68–17–3 and Chicago: 65 and 8, two of those losses coming at the hands of arch rival New York). Once the truth about professional players and teams was confronted with the candor that was necessary to sort out the game's "new order of things," it became evident that the cream of the crop among professionals would soon move on to a more advanced confederation of teams, leaving behind the more tradition-bound National Association, which kept right on demanding a "purer" and "more enlightening" competition among amateurs. It wasn't to be. The New Yorks, Chicagos, Brooklyns, Cincinnatis, Philadelphias and Bostons, among others, soon pioneered the game's first foray into a world that would ultimately be recognized as Organized Baseball. The 1870 season was the bridge that enabled the professionally-minded to collect their resources and set the rudder of pro ball in the direction of a completely professional schedule of games played within the parameters of league play.

During that partially transitional season of 1870 the Mutuals and their most feared opponent, the White Stockings, met four times. Most feared? This Johnny-Come-Lately from the hinterlands? Indeed. New Yorkers needed no primer to catch on to what was at stake in a Chicago-Big Apple rivalry. In fact it was already there in various forms and guises. Consequently, on reading the *Chicago Tribune*'s call for a professional team in 1869, and with its formation in October of that year, a wary eye was cast toward the midwest, where a new baseball titan was a-borning. At least that was the perspective from the nation's number one metropolis.

So the Chicagoans made their first trip eastward, and starting with a game at Cleveland on June 20, reeled off 10 straight victories before being humbled by the Atlantics in Brooklyn, 30–20, on the nation's birthday. Two days later their defeat at the hands of the Mutes was even more humiliating. Their loss, deemed as appropriate as it was convincing by New Yorkers, was reported in the Chicago papers as disgusting, embarrassing, and probably a harbinger of the end times. Here's the way the *Chicago Tribune*'s correspondent, in morose and tart terms, reported the 13–4 drubbing:

> There may have been clubs worse beaten than the White Stockings today, but not much. The Mutuals out-played them at every point and their play of the game was almost absolutely free from errors…. Suffice it to say that there is the material in the Chicago nine to make the best club in America. That material has not been shown to advantage in this trip, nor will it ever be until the White Stockings know what it is to have discipline and be made to do that which they have the ability to do. [*Chicago Tribune*, July 7, 1870]

The *Tribune* correspondent put it quite plainly: the sting of being cut down by the New Yorkers, combined with the inadequacies of the Whites, inexcusable in a New York–Chicago encounter, was absolutely unacceptable. Simply put, the New York thrashing was, for Chicagoans, unbearable. And that imposing 31–0 log before the losses to Brooklyn and New York meant absolutely nothing in the face of such humiliation. The game, and the report following the game, set the tone for what was to come—year after year after year. A rivalry featuring both metropolitan and athletic titans had been born.

This is the box score as reported in the July 7, 1870, *Chicago Tribune* for the inaugural clash between Chicago and New York on July 6, 1870:

New York	R	H	PO		Chicago	R	H	PO
Hatfield, ss	2	2	3		McAtee, 1b	2	1	2
Eggler, cf	3	1	2		Hodes, ss	0	1	4
Patterson, lf	1	1	4		Wood, 2b	1	1	3
Nelson, 3b	4	2	0		Cuthbert, rf	0	0	4
E. Mills, 1b	1	2	4		Flynn, cf	0	1	3
Martin, rf	0	1	4		Treacy, lf	0	0	4
C. Mills, c	0	1	3		Meyerle, p	1	1	2
Wolters, p	0	1	4		Craver, c	0	0	3
Swandell, 2b	2	2	3		Pinkham, 3b	0	1	2
Totals	13	13	27		Totals	4	6	27

Line Score:	Chicago	101 011 000	4 runs,	6 hits
	New York	104 110 024	13 runs,	13 hits

Winning Pitcher, Wolters
Losing Pitcher, Meyerle
2BH, E. Mills, Nelson
HR, Wood

Chicago's fortunes dipped even more with a crushing, 9–0 devastation that took place on July 24 in Chicago. That one cast the Chicago faithful into fits of despair. New Yorkers, on the other hand, were ecstatic.

However, New York's fears concerning the sleeping midwestern leviathan were confirmed in the last two encounters of the season when the "Whites," as they were also known, took apart the slick Easterners by scores of 21–11 and 7–5. That evened the season series at two apiece. And so tightly knotted was the intense competition between the two over the years, that by the end of their era of domination, in 1940, they had almost split some 1,152 ballgames evenly, New York leading by the thinnest of margins, 581 wins to Chicago's 571!

The starting point for that storied rivalry came during the winter of 1870–71, when baseball's more knowledgeable determined that the time had come to make a complete break from the existing mixture of amateur and professional players and teams. That step was taken at the historic Collier's Rooms meeting in New York on March 17, 1871, when the National Association of Professional Base Ball Players was organized and a schedule of games was drafted. By May 1, nine teams anted up a $10 entry fee and play began with the National Association's first game on May 4. Though neither Chicago nor New York would have the honor of playing in the new league's first game (that honor went to Cleveland and host Fort Wayne, Indiana), they not only started the season, but finished it! That was an accomplishment of rather major proportions, considering the instability of the National Association's loosely knit configuration, struggling mightily to take on the air of a professional baseball association as teams were leaving as well as joining the league throughout the season.

As for the transitional season of 1870, the Mutuals (the more familiar "Giants" was first adopted as a team name in 1883) and White Stockings, whose team name, "Cubs," was officially adopted in 1907, played each other four times with the following results:

July 6, 1870	NY	13	Chi	4	Wolters, WP	Meyerle, LP
July 23, 1870	NY	9	Chi	0	Wolters, WP	Burns, LP
Sept 27, 1870	Chi	21	NY	11	Pinkham, WP	Wolters, LP
Nov 1, 1870	Chi	7	NY	5	Pinkham, WP	Wolters, LP

II

THE NATIONAL ASSOCIATION ERA: SHORT AND BITTERSWEET

Like a newborn colt, the National Association took its first unsteady steps in Boston, Troy (NY), Philadelphia, Washington (with two teams), Rockford (IL), Fort Wayne (IN), Cleveland, and its anchor points in the East (New York), and West (Chicago). As the season wore on Fort Wayne's Kekiongas dropped out, replaced by the Brooklyn Eckfords. Thus, professional baseball's first season became a ten-city venture with what amounted to a 30 game schedule of games played by the league's teams against one another.

Like any organization trying to find its way in uncharted territory, the National Association encountered difficulties—and they were daunting to say the least. Unforeseen structural problems, dysfunctional franchises and self-serving players, financial irregularities, and untold numbers of pesky legalities (and illegalities) challenged the Association from its formation on St. Patrick's Day, 1871, forward.

Nor were the Mutuals and White Stockings spared the first year miseries suffered by the league's other entries. Chicago, in particular, though opening its season in the league's newest and very best baseball facility, Lake Front Park, suffered the utter devastation wreaked on Chicagoans by the disastrous, all-consuming fire of October 7–8, and was forced to complete its schedule in borrowed togs, playing out its remaining games on the road.

The very mention of New York's Boss Tweed and his heavy hand in the Mutuals' affairs suggest that the New Yorks were pre-ordained to problems of their own. And indeed there were problems, though not all of them could be laid at the doorstep of City Hall. The most serious involved the players in dumping games, an unsavory evil that bedeviled Organized

Baseball from the outset, bubbling to the surface regularly, especially during the game's formative years. Although New York was not alone in this dark and loathesome "enterprise," it was a hub for bookies, back-parlor betting emporiums, and the crimes that inevitably accompany the fast buck. And many of the Mutes made the most of the numerous offers that came their way.

Through it all, however, games were played and a championship was at stake. Both New York and Chicago enjoyed the plaudits and prestige of occupying first place during the course of the National Association's inaugural season. During the 1871 season one of the more crucial contests with bearing on first place was played between New York and Chicago at the Union Grounds on June 5. That day the Mutes bested the Whites 8 to 5, moving into first place. The battle royal continued on into July, when Chicago

Chicago's first professional team, the 1870 White Stockings. Top row: Fred Treacy; Joe Simmons; Ed Pinkham. 2nd row: Ed Duffy; Capt. Jimmy Wood, Chicago's first professional baseball player; Bub McAtee. 3rd row: Charlie Hodes and Mart King. Bottom row: Ed Atwater; George Zettlein; Tom Foley.

got its revenge at Lake Side Park with a 17 to 6 whipping of the New York nine on the 28th, regaining first place.

Neither would win baseball's first professional championship. That honor went to the Philadelphia Athletics, who edged past Chicago with a 4 to 1 victory on October 30 that captured the NAPBP's first flag. The final standings showed the A's with a 21 and 7 record; Boston, 20 and 10; Chicago, 19 and 9; and then New York with a 16 and 17 mark.

The White Stockings, however, had suffered, at least for the time being, a near fatal blow as a result of the "Great Fire's" aftermath. The franchise was in fact shut down for the next two seasons while the National Association moved on to its second and third campaigns. During that time the New York entry finished in third place in 1872, and fourth in 1873, while the best Chicago could do was to host a few exhibition games featuring some of the National Association teams to slake the thirst of its baseball denizens. But it would not be until the 1874 season that the Whites would be able to resume its rivalries within the league in general, and with the green-stockinged Mutuals in particular.

The fatal flaw in the very marrow of the National Association's bones, an organizational scheme that favored player control over the direction and fate of the league, began to make itself felt during the 1874 season, and by the time the 1875 campaign came to a close, with Boston exercising a stifling dominance over the league behind an all star cast that included professional baseball's first bigger-than-life superstar, Al Spalding, fellow Hall of Famers Harry and George Wright and "Orator Jim" O'Rourke, and stars Deacon White, Ross Barnes and Cal McVey, it was clearly evident that the National Association was but a step or two away from the clutches of the "Grim Baseball Reaper," and that a new direction for professional baseball was in order.

During those last two years the Chicago–New York rivalry continued apace, building, in fact, toward the early 1900's when it would become baseball's first five-star attraction. In 1874 the Mutuals placed second behind Boston, 7 1/2 games off the championship pace, while the recovering White Stockings managed an almost .500 mark with a 28 and 31 record. The 1875 figures were: Chicago, 30 and 37; New York, 30 and 38. Neither offered Boston any competition to speak of, but then, they were no different than any other team in the league. All fell by the wayside to Boston's unbelievable 71 and 8 record. As for New York and Chicago championship hopes, they would have to be shelved until a far better combination of talent, leadership and direction from the front office came along.

The Seasonal Record

THE 1871 STANDINGS

Team	Pos	Won	Lost	Pct.
Philadelphia[1]	1	21	7	.750
Chicago	3	19	9	.679
New York	4	16	17	.485

White Stocking fans waited well into the summer of 1871 to see their idols play a home game that would count for something in the National Association standings. That day came on July 28, when the first place New Yorks came to town. Much to the delight of the enthusiastic throng gathered at Lake Front Park, the Whites, led by captain Jimmy Wood, who held the honor of being "The First Cub," left fielder Fred Treacy, 1st baseman

Bub McAtee, and pitcher George Zettlein scorched the New Yorks by a 17 to 6 count, taking over first place and sending Chicago's citizenry into spasms of ecstasy. The box score follows:

New York	AB	R	H	PO		Chicago	AB	R	H	PO
Pearce, ss	5	2	3	0		Simmons, cf	6	2	2	0
Hatfield, lf	5	1	1	4		Wood, 2b	6	3	2	3
Smith, 3b	4	1	2	1		Treacy, lf	5	2	3	4
Wolters, p	4	2	1	1		King, ss	6	2	1	3
Start, 1b	4	0	2	10		McAtee, 1b	6	3	3	12
Mills, c	4	0	1	4		Foley, c	6	2	3	2
Ferguson, 2b	4	0	0	2		Pinkham, rf	5	2	3	1
Patterson, rf	4	0	0	1		Hodes, 3b	5	1	1	1
Eggler, cf	4	0	1	4		Zettlein, p	5	0	2	1
Totals	38	6	11	27		Totals	50	17	21	27

Line Score: White Stockings   021 082 012   17–21–3
              Mutuals   200 001 030   6–11–10

Home Runs—Treacy, Wood
Umpire—Bomeisler, Newark, NJ
Time of Game—1 hour 45 minutes
Scorers—Atwater and Higham

THE 1871 SEASON SERIES

June 5	NY	8	Chi	4	Wolters, WP	Zettlein, LP
July 28	Chi	17	NY	6	Zettlein, WP	Wolters, LP
August 1	Chi	15	NY	4	Zettlein, WP	Wolters, LP
August 28	Chi	6	NY	4	Zettlein, WP	Wolters, LP

THE 1872 STANDINGS

Team	Pos	Won	Lost	Pct.
Boston	1	39	8	.830
Baltimore	2	35	19	.648
New York	3	34	20	.630

THE 1873 STANDINGS

Boston	1	43	16	.729
Philadelphia	2	36	17	.679
New York	4	29	24	.547

During these two seasons New York finished a creditable third in 1872, battling the Baltimore Canaries (they were to become the Orioles when they became part of the newly enfranchised American Association in 1882) for second place honors, before finally settling for a third place finish, a game behind the Canaries. The Mutuals' effort in 1873 was less successful as they dropped to fourth in the standings. Joe "Old Reliable" Start, a native New Yorker, whose name had already appeared on the roster of the Brooklyn Enterprises in 1860, spearheaded the Mutes' attack during those years. In 1872, William Cummings, better known among baseball buffs as "Candy," was the winning pitcher in 33 of New York's 34 victories, using his famous curveball (there is still some question whether Cummings actually originated the pitch) to befuddle National Association hitters.

Chicago's players found their way to other ballclubs during the Whites' two year hiatus from the baseball wars. Captain Wood and pitcher George Zettlein played first for Troy and later finished the 1872 season with Brooklyn's Eckfords. Bub McAtee and Charlie Hodes also went to Troy, while Fred Treacy, another veteran of National Association days dating back to the Brooklyn Excelsiors of 1867, was signed to play center field for the Philadelphia Athletics. By the time the 1873 season had ended, Chicago was already drafting its re-entry strategy, determined to sign as many top players as possible, no matter where they came from. The franchise was reorganized and began to assemble the roster, get Lake Front Park ready, and return Chicago to the ranks of professional baseball's top teams. Top teams perhaps, but pennant winners—not quite yet. The Mutes and other National Association ball clubs would have something to say about that.

The 1874 Standings

Team	Pos	Won	Lost	Pct.
Boston	1	52	18	.743
New York	2	42	23	.646
Chicago	5	28	31	.475

The New York Mutuals took care of any 1874 pennant aspirations the re-entering White Stockings might have been harboring with a season-long assault that netted them nine conquests out the ten games played. The Mutes' scorched earth policy was at its most devastating at Brooklyn's Union Grounds on June 18, when the Gothamites annihilated the Chicagoans by a monstrous 38 to 1 score, running up the most staggering winning margin in the long history of the New York–Chicago rivalry. Furthermore, Bobby Mathews, winner of the National Association's first game as a pitcher for the Fort Wayne Kekiongas, who authored a 2–0 whitewashing of Cleveland's Forest Citys on May 4, 1871, gave up but one hit, a home run to Levi Meyerle, which also provided Chicago's only run. The

Bobby Mathews, Mutuals pitcher, who came to New York in 1873. He threw the first pitch in baseball's first National Association game on May 4, 1871, at Fort Wayne, Indiana.

massacre was one of Mathews's 42 triumphs (New York beat Chicago nine times, Mathews winning every one), as he led the Mutuals to second place. Once again, "Old Reliable," first sacker Joe Start, led the club in homers, RBIs, and batting average.

Chicago's lone victory came on August 5, when George Zettlein beat the Mutes 5 to 4. Even that one was suspect because of heavy betting before and during the game, and although no one was caught red-handed, there was rather well-founded "circumstantial evidence" to validate the wagering claims on every hand. In 1874, it seems, Chicago just couldn't beat New York on the up and up.

The June 18, 1874 box score:

New York	R	H	PO	E	Chicago	R	H	PO	E
Higham, c	5	5	5	1	Force, ss, p	0	0	1	1
Allison, rf	4	3	7	0	Meyerle, 3b	1	1	2	4
Start, 1b	5	5	4	0	Malone, c	0	0	1	2
Mathews, p	4	3	1	0	Devlin, 1b	0	0	8	0
Hatfield, lf	4	3	3	0	Treacy, lf	0	0	3	2
Nelson, 2b	4	3	1	0	Hines, cf	0	0	3	1
Burdock, 3b	2	2	3	1	Peters, 2b	0	0	5	2
Remson, cf	4	3	3	0	Glenn, rf	0	0	2	3
Carey, ss	6	6	0	0	Collins, p, ss	0	0	2	10
Totals	38	33	27	2	Totals	1	1	27	25

Line Score:	New York	815 358 521	38–33–2
	Chicago	000 000 100	1–1–25

The Chicago routing hiked New York's record to 13 and 9 in league play, while dropping the White Stockings under .500 with a 6 and 7 mark. Although the remainder of the season's games were much, much closer, the results were similar. As matters Chicago–New York went, it was clearly a New York year.

THE 1874 SEASON SERIES

May 21	NY	11	Chi	10	Mathews, WP	Zettlein, LP
May 23	NY	7	Chi	4	Mathews, WP	Zettlein, LP
June 18	NY	38	Chi	1	Mathews, WP	Collins, LP
June 30	NY	8	Chi	2	Mathews, WP	Zettlein, LP
August 2	NY	6	Chi	2	Mathews, WP	Zettlein, LP
August 5	Chi	5	NY	4	Zettlein, WP	Hatfield, LP
August 8	NY	3	Chi	2	Mathews, WP	Zettlein, LP
September 8	NY	6	Chi	2	Mathews, WP	Zettlein, LP
September 21	NY	14	Chi	7	Mathews, WP	Zettlein, LP
September 26	NY	2	Chi	1	Mathews, WP	Zettlein, LP

THE 1875 STANDINGS

Team	Pos	Won	Lost	Pct.
Boston	1	71	8	.899
Chicago	6	30	37	.448
New York	7	30	38	.441

The New York–Chicago season series in 1875 resulted in a flat-footed tie, each club garnering three wins. But as far as the pennant race, if it could even be called that, was concerned, *where* any team finished, or how many games they won or lost, mattered little as Boston mercilessly stomped through the National Association with an incredible winning percentage of .899. The Red Stockings whipped the New Yorks 10 straight and polished off Chicago's Whites eight out of 10. 12 other teams, some of whom played less than 20 league games, could muster but eight victories all season long against the best team in the short-lived history of the NAPBP. In a sense, that made two victories by the Philadelphia A's, the St. Louis Brown Stockings, and the White Stockings a significant accomplishment.

Boston's overwhelming superiority aside, the struggle for sixth place was a far different story. The chase was tight, intense, and ever so closely fought between the Mutes and the Whites, and it all came down to the final game of the season between the two on October 20, resulting in a 12 to 3 win for Chicago that provided the 1/2 game edge the White Stockings carried to a sixth place finish. Although the victory provided a tiny season edge, it wasn't the best Chicago exhibition against New York of the season. That came on June 12 at the 23rd St. Grounds when George Zettlein, who shared the league's leadership in shutouts with Candy Cummings at seven, shut down the Mutes on five hits in a 14 to 0 calcimining. The box score:

New York	R	H	PO	A		Chicago	R	H	PO	A
Holdsworth, ss	0	1	2	1		Higham, 2b	3	2	3	4
Start, 1b	0	1	10	0		Hastings, c	3	3	3	1
Gedney, lf	0	1	4	0		Devlin, 1b	2	3	16	2
Metcalfe, 3b	0	0	1	0		Hines, cf	1	0	0	0
Hicks, c	0	1	5	1		White, 3b	2	3	2	3
Booth, rf	0	0	0	0		Peters, ss	1	3	1	6
Nelson, 2b	0	1	3	1		Glenn, lf	0	1	2	0
Mathews, p	0	0	1	5		Zettlein, p	1	3	0	7
McGee, cf	0	0	1	0		Bielaski, rf	1	0	0	0
Totals	0	5	27	8		Totals	14	18	27	23

Line Score: Chicago   420 232 001   14–18–7
             New York   000 000 000   0–5–13

LOB—Chicago, 5; New York 7
Passed Balls—Hicks, 5
Time of Game—One hour, 40 minutes
Umpire—Nick Young of Washington D.C.
Attendance—Over 3,000

The victory proved to be "The Charmer's" last in Chicago livery. The next time the two teams met, on July 24, Mathews beat his Chicago rival, and by the time the two played their next game a week later on the 31st, George Zettlein was wearing a Philadelphia Centennials uniform. Zettlein had "resigned" from his Chicago contract over charges and countercharges about game fixing and promptly headed for the City of Brotherly Love with teammate Dick Higham.

But that was probably the lesser of causes that prompted big George's hasty departure. In mid–July of 1875 Mr. William Ambrose Hulbert, the White Stockings' CEO, was busily attending to several irons in the fire, one of which was convincing Al Spalding to "come back home" to the midwest to play for Chicago in 1876. When that kind of news leaked to several influential movers and shakers on the Chicago baseball scene, big George saw the handwriting on the wall. Literally translated, it said: Philadelphia.

And so the careers of a number of White Stocking and Mutuals players came to an end as the teams still left in the league at season's close, put their equipment in the clubhouse shed for the winter. Although there were tell-tale indications and strong suspicions on every hand, most were unaware that the demise of the National Association was just around the corner. Indeed, the afore-mentioned Mr. Hulbert had already cast a die that would provide followers of the national pastime with a "new and improved" version of professional baseball destined for 1876 delivery. Why not celebrate the nation's centennial with it?

The 1875 Season Series

June 3	Chi	8	NY	0	Zettlein, WP	Mathews, LP
June 5	NY	6	Chi	5	Mathews, WP	Zettlein, LP
June 7	Chi	14	NY	0	Zettlein, WP	Mathews, LP
July 24	NY	7	Chi	1	Mathews, WP	Zettlein. LP
July 31	NY	15	Chi	3	Mathews, WP	Devlin, LP
October 20	Chi	12	NY	3	Devlin, WP	Mathews, LP

III

FROM THE ASHES OF THE NATIONAL ASSOCIATION: A NEW LEAGUE AND BASEBALL'S FIRST DYNASTY

In a summative paragraph explaining the passing of the National Association and the emergence of the National League, the astute baseball historian David Quentin Voigt explained the causes at the root of the demise of "the Gentleman's League" this way:

> ...in 1875 the Association's weaknesses were painfully evident to thoughtful baseball men. In the East, Chadwick exposed the pernicious influence of gamblers, the selling of games by players, the mismanagement of directors, and the generally hostile reaction of the public. In demanding reform, he called for a convention that would stop fraudulent play by punishing crooked officials and blacklisting corrupt players. After the rotten timbers had been torn out, his next recommendation called for elimination of profitless, small-town franchises." *American Baseball*, Vol. 1, D. Q. Voigt, University Park, PA and London, The Pennsylvania State University Press, 1992, p. 61.

Whatever people, even those as influential as Henry Chadwick, referred to deferentially as "The Father of Baseball," and its "Dean of Sportswriters," were thinking about revamping the national pastime, they were upstaged, as well as out-witted by the busy, no-nonsense major domo of Chicago's baseball fortunes, William A. Hulbert. You will recall that his mid-summer meeting with Boston's star hurler and team leader afield, Al Spalding, set the stage for a radical overhaul that went much farther than merely the Chicago team, per se. Bringing Spalding, and by association

21

William A. Hulbert, White Stockings president, who became the first president of the National League in 1876.

through his persuasive efforts the cream of the Boston National Association juggernaut, none other than catcher James "Deacon" White, Cal McVey, one of the most able and versatile players in the old league, and Roscoe Conkling Barnes, better known as Ross to his teammates, was only the beginning of a series of moves that: 1) lifted the Chicago nine to pennant contention in any league that might be formed in the next few months (it took a little longer, but before the winter was out, Hulbert and Spalding had corralled Adrian Anson, the young and gifted third baseman of the Philadelphia Athletics to complete the Whites' roster revision from stem to stern); and 2) Hulbert, with the perceptive Spalding at his side, aimed at totally revising the terms and regulations that would govern play in a new league.

Back to New York, the birthplace of the National Association, went Hulbert, who called for a meeting of a number of representatives from among professional baseball's teams at the Grand Central Hotel on February second of the nation's centennial year. For such a year, Hulbert informed those assembled that a new league of professional teams was about to be formed. Some were enthusiastic, but most were stunned at the audacity, as well as the completely contoured outline Hulbert presented them. But before it was over, the *coup d'état* was complete, and by Opening Day, when the honor of opening the new league on Saturday, April 22, was conferred on Boston's Red Caps and the Philadelphia Athletics at the A's Jefferson Street Grounds, an eight-team league, now known as The National League, began play. And they're still at it, the years and manifold changes in all aspects of the game and its governance notwithstanding.

The primary reason for reviewing, in a cursory way, the well covered and exhaustively documented history of the birth of the National League, is the pivotal role played by the Chicagoans, who, with New York, were not only to provide baseball fans with a white-hot rivalry during those telling and momentous early years, but who also happened to be the league's blue chip drawing cards. During the three score and ten years encompassed by the 1870 to 1940 era, these two metropolitan centers became and remained the focal point of East and West in the Senior Circuit. Even though New York foundered in its early years, continuing to search out the talent, front office personnel, distinctive style and stability it eventually acquired, it was still an anchor, a *sine qua non* for the baseball enterprise, and the cognoscenti among baseball people, including William Hulbert, knew it.

During the league's first season the powerhouse assembled by Hulbert in Chicago rumbled roughshod over the seven other ball clubs to run up a 52 and 14 record. On the other hand, New York could muster only a 21 and 35 record, losing to the White Stockings seven times in eight tries, and, as a matter of fact, the Mutuals had fallen on such hard times that by mid–September they forfeited their remaining games, bringing their first National League season to a close right then and there. Philadelphia, in similar straits, followed suit. Both had responded to their situation in typical National Association style, concerning themselves first with their own plight, and without concern for the league. That, however, would not do this time around, not with William Ambrose Hulbert and Morgan G. Bulkeley, the 1876 league president, presiding over National League business.

At the December league meeting Hulbert rallied enough support to summarily dismiss the proud New Yorkers and Philadelphians from the league. Therewith, a precedent was established that would continue through the years: the league and its governing powers was more important than an individual player or a single franchise. Not until 1976, exactly a century later, would major league baseball abolish one of the primary tenets of its governing power, the Reserve Clause.

And that was not all. Mr. Hulbert was elevated to the league presidency, a position he held from 1877 until his untimely death (not all were to see it that way) in 1882. More than a little significance can be attached to Hulbert's passing and New York's National League reentry in 1883. The intervening years only provided Chicago and New York fans with exhibition games, but in the interim the intensity of their rivalry grew rather than diminished, and by 1883 the franchises and their supporting fandom were more than ready for head to head combat.

After winning the National League's first championship in 1876, it took four years for Chicago to regain the league flag. But when the Whites broke through again, they proceeded to put together five championships in seven years, starting with baseball's first, three-straight pennant run in 1880, thus becoming baseball's first dynasty. Powered by Adrian "Cap" Anson, who succeeded Al Spalding as Chicago's team leader after Spalding's move into the Whites' front office and the sporting goods business, this dynasty featured baseball's first pitching rotation, a two and sometimes three man affair, to go along with what soon became known as "inside baseball," adding to the game fine touches like hit-and-run plays, heady baserunning, and smart play afield, and, not least, powerful hitting. On their best days, these boys could play with anyone in any age. And even on the subpar days, which came up and down the lineup regularly because players like Whites' stars King Kelly, Silver Flint, and Ned Williamson, to mention but three who chased "John Barleycorn" all over the league frequenting their favorite watering holes, they were still a daunting challenge for all comers.

Meanwhile, in New York baseball moguls and aficianados were not merely standing by. Although on the outer rim of professional baseball, in 1880 the Gothamites put together a ball club under Jim Mutrie and John B. Day. Named the Metropolitans, the club scheduled as many games as possible with major league teams, and on September 8 they leased a playing field popularly known as the Polo Grounds for an exhibition against the Washington Nationals, which they won 4 to 2 with excess of 2,500 in attendance. They also booked three post-season games with the champion White Stockings in October, and though the champs took the measure of the Metropolitans, sizeable crowds were on hand to provide Mutrie and Day with the incentive to keep at it until major league ball would once again come to the nation's number one metropolis. By 1882 the Mets and Whites managed to find scheduling dates for ten tilts, four of them won by New York, and furthermore, by that time both the league and New York were ready for a return to major league baseball in 1883. That was formalized during the off season when the Gothams, as they would at first be known, (later that summer "Giants," a name that was actually prompted by Jim Mutrie himself, became the now familiar franchise team name) were readmitted to the National League.

The era we have entitled "A New League and Baseball's First Dynasty," extended from 1876 through the 1887 season, and came to a close with New York's ballclub clearly on the rise, as the Giants, whose 85 and 27 record was second by a scant two games to Chicago's championship team in 1885, put together the makings of a challenger that would soon overcome the front-running Chicagos and Detroits of the mid–'80s. And by October of 1888 there would be a championship to celebrate in The Big Apple.

The 1876 Standings

Team	Pos	Won	Lost	Pct.
Chicago	1	52	14	.788
St. Louis	2	45	19	.703
New York	6	21	35	.375

Albert G. Spalding, professional baseball's guiding light during its pioneer years, a pitcher turned sporting goods entrepeneur and star hurler for the 1876 champion White Stockings.

The White Stockings humbled Cincinnati's Red Stockings ten straight times, both Boston and Louisville nine out of ten, and both the New York and Philadelphia teams seven out of the eight games played before both called it quits for the season in September. The only season series Chicago lost was to St. Louis by a six to four margin. The ballclub, stacked by Hulbert at every position, showcased the best pitcher in the league by far, Al Spalding, who not only won 47 games but hit a steady .312. Around the infield first baseman Cal McVey hit .347 (he also played at least one game at every position except second and short), Ross Barnes hit a league-leading .429 as well as playing the best defensive second base in the circuit, shortstop John Peters hit .351 and third baseman Adrian Anson chipped in with a solid .356 and 59 RBIs. Together this infield set a still-standing hitting record, combining for a towering .371 average. They were particularly destructive on July 25, when they flattened hapless Cincinnati 23 to 3. McVey, that day stationed behind the plate, banged out six hits, the second game in succession he had turned the trick.

Cincinnati	AB	R	H	PO		Chicago	AB	R	H	PO
Jones, lf	4	1	0	4		Barnes, 2b	7	3	2	4
Booth, 3b	4	0	1	3		Peters, ss	7	5	4	2
Gould, 1b	4	0	0	7		McVey, c	7	4	6	6
Kessler, ss	4	1	1	2		Anson, 3b	7	4	3	2
Pierson, rf	4	0	0	1		White, 1b	7	2	3	8
Dean, p	4	0	3	1		Hines, cf	7	2	2	2
Sweasy, 2b	5	0	11	4		Spalding, p	6	1	2	0
Foley, c	4	1	1	4		Andrus, rf	6	1	2	1
Snyder, cf	3	0	0	1		Glenn, lf	6	1	2	2
Totals	36	3	7	27		Totals	60	23	26	27

Line Score: Chicago   456 021 030   23–26–8
                Cincinnati   012 000 000   3–7–21

2BH—Barnes, Peters, McVey, Andrus, Dean 2, Foley
3BH—Peters, Hines, Glenn
LOB—Chicago 9, Cincinnati 6
Umpire—M. Walsh, Louisville
Time of Game—2 hours, 30 minutes

In the National League's inaugural season the White Stockings outscored their opponents 624 to 257, an average of 5.56 runs per game more than their opponents were able to score. Outfielders John Glenn, Bob Addy and Paul Hines, seasoned and canny defensive players, contributed significantly to Chicago's sturdy defensive unit. Rounded out capably by catcher Deacon White, who was as effective behind the plate as he was with a bat in his hands, with a .343 average and a league-leading 60 ribbies, this team hit a still unsurpassed .337, posting a record that would withstand any and every assault down to the present day.

During the course of the season the Chicagoans managed to avenge New York's eight games to one trimming in 1874, outscoring them 75 to 22, the most lopsided match coming on September 8, when Spalding "Chicagoed" the Mutes, 16-nil. At that time calling a shutout a "Chicago" stemmed from the Whites' embarrassing 9 to 0, 1870 loss to those self-same New Yorks, so it seemed appropriate that Spalding would include New York among his seven victims that season. The 16 to 0 humiliation caused the *New York Times* sports writer to report on the slaughter in icy tones:

> During the first three innings they (Chicago) batted with terrific effort, and, of course, the Mutuals had to indulge in the customary amount of muffing, the result being ten runs scored for Chicago... The unhappy New Yorkers looked quite disconsolate as they went to the last inning, and seemed to have no hope of scoring at all. And such was their fate [*New York Times*, Sunday, September 9, 1876].

The 1876 Season Series

June 15	Chi	5	NY	1	Spalding, WP	Mathews, LP
June 15	NY	6	Chi	5	Mathews, WP	Spalding, LP
June 17	Chi	10	NY	3	Spalding, WP	Mathews, LP
June 20	Chi	4	NY	2	Spalding, WP	Mathews, LP
June 22	Chi	6	NY	4	Spalding, WP	Mathews, LP
June 24	Chi	16	NY	2	Spalding, WP	Mathews, LP
September 8	Chi	16	NY	0	Spalding, WP	Mathews, LP
September 9	Chi	13	NY	4	Spalding, WP	Mathews, LP

The 1877 to 1882 Season Standings

	Team	Pos	Won	Lost	Pct.
1877	Boston	1	42	18	.700
	Louisville	2	35	25	.583
	Chicago	5	26	33	.441
1878	Boston	1	41	19	.683
	Cincinnati	2	37	23	.617
	Chicago	4	30	30	.500
1879	Providence	1	59	25	.702
	Boston	2	54	30	.643
	Chicago	4(t)	46	33	.582
1880	Chicago	1	67	17	.798
	Providence	2	52	32	.619
	Cleveland	3	47	37	.560
1881	Chicago	1	56	28	.667
	Providence	2	47	37	.560
	Buffalo	3	45	38	.542
1882	Chicago	1	55	29	.655
	Providence	2	52	32	.619
	Boston	3(t)	45	39	.536
	Buffalo	3(t)	45	39	.536

With the banishment of New York and Philadelphia from the National League, a league still very much in its infancy, came some predictable consequences. Not only had Hulbert and Co. ousted the league's most populous cities by imposing the ultimate disciplinary measure on them, it also made

The 1876 National League Champion White Stockings: Ross Barnes, John Peters, Adrian "Cap" Anson, George Bradley, Charles Waitt, Paul Hines, Calvin McVey, John Glenn, and Al Spalding.

inevitable an instability that might well have proven disastrous. But the league survived—barely—though with trimmed sails, playing out the 1870s with a six team circuit. Chicago's 1876 champions underwent similar adversities, dropping out of pennant contention when confronted with a rebuilding challenge occasioned by the departure of key players and wholesale changes in management and among the governing directors. Consequently, between 1877 and the dawning of the '80s the White Stockings finished out of the money. Further, those much anticipated battles with New York would not be a part of the summer scene, and that would take some getting used to.

But in Chicago the Spalding-Anson tandem was intact, Spalding having moved into the front office replacing William Hulbert, while moving full time into the sporting goods and sports publication business, and in New York Jim Mutrie and John Day, another pair of front office and on-the-field dynamos, were on hand to give both cities the hope of brighter days ahead. They weren't long in coming.

The White Stockings' lineup for 1880 was once again stacked with power, good pitching and an able defense that would improve with each passing year. Meanwhile, in New York Mutrie and Day were busily engaged in reconstructing the city's baseball presence. In their book *The Giants: Memories and Memorabilia from a Century of Baseball*, Bruce Chadwick and David Spindel explain it this way:

> Right around this time (Ed: 1879-80, when New York and Philadelphia were not league members, but small cities like Troy, Syracuse and Worcester were, causing no little financial stress around the league) two wealthy New York fans named Jim Mutrie and John B. Day formed their own team, the Metropolitans... The Metropolitans played a 24-game season against independents in 1880 and 151 games the next year against independents, colleges, and National League teams in exhibitions. By 1883 the team had gained admittance into the upstart American Association, and in 1884 they won the league's pennant [Abbeville Press, NY. 1993].

"Just a few good men," as the Marines have been wont to say, can make a huge difference, and Spalding, Anson, Mutrie, Day, and a bright young talent, John Montgomery Ward, who was brought to New York for its reentering season in 1883, were those men. Baseball fortunes in New York and Chicago were about to change. The 1880s, in fact, would belong to these two, baseball's Mecca and Medina.

Baseball's first three-peat, won by the versatile and multi-talented White Stockings, was put into the record books by a ballclub that was exciting to watch as they finessed, stole, bludgeoned, defensed, or pitched their way to pennants won in 1880 by 15 games, in 1881 by nine, and in 1882 by three, each time over a game but out-manned Providence team. A few of the more interesting highlights from those seasons follow:

>> Except for Adrian Anson, by 1880 a Chicago fixture aptly tagged with the nickname "Cap," an entirely new team wore the Chicago uniform: Abby Dalrymple, superstar Michael "King" Kelly and powerful George Gore were the team's primary outfielders; Cap Anson, of iron fist and heavy lumber, Joe Quest, Tommy Burns and William "Ned" Williamson, one of the game's great naturals, were the infielders; ham-handed, rough-hewn Silver Flint did the catching; and a two-man pitching rotation consisting of flame-thrower Larry Corcoran and an off-speed, curve balling lefty, Freddy Goldsmith, comprised Anson's hurling corps.

John Ward, New York Hall of Famer, pitcher, infielder and legal expert/organizer during the players' revolt that eventuated in the 1890 Players' League.

>> On April 4 the Whites greeted the 1880 season with a Kelly home run and George Gore's 4-for-4, winning the season opener for Larry Corcoran before 9,000 wildly cheering Chicagoans.

>> During the 1880 season the Whites reeled off winning streaks of 13, from May 5 to the 27th, and then a pennant-sealing 21-gamer between June 2 and July 8. Corcoran ran off 13 wins

White Stockings ace Larry Corcoran, who signalled his pitches to catcher Silver Flint by shifting the wad of tobacco in his mouth. He tossed Chicago's first three no-hitters.

in a row and on August 19 no-hit Boston, 6 to 0, to record the franchise's first no-hitter:

Chicago	AB	R	H	PO		Boston	AB	R	H	PO
Dalrymple, lf	3	2	0	0		Jn. O'Rourke, cf	2	0	0	1
Gore, cf	4	0	4	2		Richmond, ss	2	0	0	0
Williamson, 3b	4	0	1	0		Ja. O'Rourke, cf, ss	4	0	0	1
Anson, 1b	4	0	1	21		Burdock, 2b	4	0	0	2
Kelly, rf, c	4	0	0	0		Jones, lf	3	0	0	5
Burns, ss	4	1	2	0		Morrill, 1b	3	0	0	10
Corcoran, p	4	1	1	1		Foley, rf, p	3	0	0	2
Flint, c, rf	4	0	0	1		Sutton, 3b	3	0	0	2
Quest, 2b	4	2	2	2		Bond, p, rf	3	0	0	0
						Trout, c	3	0	0	1
Totals	35	6	11	27		Totals	30	0	0	24

Line Score: Boston   000 000 000   0–0–5
               Chicago   102 003 00x   6–11–4

2BH—Gore
2 LOB—Chicago 6, Boston 3
DP—Quest and Anson
Umpire—Doescher
Time of Game—2:36

>> On September 30 the red-hot Whites finished the 1880 season with their 67th victory, establishing a still-standing winning percentage record at .798.

>> The 1880 Troy pitching staff consisted of two future Hall of Famers, rookies Tim Keefe and Mickey Welch, both of whom starred for the New York Giants on their pennant-winning 1888 and '89 teams.

>> On June 25, 1881, George "Piano Legs" Gore, Chicago's star center fielder, stole seven bases against the Providence Grays (second base five times, and third, twice). That established a record tied by Billy Hamilton in 1894, but never surpassed.

>> With one more hit Cap Anson, who led the N.L. in BA, Hits, TB, RBI, OB%, SA, Runs Created, FA, PO, and Assists, would have added his name to the ranks of the game's .400 hitters. His 137 hits in 343 AB produced a .3994 average.

>> The 1881 Metropolitans included 61 exhibition games against National League teams in their 151 game independent schedule, winning 18 of them. One of their 18 victories came on October 31 against Chicago, 7 to 4.

>> Although the American Association was organized during the 1881-82 off season, Day and Mutrie chose to bide their time before getting back into the National League. Instead they marshalled forces to make an entry into the American Association.

>> After overcoming a shaky start in 1882, the White Stockings won 10 out of 11 in late June to hike their won-loss record to 22 and 15, moving into second place behind Providence and Buffalo. Another 10 game streak put them atop the league standings shortly after the July 4 mid-point of the pennant chase. But the 1882 race was a tight one, and in late September Providence was still in a position to win the flag. However, a surge by the Whites produced their third straight pennant when they won the season's final series against Buffalo.

The gifted Michael "King" Kelly, one of the most popular 19th century baseball players. Chicago hero, bon vivant, and base stealer supreme.

>> The Chicagos and New Yorks found time during their busy 1882 schedules to stage a 10-game exhibition series with games at the Polo Grounds and the Whites' Lakefront Park. The games were well played, seven of them decided by two or less runs. New York won four. The April 28, 1882 game was typical in two respects: 1) it was closely contested; and 2) George Gore and King Kelly, customarily in the thick of every game, starred. The box score:

Chicago	R	H	PO	A	Metropolitans	R	H	PO	A
Dalrymple, lf	0	0	1	0	O'Neill, cf	0	0	0	0
Gore, cf	2	2	1	0	Nelson, ss	2	2	0	2
Kelly, rf	1	3	2	1	Hankinson, 3b	1	1	1	0
Anson, 1b	1	1	12	0	Mansell, lf	1	2	2	0
Williamson, 3b	0	0	1	2	Clapp, c	0	1	5	0
Burns, ss	0	1	2	3	Reilly, 1b	0	0	14	0
Corcoran, p	1	0	0	1	Kennedy, rf	0	0	3	0
Flint, c	1	2	6	2	Foster, 2b	0	0	1	7
Quest, 2b	0	0	2	3	Lynch, p	0	1	0	1
Totals	6	9	27	12	Totals	4	7	26^2	10

Line Score   Chicago   301 100 100   6–9–5
              New York   200 020 000   4–7–4

LOB—Chicago 3; Metropolitans, 9
Umpire—Mr. John Kelly
Attendance—More than 2,000 people
Time of Game—One hour, 55 minutes

The '80s were astir with rapid-fire, cataclysmic changes in the national pastime. New leagues debuted, baseball magnates had financial interests in more than one league, and players shifted, or *were* shifted from franchise to franchise. By the time the 1883 to 1893 era in major league baseball had come and gone, three major leagues (there was almost a fourth) had risen and wilted under a multitude of pressures brought about by administrative and financial burdens, as well as by the temper of the times, which mightily affected fan support, causing that particular ten year period to be one of the most eventful, yet simultaneously stressful, in the game's history.

In the midst of this '80s angst New York reappeared on the major league scene with not only one, but two teams. With their reentry, accompanied by Philadelphia, the revamped National League now had an eight team alignment that was at last composed of metropolitan centers that might reasonably be expected to be able to sustain top flight professional baseball. Indeed, many presently would use that 1883 date as the beginning point for what today would be called "real time baseball." Giants fans would no doubt agree.

The return of the New York-Chicago rivalry also helped stir up a perceptible rise at the gate. Despite upsetting and constant reorganization, franchise shuffling and other assorted ills, baseball's fandom didn't stay away from the park, and by the end of the era 350,000 clicks of the turnstile in a season seemed a reasonable goal both at the Polo Grounds and at the Cubs' West Side Park.

The 1883 and 1884 Standings

	Team	Pos	Won	Lost	Pct.
1883	Boston	1	63	35	.643
	Chicago	2	59	39	.602
	New York	6	46	50	.479
1884	Providence	1	84	28	.750
	New York	4(t)	62	50	.554
	Chicago	4(t)	62	50	.554

Subsequent the dissolution of the small town Troy and Worcester franchises at the National League's December 6, 1882 meeting, New York and Philadelphia were officially welcomed back into the fold. New York, in particular, availed itself of one of the most astounding windfalls of talent in the game's history, landing four eventual Hall of Famers including Roger Connor, Mickey Welch, "Sir Timothy" Keefe and a born leader endowed with prodigious abilities whose name was just made for New York society's upper crust, William Buckingham Ewing, who would, of course, be called "Buck." Remarkably, all four had played together at Troy, and all four would some day find their way to baseball's pantheon at Cooperstown. A fifth from that ball club, shortstop Fred Pfeffer, would make his way to Chicago, where he would anchor the Whites' famous "Stonewall Infield." And can someone please explain how that Troy ball club finished in the National League's seventh spot, some 19½ games off Chicago's winning 1882 pace?

WM EWING,
CATCHER – NEW YORK.

Buck Ewing, New York's brilliant all-around player. He led the Giants to two consecutive NL championships in 1888 and 1889, and was named to the Hall of Fame in 1939.

The cumbersome New York arrangement, with its forces divided among two leagues, though under single management, lasted through the 1887 season, but after the Mets brought New York its first professional baseball championship by dint of seizing the American Association title in 1884 behind Tim Keefe's superlative pitching, Jim Mutrie moved Keefe to the Giants' roster, thus signalling his intent to cast his lot with the National League, and by 1888, his forces fully concentrated in one, National League ball club, the Giants would be ready for a strong drive to the Senior Circuit's pennant.

1883 and 1884 were disappointing seasons, and not only for Cap Anson's White Stockings, who, after a hectic season in which they were in contention for the N.L. crown, came up short of the big prize. There would be no "4-Straight" for Chicago. New York's revised lineup struggled to a sixth place finish, some four games below the .500 mark. But there was at least some balm in Gilead. When the 14 game season series with Chicago ended in late September, the New Yorkers, now hailed as the Giants, had left a calling card for the years ahead. Even though they managed only five wins in 14 tries, the five games they did win were pounded out to the tune of 22 to 7, 10 to 3, 18 to 8, 5 to 0, and 10 to 1, each a decisive conquest of their old rivals. Four others were decided by two runs or less in Chicago's favor. Of the six shutouts recorded by Giant pitchers in 1883, the 5 to 0 Welch masterpiece, a three-hitter in which he was in command all the way, was by far the most satisfying.

William "Ned" Williamson, one of the greatest natural athletes of the 19th century. A Chicago favorite, he was a part of the White Stockings' famed "Stonewall Infield."

And, an interesting Chicago side note: the famed "Stonewall Infield," with Anson, Burns, Williamson, and Fritz Pfeffer combining to play the best inner defense in the league, is in evidence this game, with the brilliant Pfeffer ranging far afield to convert two smashes headed for base hits into 4–3 putouts. Here is the box score of that August 1, 1883 game, played at the remodeled Lakefront Park in Chicago with its rectangular configuration and its 41 uniformed attendants to attend to Chicago's growing fandom:

Chicago	AB	R	H	A	New York	AB	R	H	A
Dalrymple, lf	4	0	0	0	Ewing, c	4	0	0	1
Gore, cf	4	0	2	0	Connor, 1b	4	1	2	1
Kelly, rf	4	0	0	2	Ward, rf	3	1	0	0
Anson, 1b	2	0	0	1	Gillespie, lf	4	0	1	0
Williamson, 3b	3	0	0	2	Caskins, ss	4	1	1	1
Burns, ss	3	0	0	4	Welch, p	4	0	1	3
Pfeffer, 2b	3	0	1	2	Troy, 2b	4	1	1	2
Flint, c	3	0	0	1	Hankinson, 3b	4	1	2	0
Corcoran, p	3	0	0	1	Pierce, cf	4	0	1	0
Totals	29	0	3	13	Totals	39	5	9	8

Line Score: New York   000 030 020   5–9–3
              Chicago   000 000 000   0–3–3

2BH—Connor, Troy
LOB—Chicago 3; New York 4
DP—Corcoran, Anson, Williamson; Kelly, Flint
Umpire—Frank Lane
Time of Game—Two hours

The 1883 Season Series

May 15	Chi	8	NY	7	Corcoran, WP	Welch, LP
May 16	Chi	6	NY	2	Goldsmith, WP	O'Neill, LP
May 17	Chi	15	NY	2	Corcoran, WP	Welch, LP
June 2	NY	22	Chi	7	Welch, WP	Corcoran, LP
June 4	Chi	5	NY	2	Corcoran, WP	Ward, LP
June 5	NY	10	Chi	3	Welch, WP	Goldsmith, LP
June 8	NY	16	Chi	8	Welch, WP	Corcoran, LP
July 31	Chi	6	NY	5	Corcoran, WP	Ward, LP
August 1	NY	5	Chi	0	Welch, WP	Corcoran, LP
August 2	Chi	5	NY	2	Corcoran, WP	Ward, LP
August 4	Chi	5	NY	3	Goldsmith, WP	Welch, LP
September 21	NY	10	Chi	1	Ward, WP	Goldsmith, LP
September 22	Chi	5	NY	3	Goldsmith, WP	Ward, LP
September 25	Chi	11	NY	10	Goldsmith, WP	Welch, LP

The 1884 season brought more bad news for the Chicago faithful. As one of the most bizarre of professional baseball years unfolded, during which three leagues stormed belligerently through chaotic seasons, the White Stockings found themselves out of contention, stumbling all the way down to fourth place, light years behind a Providence team that had unsuccessfully threatened to capture league honors several times before crashing through with a decisive championship. Forged on the strong arm of Charles "Old Hoss" Radbourn, the Grays swept aside all contenders with a sparkling 84 and 28 record, at one time streaking to ten straight victories before a Larry Corcoran no-hitter, his third, ended the skein with a 6 to 0 win. As impressive as Corcoran's no-no was, the "Old Hoss" outdid him, though in a different way, by stringing together 18 straight victories in a season that saw him win no less than 60 ballgames. His 1939 election to the Hall confirmed the immensity of that singularly awesome year.

As for the 1884 New York Giants, there was no little satisfaction in bringing about the only flat-footed tie to date in the century-plus history of the Cubs-Giants rivalry. At 62 and 50 they managed a fourth place standoff, though 22 games off the top mark. By whipping Buffalo, Philadelphia and Cleveland 11 times each and Detroit 14 times, the Giants more than compensated for a disastrous season series with Chicago in which they dropped 12 of the 16 games played. That remained to be atoned for, and the atonement was not long in coming.

On July 9, 1884, at Lakefront Park, Cap Anson, with two, and Fred Pfeffer and Ned Williamson, with one apiece, homered to lead the Whites past the Giants, 9 to 1. Not only did these three White Stockinged heavies play great defensive ball, they pounded those deadened 1880s pellets to a fare thee well. In 1884, it will be remembered, big Ned, working in an admittedly homer-friendly ball park with a right field fence somewhere in the neighborhood of 230 to 250 feet beckoning, sent 27 round trippers into orbit, three of them coming on Memorial Day, marking him as the first player to hit three homers in one game. Though much maligned as a power hitter, or even as a hitter for that matter, the agile, powerfully built Williamson was one of the better batsmen of his day and especially dangerous in the clutch. The box score of that Cubs-Giants game follows:

New York	R	H	PO	A	Chicago	R	H	PO	A
Ewing, c	0	0	2	1	Dalrymple, lf	2	2	5	2
Ward, cf	0	0	1	0	Gore, cf	0	0	1	0
Connor, 2b	0	1	2	4	Kelly, rf	0	0	1	1

Lake Front Park, quartered between Chicago's famous Michigan Boulevard and Lake Michigan. The home of the White Stockings between 1878 and 1884 (from a newspaper sketch).

New York	R	H	PO	A	Chicago	R	H	PO	A
Gillespie, lf	0	1	1	0	Anson, 1b	4	3	12	0
Dorgan, rf	0	0	2	1	Pfeffer, 2b	2	2	1	2
McKinnon, 1b	1	2	12	1	Williamson, 3b	1	4	0	3
Hankinson, 3b	0	1	0	2	Burns, ss	0	2	2	1
Begley, p	0	0	0	1	Corcoran, p	0	0	2	5
Caskins, ss	0	1	4	3	Flint, c	0	0	3	1
Totals	1	6	24	13	Totals	9	13	27	15

Line Score: New York   000 000 010   1-6-8
             Chicago   000 301 32x   9-13-2

3BH—Dalrymple
HR—Anson 2, Williamson, Pfeffer
LOB—Chicago 8, New York
3 DP—Williamson, Pfeffer, Anson; Dalrymple and Anson
PB—Ewing
Umpire—Van Court
Time of Game—Two hours
Attendance—More than 2,200

The 1884 Season Series

May 1	NY	15	Chi	3	Welch, WP	Corcoran, LP
May 2	NY	13	Chi	6	Welch, WP	Corcoran, LP
July 5	Chi	7	NY	6	Corcoran, WP	Welch, LP
July 7	Chi	7	NY	0	Corcoran, WP	Begley, LP
July 8	NY	11	Chi	4	Welch, WP	Goldsmith, LP
July 9	Chi	9	NY	1	Corcoran, WP	Begley, LP
August 16	Chi	13	NY	9	Brown, WP	Welch, LP
August 18	NY	5	Chi	3	Dorgan, WP	Corcoran, LP
September 2	Chi	8	NY	3	Corcoran, WP	Welch, LP
September 3	Chi	8	NY	3	Brown, WP	Begley, LP
September 4	Chi	7	NY	5	Corcoran, WP	Ward, LP
September 6	Chi	3	NY	2	Clarkson, WP	Ewing, LP
September 30	Chi	17	NY	2	Clarkson, WP	Dorgan, LP
October 2	Chi	9	NY	5	Brown, WP	Welch, LP
October 3	Chi	13	NY	5	Clarkson, WP	Dorgan, LP
October 4	Chi	7	NY	5	Clarkson, WP	Welch, LP

The 1885 to 1887 Season Standings

	Team	Pos	Won	Lost	Pct.
1885	Chicago	1	87	85	.777
	New York	2	85	27	.759

	Team	Pos	Won	Lost	Pct.
	Philadelphia	3	56	54	.509
1886	Chicago	1	90	34	.726
	Detroit	2	87	36	.707
	New York	3	75	44	.630
1887	Detroit	1	79	45	.637
	Chicago	3	71	50	.587
	New York	4	68	55	.553

There are those who claim that the 1885-86 White Stockings rank among baseball's top ten teams in National League history. Of course, there are arguments to the contrary, some of them quite persuasive. But there is no argument against their lofty status among 19th century ball clubs. During the dynastic, 1880–86 span, Cap Anson's 1885 team was arguably better than any of his others, succeeding in a spine-tingling race to the wire over some of the National League's better entries, New York's Giants, the Philadelphia Phillies and the Detroit Wolverines among them. Especially those Jim Mutrie Giants, who let it be known particularly in Chicago that New York was going to be a force to be reckoned with. And they were, pressing the Whites doggedly throughout the summer of 1885 with a star-studded lineup that would soon emerge at the National League's summit. Faltering momentarily in 1886 as they dropped into third behind the onrushing Wolverines, they regrouped after the 1887 Detroit championship to bring New York its first pennant flag in 1888.

Chicago's fearless leader, Adrian "Cap" Anson, greatest of the 19th century hitters.

Some of the stellar Whites during the final years of Chicago's championship run included pitchers John Clarkson, a finicky Bostonian with a crackling heater, and the stout Scot, "Big Jim" McCormick, who were added to the roster by Al Spalding just in time to pick up the slack left by the departing Larry Corcoran and Freddy Goldsmith, both worn to a nub by excessive use. Another, whose speed and verve attracted attention, was the famed Billy Sunday, who would later turn to the "Sawdust Trail," evangelizing the wayward with his Gospel message in baseball lingo.

Meanwhile, out there on Coogan's Bluff, Roger Connor, the 1885 batting

Left: John Clarkson, ace of Chicago's pennant winning teams of 1885 and 1886. He won 53 ballgames in 1885 and followed that with another 35 in 1886. Elected to the Hall of Fame in 1963. *Right:* "Orator Jim" O'Rourke, hard-hitting New York Hall of Famer who, like "Cap" Anson played in both the NAPBP and the NL. He made the first hit in National League history on April 2, 1876. His last came in his 54th year, in a cameo appearance with the Giants in 1904.

champ, "Orator Jim" O'Rourke, John Ward, Buck Ewing, Tim Keefe and Mickey Welch, each a future Hall of Famer, formed a powerful nucleus for the New Yorkers. O'Rourke, who hit for a lifetime .311 average, Connor, who crunched National League pitching at a .371 clip while also leading the league with a .435 on base percentage, and Ewing led the New York attack. Mickey Welch, who subdued Chicago seven times while piling up 44 wins, engineered a 17 game winning streak to pace the Welch-Keefe tandem that won 56 between them, complimenting the

Fred "Fritz" Pfeffer, both the brains and the glue of Chicago's infield. He was a White Stockings hero for a decade and prominent organizer/player in the Players League. (George Brace photograph)

Giants' offense ably, as the Mutriemen ground out 10 victories over the Whites, losing but six times to the champions.

The pennant in 1885 hinged on a final New York-Chicago showdown in the Windy City, September 29-October 2. Unfortunately for the New Yorkers, John Clarkson and Jim McCormick won the first three in the four game set, icing the flag for Chicago. In the second game of that series Fritz Pfeffer tied into one of Keefe's better fastballs, driving it out of sight in the seventh stanza to win the pivotal game, a white-knuckle special, 2 to 1. The last game of the series, though inconsequential in the final standings, was won by a determined New York nine that was not about to wrap up a season with a defeat at the hands of the Chicagoans. They didn't, winning 10 to 8, on the strength of some strong stickwork by Roger Connor and Jim O'Rourke. The box score of that October 3, 1885, game:

New York	R	H	PO	A	Chicago	R	H	PO	A
O'Rourke, c	3	3	0	0	Dalrymple, lf	1	1	1	0
Connor, 1b	2	2	3	1	Gore, cf	2	1	4	1
Ewing, c	1	1	4	2	Kelly, c	2	2	6	1
Gillespie, lf	1	1	3	0	Anson, 1b	0	0	6	0
Dorgan, rf	1	0	2	0	Pfeffer, 2b	0	0	3	3
Richardson, 3b	0	1	1	1	Williamson, 3b	1	0	1	1

New York	R	H	PO	A	Chicago	R	H	PO	A
Keefe, p	1	0	1	4	Burns, ss	1	2	0	1
Gerhardt, 2b	1	1	5	2	Clarkson, p	0	1	0	10
Ward, ss	0	0	2	1	Sunday, rf	1	0	0	0
Totals	10	9	21^3	11	Totals	8	7	21	17

Line Score	New York	200 125 0	10–9–10
	Chicago	242 000 0	8–7–15

2BH—Burns, Ewing
3BH—Gillespie
HR—Connor, Kelly
DP—Pfeffer and Anson
Umpire—Mr. Curry
Attendance—Approximately 8,000

The 1885 Season Series

May 11	NY	8	Chi	4	Welch, WP	Clarkson, LP
May 12	Chi	10	NY	2	Corcoran, WP	Keefe, LP
May 15	NY	4	Chi	3	Welch, WP	Clarkson, LP
May 16	NY	13	Chi	4	Richardson, WP	Corcoran, LP
July 3	NY	6	Chi	2	Welch, WP	Clarkson, LP
July 4	NY	6	Chi	3	Keefe, WP	Pfeffer, LP
July 4	Chi	6	NY	3	Clarkson, WP	Ewing, LP
July 6	NY	7	Chi	4	Welch, WP	Clarkson, LP
August 1	NY	7	Chi	6	Welch, WP	Clarkson, LP
August 6	NY	1	Chi	0	Welch, WP	Clarkson, LP
August 7	Chi	8	NY	3	McCormick, WP	Keefe, LP
August 10	NY	12	Chi	0	Welch, WP	Clarkson, LP
September 29	Chi	7	NY	4	McCormick, WP	Welch, LP
September 30	Chi	2	NY	1	Clarkson, WP	Keefe, LP
October 1	Chi	8	NY	3	McCormick, WP	Welch, LP
October 3	NY	10	Chi	8	Keefe, WP	Clarkson, LP

The 1886 race was another down-to-the-wire affair involving Chicago, the fast-improving Detroit club and, once again, New York. This time the Whites tucked away the championship by virtue of a strong August, during which they won 17 of 23 while the league's leader all summer, Detroit, was losing 13 of 23. Rookie John "Jocko" Flynn, one of baseball's most intriguing ballplayers,[4] added 23 wins to the artistry of Clarkson and McCormick, while Keefe and Welch were winning every last game the Giants put in the victory column, with Welch notching 33 and "Sir Timothy" Keefe another 42 to lead the league. King Kelly's .388 led all hitters

(Anson's .371 wasn't far behind), and his 53 stolen bases sparked the Chicago attack. Clarkson, with 36 wins, a 2.41 ERA and 313 whiffs, became the fourth of the White Stockings to merit Hall of Fame honors, the others included Al Spalding, Cap Anson and King Kelly. A fifth, William Hulbert, was elected to the Hall in 1995 as a baseball executive.

The 1886 White Stockings: left to right, John "Jocko" Flynn, Michael "King" Kelly, Tom Burns, Abner Dalrymple, John Clarkson, "Cap" Anson, Billy Sunday, Fred Pfeffer, George Gore, "Silver" Flint, "Ned" Williamson, "Jimmy" Ryan, "Big Jim" McCormick and George "Prunes" Moolic.

The 1886 Season Series

May 13	Chi	7	NY	3	McCormick, WP	Welch, LP
June 5	Chi	4	NY	0	McCormick, WP	Keefe, LP
June 8	Chi	3	NY	2	McCormick, WP	Keefe, LP
June 9	NY	4	Chi	1	Welch, WP	Flynn, LP
July 1	Chi	7	NY	3	McCormick, WP	Welch
July 2	NY	11	Chi	1	Keefe, WP	Clarkson, LP
July 3	NY	7	Chi	3	Welch, WP	McCormick, LP
July 7	Chi	21	NY	9	McCormick, WP	Welch, LP
July 31	NY	3	Chi	2	Welch, WP	McCormick, LP
August 2	NY	10	Chi	4	Keefe, WP	Clarkson, LP
August 3	NY	7	Chi	6	Welch. WP	Clarkson, LP
September 6	Chi	7	NY	4	McCormick, WP	Welch, LP
September 7	Chi	13	NY	11	Flynn, WP	Keefe, LP
September 8	Chi	12	NY	3	McCormick, WP	Welch, LP
September 8	Chi	9	NY	4	Flynn, WP	Keefe, LP
October 4	Chi	9	NY	7	McCormick, WP	Welch, LP

| October 5 | NY | 7 | Chi | 4 | Keefe, WP | Flynn, LP |
| October 6 | NY | 4 | Chi | 1 | Welch, WP | McCormick, LP |

Although the Giants, Phillies and White Stockings threatened Detroit's precarious grip on first place throughout the summer of 1887, the championship flag wound up in the Wolverines' trophy case, lowering the curtain on the Chicago dynasty. It would take another 20 years before the Chicagoans, by that time known as the Cubs, would win another title. However close they would come (they finished in the second spot three times during the next five seasons), the Ansonmen, stripped of super stars King Kelly, who was peddled to Boston after the 1886 season for the then monstrous sum of $10,000, Famer John Clarkson, for another 10 grand, also to Boston, and hard hitting George Gore, shipped off to, of all places, New York, lost the magic touch that had made their name synonymous with first class baseball superiority.

Detroit, spearheaded by future Hall of Fame outfielder "Big Sam" Thompson who led the league in hitting, lefty Charles Baldwin, curiously nicknamed "Lady," Ned Hanlon, Charlie Bennett, the league's best catcher, and a fearsome foursome that arrived from Buffalo after the 1885 season, handyman Hardy Richardson, another future Famer, Dan Brouthers, shortstop Jack Rowe, and the "Deacon," James White, took 1887 honors and then bested Charlie Comiskey's American Association St. Louis champ, for the post-season title that had already taken on World Series prestige, and was in fact hailed as just that.

Detroit's reign atop the National League was fated for a short run, as was the franchise itself, which after another season's play, was history. Into the void stepped New York, which finally, after years of membership in a league Gothamites sometimes loved, sometimes hated, and most always felt they should dominate, swept all comers aside and won their first professional championship. A new era had begun...

The 1887 Season Series

May 30	Chi	12	NY	11	Baldwin, WP	George, LP
May 30	Chi	3	NY	2	Clarkson, WP	Keefe, LP
June 1	NY	11	Chi	8	Welch, WP	Baldwin, LP
July 4	Chi	5	NY	1	Clarkson, WP	Keefe, LP
July 4	Chi	4	NY	2	Baldwin, WP	Welch, LP
July 5	Chi	15	NY	8	Van Haltren, WP	Keefe, LP
July 15	Chi	5	NY	4	Clarkson, WP	Keefe, LP
July 16	Chi	9	NY	4	Van Haltren, WP	George, LP
July 18	NY	6	Chi	2	Keefe, WP	Baldwin, LP

August 5	Chi	7	NY	3	Clarkson, WP	Keefe, LP
August 6	NY	9	Chi	8	Welch, WP	Van Haltren, LP
August 8	Chi	12	NY	6	Clarkson, WP	Keefe, LP
August 25	NY	9	Chi	1	Welch, WP	Clarkson, LP
August 26	Chi	5	NY	2	Van Haltren, WP	Keefe, LP
August 27	NY	5	Chi	1	Welch, WP	Clarkson, LP
September 15	NY	4	Chi	3	Welch, WP	Van Haltren, LP
September 16	Chi	12	NY	8	Clarkson, WP	Titcomb, LP

IV

LOSING IT AND PUTTING IT BACK TOGETHER

Prior to an era marked off by the years 1888 to 1901, competition between the Giants and the Cubs quickly grew into a hotly contested rivalry after the Giants' 1883 re-entry into the National League. The new era started off with a smash hit in New York when at long last Jim Mutrie's boys brought Gotham a championship. However, the championship express soon lost its steam. After a second straight pennant winner in 1889, the spiral downward from the heights brought with it a span of years for both the Giants and the White Stockings that tried the spirit and determination of both teams. The league as both franchises had known it was about to undergo, if not soon then most assuredly later, some changes that the Spaldings and Days of the baseball world were quite clearly unwilling to entertain.

Even as the Giants were celebrating their 1888 and 1889 pennant and World Series conquests, trouble was brewing. The rumblings around the league came to a crescendo prior to the 1890 season when two of the Giants' pillars, Monte Ward and Buck Ewing, along with the Whites' Fred Pfeffer and a number of other veteran stars, disgruntled over their chattel status in a circuit thoroughly and oppressively dominated by management and baron-like owners, began to put together the makings of what would be called the Players' League. With support from willing backers like Cleveland street railway owners Albert and Tom Johnson, prime movers among the proposed league's magnates, the owners and players drafted a constitutional framework whose major operational tenet struck at the heart of the owners' complete control of the players through the Reserve Clause and its Limitation Rule which, most effectively, deprived players of negotiation rights and bound them by contract to their teams unless or until management decreed otherwise. That meant war. Three major leagues would now

45

vie for the available playing talent. None of the three could, or would become a clear-cut winner in the ensuing battle, although when the smoke of the 1890 battlegrounds had cleared the National League staggered to its feet, somewhat less damaged than the American Association, and resumed its former ways. The Players' League went down in flames and the moguls of the Senior Circuit, who apparently hadn't learned a thing from the fracas, clamped down once again, reasserting their iron grip on the fortunes and fate of Organized Baseball.

The New York Players' League franchise featured no less than ten former National League Giants, and the 1890 N.L. Giants? Their makeshift roster, with returning star Mike Tiernan and newly signed "Pebbly Jack" Glasscock, an N.L. shortstop of all star caliber who led the senior circuit in hitting, could achieve but second division scrapings with a 63 and 68 record. Mickey Welch stayed on, but his sidekick over the many Troy and New York seasons, Tim Keefe, cast his lot with the New York Players' League team, supplying the new league with a lighter and livelier ball inasmuch as he was also in the baseball equipment business. Keefe recorded 17 wins against 14 losses in his last good season, but neither the pitching nor the New York defense was up to pennant contention. The White Stockings spent the first several seasons of their post-dynasty years chasing the league's front runners. Though they were able to knock off the rival Giants in season series encounters, winning, for example, 11 of 17 in 1887, 13 of 19 in 1890, 9 of 14 in 1898 and 12 of 20 in 1900, their days of dominating the senior circuit's ball clubs were over. The best they could come up with was a second place finish in 1891 to the Boston Beaneaters, who won the title by 3½ games over the Chicagoans, by that time called, simply, "Anson," or "The Ansons," so completely was the Chicago franchise associated with the irrepressible Chicago star's name.

Mickey Welch, workhorse righthander, who won 238 ball games for the Giants in nine seasons. He was elected to the Hall of Fame in 1973. (George Brace photograph)

The 1888–1901 era also marked the passing of most of the great stars of 19th

Roger Connor, .325 lifetime hitter, a Hall of Famer, who scored 117 runs and hit a league-leading 17 triples for the New York champions of 1889.

century play. Chief among them was Captain Adrian Anson, who played his last game in 1897, winding up a brilliant Hall of Fame career as the National League's first larger-than-life superstar. Other New Yorkers and Chicagoans whose careers ended with the last years of the 19th century included Hall of Famers Buck Ewing, King Kelly, Jim O'Rourke, John Clarkson, Tim Keefe, Monte Ward, Jake Beckley, Mickey Welch, Roger Connor, Amos Rusie and Ned Hanlon. With King Kelly behind the plate, Jake Beckley, 1b, Cap Anson (who played each of the infield positions at one time or another) 2b, Monte Ward, ss, Buck Ewing, 3b, a position he often played, and an outfield of Roger Connor, Jim O'Rourke and a playing-manager in Ned Hanlon, supported by a pitching staff of Keefe, Welch, Clarkson and Rusie, one would suspect this combined New York-Chicago outfit could take on just about anybody—in any era. Of more than passing interest—and significance—is the total number of baseball's Hall of Fame heroes whose association with the game in either playing or executive capacities was *not* a part of New York's or Chicago's 19th century baseball history. Their numbers include six players, George Wright, Candy Cummings, Old Hoss Radbourn, Tommy McCarthy, Dan Brouthers and Pud Galvin; two executive/managers, Harry Wright and Charlie Comiskey; two of the game's early pioneers and promoters, Alexander Cartwright and Henry Chadwick; and Morgan Bulkeley, the National League's first president. William Hulbert and Albert Spalding, both associated with Chicago's franchise, were elected as executives. With the latter two, the Chicago total comes to 15, as compared to the 11 who were *not* New Yorkers or Chicagoans. That makes its own statement about the stature, power and notoriety of these two pivot points in the 19th century baseball world. That would not diminish in the century to come.

By 1893 the American Association, the National League's last surviving rival, had played out its last ball game, leaving the senior circuit as the only viable enterprise in Organized Baseball. Those who wanted to play ball now had but one recourse: sign—or sit. The players signed.

Between 1893 and 1900, seasons of New York and Chicago discontent, a bloated National League of 12 teams monopolized professional baseball. In 1894, New York, with its pre–Players' League roster back in the fold at the Polo Grounds, wound up its season in second place, a scant three games behind pennant winner Baltimore. The O's' championship lineup included a tautly-wired, hyper-sensitive third baseman by the name of John Joseph McGraw who would wind up in a Giants uniform some years later, after having pulled off the kind of deal that players in the late 1890s would only dare to fantasize about. That's a story that merits at least a brief review further on.

As the new century neared, New York joined Chicago on the slippery slope to second division inferiority, and by 1901, when the National League could no longer avoid or disregard yet another professional baseball enterprise, known this time as the American League, which was immediately and derisively branded "The Junior Circuit," both teams were wallowing at sub-.500 levels that produced inevitable grousing in the nation's number one and two cities, reflected in rapidly diminishing turnstile numbers.

But there was light at the end of the tunnel, that is to say, with a new century the darkness of the 1890s was about to give way to news stars and an altogether new level of baseball summitry. The first precursor of things to come arrived in 1898 when there appeared on the Chicago scene a determined young man with Anson-like leadership capabilities. His name was Frank Leroy Chance. A Californian with a pugilistic background, he was used initially as a catcher and occasionally in the outfield. But by 1902 he was primarily a first baseman, put there by Frank Selee who, after serving the Boston Beaneaters brilliantly for a dozen years during their championship run, moved over to Chicago to lead an "orphaned" ball club with Hall of Fame sagacity and class. Two of Chicago's most vital foundation pieces were now in place. Others would soon arrive and Selee would make utmost use of each of them.

In New York, meanwhile, two pitchers of Everest-like stature made their way from the minors to the Giants, though by differing routes, to join the third "M," John McGraw, as anchor points for New York's ascendancy to National League power and prestige. The other two "M's": McGinnity and Mathewson, who throughout the first decade of the 1900's provided baseball's fandom with some of the game's most amazing achievements.

The 1888 and 1889 Standings

	Team	Pos	Won	Lost	Pct.
1888	New York	1	84	47	.641

	Team	Pos	Won	Lost	Pct.
	Chicago	2	77	58	.570
	Philadelphia	3	69	61	.531
1889	New York	1	83	43	.659
	Boston	2	83	45	.648
	Chicago	3	67	65	.508

On August 14, 1888, the Giants welcomed 10,200 fans and the Chicago White Stockings to the Polo Grounds, where they sought to extend the beloved "Sir Timothy" Keefe's 19-game winning streak. There to challenge both the throng and the Mutriemen were Cap Anson & Co. On that particular day the Whites sent a rookie left-hander, in the midst of a 25-victory summer, Gus Krock by name, to the mound.

In a clever piece about that day, which would turn out to be more famous as far as baseball lore is concerned than the Krock-Keefe confrontation, Tim Wiles[5] introduced the story about the day's events this way:

> The city is abuzz with baseball excitement, as the visiting Chicago White Stockings (known today as the Cubs), winners of the National League pennant five of the last eight seasons, are in town to play the ascendant New York Giants, who will win the next two. The pennant chase is on, and the New York fans are hoping to steal a little bit of the Chicagos' glory at the old Polo Grounds, home of the Giants. Pennants and flags flap in the breeze atop the old double-decked wooden grandstand. The sound of brass bands pervades the festive atmosphere.
>
> Among the many fans in attendance are two of New York's gifted young actor-comedians, Digby Bell and DeWolf Hopper, both of the McCaull Opera Company. Both men are spirited baseball "cranks" as fans were then known, and they have persuaded their boss, Colonel John McCaull, to take the entire company on an outing to the baseball game. The flip side of their idea will take place later, as the ball clubs have been invited to take in the evening's performance, which will be dedicated to them.

The game that afternoon resulted in a 4 to 2 Krock victory, preventing Tim Keefe from notching his 20th straight, and that 4 to 2 score was, coincidentally, the same score of the game lost by the Mudville nine on the fateful day Casey came to bat. The connection between the real and the fictitious games would become increasingly palpable as the evening's entertainment unfolded.

The Chicago victory didn't derail the Giants' pennant parade, at that point cruising along at a 7½ game lead before game time, but the New York

In five full seasons with the Giants Tim Keefe averaged 34 wins, peaking with a 42 and 20 record in 1886. "Sir Timothy" was enshrined in the Hall of Fame in 1964.

faithful were chagrined that it took place at the expense of Keefe's bid for glory. No less disappointed were the members of the McCaull Opera Company who that evening would entertain both teams as special guests at Wallack's Theater in return for having been the guests of the Giants.

Here's the way Tim Wiles[6] describes the gala evening:

The crown jewel of the evening's performance was (DeWolf) Hopper's world premier performance of "Casey At the Bat," which, according to the New York World newspaper, was an unqualified hit ... Hopper himself, in his memoir "Once a Clown Always a Clown,"[7] recalled the memorable scene:

"When I dropped my voice to B flat, below low C, at 'but one scornful look from Casey, and the audience was awed,' I remember seeing Buck Ewing's mustachio give a single nervous twitch. And as the house, after a moment of startled silence, grasped the anticlimactic denouement, it shouted its glee. They had expected, as anyone does on hearing Casey for the first time, that the mighty batsman would slam the ball out of the lot, and a lesser bard would have had him do so...

Whether it was the grandeur of that evening, or Marcus "Fido" Baldwin, called by the New York Times "that clever pitcher," and his assortment of clever pitches, the Giants fared no better the next day, taking a whitewashing at the hands of Mr. Baldwin and his white stockinged compadres. But though the Whites won the season series in 1888, the Giants went on to capture the flag.

Prime movers in a lineup sporting four Famers around the diamond plus two more that formed the backbone of the mound corps, were hurlers Welch and Keefe. Particularly the latter. With 35 wins, 335 K's and a career low ERA of 1.74, to earn Triple Crown honors, "Sir Timothy" accomplished far more than winning 19 straight. He also led the league in shutouts (8), winning percentage (.745), opponents' low batting average (.196) and pitching runs (54), a linear weights measure that calculates the number of runs saved beyond what a league-average pitcher might save his team. Behind Keefe and Welch, who added 26 wins to New York's total, was the

"Cannonball Duo," Ed Crane (five wins) and Ledell Titcomb (14 and 8 on the season).

It was Cannonball Crane who put the icing on the Giants' cake in 1888, neither Keefe nor Welch having a hand in the pennant clincher on October 4th. That day Crane beat Chicago in a tight one, 1 to 0, before more than 8,000 Gothamites who whooped it up for several days in the aftermath of "The Cannonball's" one-hitter. The box score:

Chicago	R	H	PO	A	New York	R	H	PO	A
Ryan, cf	0	1	1	1	Tiernan, rf	0	0	2	0
Van Haltren, lf	0	0	1	0	Richardson, 2b	0	0	1	3
Duffy, rf	0	0	1	0	Connor, 1b	0	2	12	0
Anson, 1b	0	0	11	0	Ward, ss	0	0	0	5
Pfeffer, 2b	0	0	2	5	Foster, lf	0	0	0	0
Williamson, ss	0	0	2	2	Gore, cf	0	1	1	0
Burns, 3b	0	0	2	2	Whitney, 3b	1	1	0	1
Tener, p	0	0	0	6	Brown, c	0	0	11	0
Farrell, c	0	0	7	1	Crane, p	0	0	0	14
Totals	0	1	27	17	Totals	1	4	27	23

Line Score: New York   000 010 000   1–4–6

                Chicago   000 000 000   0–1–6

SB—Connor, Foster, Crane, Ryan 2, Anson 2, Burns
DP—Ward, Richardson and Connor
HPB—Foster, by Crane
WP—Crane 1, Tener
1 PB—Brown
Umpire—Mr. Kelly
Time—1:50
Attendance—8,000

The 1888 Season Series

May 10	NY	5	Chi	2	Welch, WP	Van Haltren, LP
May 12	Chi	9	NY	3	Baldwin, WP	Titcomb, LP
May 14	Chi	5	NY	1	Krock, WP	Welch, LP
June 8	NY	19	Chi	2	Welch, WP	Van Haltren, LP
June 9	Chi	8	NY	3	Krock, WP	Keefe, LP
June 11	Chi	4	NY	3	Krock, WP	Welch, LP
June 12	Chi	4	NY	2	Baldwin, WP	Keefe, LP
July 14	Chi	5	NY	1	Baldwin, WP	Welch, LP
July 15	NY	12	Chi	4	Keefe, WP	Baldwin, LP
July 16	NY	7	Chi	4	Keefe, WP	Krock, LP
August 14	Chi	4	NY	2	Krock, WP	Keefe, LP

August 15	Chi	2	NY	0	Baldwin, WP	Welch, LP
September 11	Chi	5	NY	3	Tener, WP	Welch, LP
September 12	forfeit to Chicago, 9–0					
September 13	Chi	9	NY	3	Tener, WP	Welch, LP
September 14	NY	7	Chi	3	Keefe, WP	Krock, LP
October 3	NY	3	Chi	0	Welch, WP	Gumbert, LP
October 4	NY	1	Chi	0	Crane, WP	Tener, LP
October 5	NY	12	Chi	3	Keefe, WP	Krock, LP

Could the Giants repeat their 1888 championship? Indeed they could, but not without a nerve-wracking, nail-biting finish that had New York's fandom holding their breath down to the very last game of regular season play. That day was October 5, a day on which three Hall of Fame pitchers would be put to work. In Pittsburgh, John Clarkson, who almost single-handedly had led Boston to championship contention, faced the Alleghenys, who had 23-game winner James "Pud" Galvin going for them. A New York loss and a Boston win would bring the flag back to Boston, while at the shores of Lake Erie, Cleveland was ready to throw sand into the Keefe-led New York machinery. The Giants, despite playing on foreign grounds, had only to win to bring home their second straight flag.

In both games, the winners got busy early. Pittsburgh produced three runs and New York two, on a home run blast by Mike Tiernan. Neither team squandered its first inning lead, Pittsburgh knocking Boston out of contention while the New Yorkers took care of business with a 5 to 3 win behind Tim Keefe's 28th season victory. With a 3 to 2 victory over Philadelphia, Chicago tied down third place, although far behind runnerup Boston.

Getting into a position to be able to win the 1889 pennant took herculean efforts on the part of the Giants, most of which took place during a 12-game winning streak in September. During the streak New York dusted off Chicago twice on the 14th, drawing them within a half game of front-running Boston, and then a victory on the 15th, combined with a Boston loss put them put them in the league's driver's seat. Doubles by Roger Connor and Jim O'Rourke came at opportune moments in New York's victory over Chicago in the second game of the September 14 doubleheader. The box score of that pivotal game follows:

New York	R	H	PO	A	Chicago	R	H	PO	A
Gore, cf	2	3	4	0	Ryan, cf	1	1	3	2
Tiernan, rf	2	0	2	0	Van Haltren, lf	0	0	2	0
Brown, c	1	3	2	1	Duffy, rf	1	1	0	1
Connor, 1b	0	1	9	0	Anson, 1b	1	2	3	1
Ward, ss	2	2	1	3	Pfeffer, 2b	0	0	2	4

The 1889 New York Giants: top row, Art Whitney, Tim Keefe, Roger Connor, Willard Brown, "Buck" Ewing; seated, Pat Murphy, "Cannonball" Crane, Monte Ward, Manager Jim Mutrie, Danny Richardson, Bill George and Jim O'Rourke.

New York	R	H	PO	A	Chicago	R	H	PO	A
Richardson, 2b	2	1	2	2	Williamson, ss	0	0	1	0
O'Rourke, lf	1	2	0	0	Burns, 3b	0	0	4	1
Whitney, 3b	2	2	1	1	Darling, c	0	0	6	0
Keefe, p	1	1	0	1	Dwyer, p	0	0	0	0
Totals	13	15	21	8	Totals	3	4	21	9

Line Score:	New York	003 082 0	13–15–2
	Chicago	200 000 1	3–4–5

2BH—Gore, Brown, Connor, Richardson, O'Rourke 2, Whitney 2, Keefe
SH—Van Haltren
LOB—New York 8, Chicago 0
SB—Tiernan, Brown, Connor, Richardson, Ryan, Duffy
HPB—Brown by Dwyer
K—Keefe 2, Dwyer 2
DP—Ryan and Darling
WP—Dwyer 2
Umpire—Mr. Power
Attendance—9,600

The 1889 Season Series

May 22	NY	11	Chi	4	Keefe, WP	Tener, LP
May 23	Chi	18	NY	17	Gumbert, WP	Hatfield, LP
May 24	NY	9	Chi	7	Welch, WP	Dwyer, LP
May 25	Chi	9	NY	8	Krock, WP	Keefe, LP
June 24	Chi	6	NY	0	Gumbert, WP	Crane, LP
June 25	NY	12	Chi	8	Crane, WP	Hutchison, LP
June 26	NY	12	Chi	7	Welch, WP	Tener, LP
June 27	NY	13	Chi	10	Crane, WP	Gumbert, LP
July 15	NY	7	Chi	4	Keefe, WP	Healy, LP
July 16	Chi	13	NY	10	Tener, WP	Crane, LP
July 17	NY	8	Chi	3	Welch, WP	Dwyer, LP
August 5	NY	8	Chi	7	Keefe, WP	Gumbert, LP
August 6	NY	10	Chi	8	Keefe, WP	Tener, LP
August 7	NY	4	Chi	2	Crane, WP	Tener, LP
September 14	NY	3	Chi	1	Welch, WP	Hutchison, LP
September 14	NY	13	Chi	3	Keefe, WP	Dwyer, LP
September 26	Chi	4	NY	3	Hutchison, WP	Welch, LP
September 27	NY	18	Chi	6	Keefe, WP	Tener, LP

The 1890 to 1894 Team Standings

	Team	Pos	Won	Lost	Pct.
1890	Brooklyn	1	86	43	.687
	Chicago	2	84	53	.613
	New York	6	63	68	.481
1891	Boston	1	87	51	.630
	Chicago	2	82	53	.607
	New York	3	71	61	.538
1892	Boston	1	102	48	.638
	Chicago	7	70	76	.479
	New York	8	71	80	.470
1893	Boston	1	86	43	.667
	New York	5	68	64	.515
	Chicago	9	56	71	.471
1894	Baltimore	1	89	39	.695
	New York	2	88	44	.667
	Chicago	8	57	75	.432

During the 1890 to 1900 seasons the Chicago White Stockings (during the post–Anson years the team took on several names before one and all decided on the team name that was to endure, the Cubs) were forced to deal with some new realities. What they might have imagined was a temporary glitch on the radar screen of their lofty National League status following their 1885 and '86 successes, soon turned out otherwise. In New York there were similar discoveries. The "Three B's," putting together a decade of league leadership, first Brooklyn with three titles, then Boston with four, and finally Baltimore with another threesome of first place spoils, let the erstwhile champs know in no uncertain terms that the old kings were dead—long live the new ones—at least through the last decade of the 19th century.

Before really heading south in the standings, the Chicagos wound up in the league's second slot (1890 and '91), and New York climbed up to the runner-up spot behind Baltimore in 1894 before heading into a franchise tailspin that would not get straightened around until the 1900s broke with new hopes and a new direction for both ballclubs. Consequently, the "Gay '90s" were not all that gay for New York and Chicago fans.

The decade of the '90s opened with New York and Chicago teams whose lineups no longer featured the names of the old stand-bys, Ewing, Connor, Ward, Keefe, Pfeffer, Ryan and Duffy. They were wearing Chicago and New York uniforms, all right, but of the Pirates and Players' League Giants. But many would be back in another year after the demise of players' rights and the Players' League itself. For both New York and Chicago the better years during this span came first. Despite the fact that Chicagoans, and in particular, New Yorkers, knew that the 1890 season would be a rough one, it was not without an awesome moment or two here and there. The downs and ups of the season:

Jimmy Ryan was a Chicago star for 16 seasons, enjoying his best year in 1888, when he led the NL in hits (182), homers (16) and slugging average (.515).

>> An astonishingly poor season at the gate opened with 4,644 on hand to see the Giants host the Phillies at the Polo Grounds. It was one of the biggest crowds of a season during which the Giants averaged but 919 per game. By July owner John Day found it necessary to call for help—and he got it. Realizing the stakes involved, not only for the New York franchise, but for the league as well, A. G. Spalding and Cap Anson launched a successful rescue effort to keep New York and the league in business.

>> In Chicago, the White Stockings, behind "Wild Bill" Hutchison, opened the season with a 5 to 4 win over Cincinnati before 6,311. He would go on to a 42–25 season, pitching 603 innings in 65 complete games (he started 66 times), while adding five relief appearances to his workhorse season. Between 1890 and '92 he pitched 1,786 innings, averaging 595.1 per season, an awesomely peerless feat.

>> On May 12, Silent Mike Tiernan's tape-measure blast in the bottom of the 13th inning beat Boston, 1 to 0. Newly arrived Amos Rusie outdueled Kid Nichols, pitching a strong three-hitter. Future Famer Nichols and manager Frank Selee, both of whom were in the

New Yorker "Silent Mike" Tiernan, whose noisy bat led helped the Giants win pennants in 1888 and 1889. He led the NL in runs scored (147) in 1889 and in slugging (.495) in 1890.

employ of Omaha in the Western Association the year before, began a long and highly successful Boston stay in 1890. Selee would take over the reins of the floundering Chicago ball club in 1902. The box score of the New York-Boston game:

New York	AB	R	H	PO	Boston	AB	R	H	PO
Tiernan, cf	6	1	2	2	Tucker, 1b	5	0	0	21
Glasscock, ss	6	0	0	5	McGarr, 3b	5	0	0	0
Esterbrook, 1b	5	0	0	14	Sullivan, lf	3	0	1	0
Bassett, 2b	5	0	0	3	Long, ss	4	0	0	1
Clarke, rf	5	0	0	0	Brodie, cf	4	0	1	2
Denny, 3b	5	0	1	3	Hardie, c	4	0	0	10
Hornung, lf	5	0	0	2	Smith, 2b	3	0	0	5
Buckley, c	5	0	0	10	Schellhase, rf	4	0	0	0
Rusie, p	5	0	1	2	Nichols, p	4	0	1	0
Totals	47	1	4	39	Totals	36	0	3	39

Line Score: Boston   000 000 000 000 0   0–3–5
                 New York   000 000 000 000 1   1–4–2

HR—Tiernan	PB—Hardie
SB—Tiernan, Glasscock	WP—Rusie (5–5)
SH—Glasscock, Tucker, Bassett	LP—Nichols (2–5)
LOB—Boston 5; New York 6	Umpires—Powers and McDermott
K—Rusie 11; Nichols 10	Time—2:00
BB—Rusie; Nichols 1	Attendance—1,000 plus

>> New York's spurt to contention in May, on the strength of an eight-game winning streak, was followed by a shabby June. The Giants never recovered, winding up under .500.

>> Rookie John Luby turned in a 20-game season for the Whites. 17 of the 20 during his streak were consecutive, culminating with a 3 to 2 conquest of the Giants on October third. The win was also Chicago's 11th straight.

The 1890 Season Series

May 24	NY	5	Chi	3	Rusie, WP	Coughlin, LP
May 26	NY	5	Chi	3	Rusie, WP	Hutchison, LP
May 27	NY	4	Chi	2	R. Murphy, WP	M. Sullivan, LP
May 28	Chi	5	NY	4	Hutchison, WP	Rusie, LP
June 21	NY	8	Chi	7	Welch, WP	Hutchison, LP
June 23	Chi	7	NY	3	M. Sullivan, WP	Burkett, LP
June 23	NY	6	Chi	4	Welch, WP	Hutchison, LP
June 24	NY	12	Chi	5	Rusie, WP	M. Sullivan, LP
July 7	Chi	4	NY	1	Hutchison, WP	Rusie, LP
July 8	Chi	3	NY	2	Luby, WP	Welch, LP
July 9	Chi	3	NY	2	Hutchison, WP	Rusie, LP
July 21	Chi	7	NY	2	Hutchison, WP	Rusie, LP
July 22	Chi	14	NY	7	Luby, WP	Welch, LP
July 23	Chi	13	NY	12	Hutchison, WP	Burkett, LP
August 25	Chi	6	NY	5	Luby, WP	Rusie, LP
August 26	Chi	4	NY	2	Stein, WP	Welch, LP
August 27	Chi	5	NY	1	Hutchison, WP	Rusie, LP
October 2	Chi	7	NY	3	Luby, WP	Rusie, LP
October 3	Chi	3	NY	2	Luby, WP	Rusie, WP

In 1891 there was a turnaround in the New York–Chicago confrontation, New York winning 13 games, as compared to their 6 and 13 showing the season before. Had they only been able to do as well against their other N.L. opponents they no doubt would have won the pennant, but Boston with 15, Pittsburgh with 12, and Philadelphia with 10, took the measure of the Giants 37 times to knock them into third place behind the Ansonmen. But if winning the flag wasn't possible, the return of Buck Ewing, fresh off a record-breaking $5,500 signing, along with George Gore, Big Jim Connor, and new pitching hero Amos Rusie, plus beating up on Chicago regularly, was a more-than-satisfying consolation. That also offset a number of mystifying moves made by manager Jim Mutrie as the season wore on down to its climactic September stages. Mutrie, it seems, refused to start his best talent against Boston as the Beaneaters, in the midst of an 18-game winning streak, swept to the pennant. While exonerated of any game-fixing mischief, the Giants decided that a new year would bring with it a new manager. Not only was there a new manager, Pat Powers, but the new manager announcement would be made each season for the next 10 straight years. The list stretched from Powers to John J. McGraw, who put an end to the Giants' annual replay of managerial musical chairs. The 1891 highlights:

>>   On June 13, 22,289 revved-up Polo Grounds fans thrilled to an 8 to 7 Amos Rusie victory over the Chicago Colts' Ed Stein. The New York crowd set a new National League attendance record.

>>   Rusie, who went on to post a 33-win season, including a league-leading six shutouts, beat the "Ansons" with a brilliant two-hitter, 5 to 0 at the Polo Grounds on June 17. The box score:

Chicago	R	H	PO	A		New York	R	H	PO	A
Ryan, cf	0	1	1	0		Tiernan, rf	1	1	3	0
Wilmot, lf	0	0	2	1		Richardson, ss	0	0	3	4
Dahlen, 3b	0	0	2	1		Gore, cf	2	1	2	0
Anson, 1b	0	0	5	1		Connor, 1b	1	1	9	1
Carroll, lf	0	1	1	0		O'Rourke, lf	0	2	0	0
Cooney, ss	0	0	3	4		Bassett, 2b	0	0	1	3
Pfeffer, 2b	0	0	8	2		Clarke, 3b	0	0	0	1
Luby, p	0	0	1	0		Buckley, c	1	1	9	0
Kittridge, c	0	0	4	2		Rusie, p	0	0	0	0
Totals	0	2	27	11		Totals	5	6	27	9

Line Score: New York   202 001 000   5–6–1
               Chicago   000 000 000   0–2–1

HR—Beckley
SB—Tiernan 2, Gore, Bassett, Wilmot, Luby
SH—Richardson, Luby, Dahlen
DP—Bassett and Connor
K—Rusie 8; Luby 2

HBP—Carroll (by Rusie)
WP—Luby
PB—Kittridge
Umpire—Mr. Powers

>> Another gem by Amos Rusie, this time a no-hitter, felled the Brooklyn Bridegrooms on July 31, 6 to 0. At age 20 and two months, he became the youngest no-hit author in baseball history.

>> Rookie John McGraw debuted with the Baltimore American Association team at shortstop on August 26 with one hit and an error as Baltimore beat Columbus 6 to 5.

>> On September 4, "Old Man" Anson, who had waited for a Boston playing date, donned a fake gray beard with long whiskers as he led his charges to a 5 to 4 victory over the Beaneaters. Nearing 40, he had already been adjudged "over-the-hill" by Boston's press.

Amos Rusie (Hall of Fame, 1977), who was traded to Cincinnati for none less than Christy Mathewson in 1900, was the N.L.'s biggest gate attraction during the 1890s. His crackling heater accounted for 345 whiffs in 1890 and he led the league in that department six straight times. (George Brace photograph)

The 1891 Season Series

May 26	NY	5	Chi	4	Rusie, WP	Hutchison, LP
May 27	NY	12	Chi	1	Sharrott, WP	Luby, LP
May 28	Chi	3	NY	2	Hutchison, WP	Rusie, LP
June 12	NY	9	Chi	6	Rusie, WP	Hutchison, LP
June 13	NY	8	Chi	7	Rusie, WP	Stein, LP
June 15	NY	14	Chi	13	Welch, WP	Hutchison, LP
June 16	NY	5	Chi	0	Rusie, WP	Luby, LP

July 10	Chi	8	NY	6	Hutchison, WP	Rusie, LP
July 11	NY	15	Chi	6	Rusie, WP	Stein, LP
July 13	NY	7	Chi	3	Rusie, WP	Hutchison, LP
August 10	Chi	4	NY	3	Hutchison, WP	Rusie, LP
August 11	NY	2	Chi	0	J. Ewing, WP	Luby, LP
August 12	NY	8	Chi	2	Rusie, WP	Hutchison, LP
September 1	Chi	4	NY	1	Vickery, WP	J. Ewing, LP
September 2	Chi	14	NY	2	Gumbert, WP	Rusie, LP
September 17	NY	3	Chi	1	Rusie, WP	Vickery, LP
September 18	NY	9	Chi	8	J. Ewing, WP	Gumbert, LP
September 19	NY	4	Chi	0	Rusie, WP	Hutchison, LP

During the 1892 to '94 seasons, at a low point in organized baseball's history that was marked by monopoly, greed and internecine warfare among the National League's 12-team circuit, neither Chicago nor New York could overcome a preoccupation with front office struggles and their direct involvement with the league's crises. That left its mark on the playing field. Aside from the Giants' second place finish in 1894, both clubs found their way into the nether regions of the bloated league's second division. That was a revolting development in both cities, but a reality. And that harsh reality would not be altered until much later. The years "in the wilderness" were upon them.

1892–1894: With a Foot on the Slippery Slope:

THE 1892 SEASON

>> Bill Hutchison, a Yale grad, fired a one-hitter to beat the Giants 8 to 0, on May 7. At season's end he led the N.L. in wins (36), games (75), CG (67), IP (627) and K's (314).

>> Between May 4 and 21 Anson's Colts ran off 13 consecutive victories.

>> June 30: Cincinnati and Chicago battled to a 7–7 tie in 20 innings, the 19th century's longest game. The Reds' Tony Mullane, a 21-game winner, and Chicago's Addy Gumbert both went the route, both pitchers shutting out their opponents the last 15 innings of the game, which was called due to darkness.

>> Jimmy Ryan hit safely in 29 straight games between July 9 and August 14, 2nd on the Cubs' all time list. Ryan leads all Cubs players with 22 career leadoff homers. One of them was hit on August 22 in a 3-for-3 day as Chicago beat New York 7 to 1.

>> Willie Keeler, eventually a Hall of Famer, debuted with the Giants on September 30, played in 14 games and ended the season at .317.

The 1892 Season Series

May 6	Chi 6	NY 3	Gumbert, WP	Rusie, LP
May 7	Chi 8	NY 0	Hutchison, WP	King, LP
May 26	NY 3	Chi 2	Rusie, WP	Hutchison, LP
May 27	Chi 4	NY 1	Luby, WP	King, LP
May 28	Chi 10	NY 4	Hutchison, WP	Rusie, LP
July 4	NY 11	Chi 2	Rusie, WP	Gumbert, LP
July 4	Chi 12	NY 5	Hutchison, WP	Crane, LP
July 20	Chi 8	NY 6	Hutchison, WP	Crane, LP
July 21	NY 5	Chi 1	Rusie, WP	Luby, LP
August 22	Chi 7	NY 1	Hutchison, WP	Rusie, LP
August 23	Chi 8	NY 7	Gumbert, WP	Crane, LP
September 5	Chi 6	NY 1	Gumbert, WP	Crane, LP
September 5	Chi 7	NY 2	Hutchison, WP	Rusie, LP
September 6	NY 12	Chi 5	King, WP	Gumbert, LP

THE 1893 SEASON

Versatile George Davis, elected to the Hall of Fame in 1999, fielded brilliantly and hit with authority. He joined the Giants in 1883 with Buck Ewing. The two became field leaders for the Giants. (George Brace photograph)

>> The game's playing rules had been in a constant of flux for 15 years, but took its most drastic step when it moved the pitcher's box back to the present-day 60'6" *and* ruled that the pitcher must deliver his pitches from a white rubber plate 12"×4". With it came an upsurge in hitting and offense that brought record crowds to the ball park. New York and Chicago doubled their 1892 attendance marks.

>> One of the finest all-around ball players in the game's history, George Davis, finally elected to the Hall of Fame in 1998, set a major league record on June 14 against Chi-

cago by slamming a homer and a triple in the same inning. In 1897 he set a still-standing record for shortstops by driving home 136 runs for the Giants. His 33 game hit streak was an 1893 Giants' highlight.

>>   In the season series New York only won five of the 12 games played against Chicago but wound up 10 games ahead of "The Ansons" with a 68–64 record, compared to Chicago's 56 and 71.

>>   The June 14 game between Chicago and the Giants at the Polo Grounds was typical of the 1893 slugfests around the league. In this game Davis cracked his homer and triple in the fourth inning. The box score follows:

Chicago	R	H	PO	A	New York	R	H	PO	A
Ryan, cf	2	1	1	0	Burke, lf	1	1	4	0
Dahlen, ss	2	3	1	2	Ward, 2b	2	1	2	3
Dungan, rf	1	2	0	0	Tiernan, rf	1	3	1	1
Anson, 1b	1	2	8	0	Connor, 1b	2	2	8	1
Lange, 2b	0	1	3	4	Davis, 3b	3	2	1	1
Wilmot, lf	1	1	2	0	Doyle, cf, c	2	3	4	0
Parrott, 3b	2	2	1	1	McMahon, c	0	0	1	0
McGill, p	0	0	0	1	Lyons, cf	2	2	2	0
McGinness, p	1	1	0	0	Crane, p	1	1	1	3
Schriver, c	1	1	8	2	Fuller, ss	1	1	3	2
					Baldwin, p	0	0	0	0
Totals	11	14	24	10	Totals	15	16	27	11

Line score: Chicago   200   110   313   11–16–9
                 New York   010 [10]22 00x   15–16–2

2BH—Dahlen, Dungan, Burke, Fuller
3BH—Davis, Wilmot
HR—Davis, Tiernan
SH—Dungan, Schriver 2, Davis
SB—Lange, Parrott, McGill, Ward, Tiernan, Connor, Davis, Doyle 2, Lyons
LOB—Chicago 13; New York 7
K—McGill 2; McGinness 4; Crane 1
BB—McGill 3; McGinness 2; Crane 10
DP—Lange, Dahlen and Anson
WP—McGill 2; Crane 2
LP—McGill
Win. P—Crane
Umpire—Mr. Hurst
Attendance—5,000

The 1893 Season Series

June 14	NY	15	Chi	11	Crane, WP	McGill, LP
June 15	Chi	9	NY	6	Mauck, WP	Baldwin, LP
June 16	Chi	10	NY	9	Mauck, WP	Rusie, LP
June 29	NY	12	Chi	6	Rusie, WP	McGinness, LP
June 30	Chi	9	NY	5	Hutchison, WP	Baldwin, LP
July 1	NY	1	Chi	0	Rusie, WP	Mauck, LP
August 22	NY	17	Chi	7	German, WP	Hutchison, LP
August 23	NY	6	Chi	0	Rusie, WP	McGill, LP
August 24	Chi	10	NY	4	Clausen, WP	Petty, LP
September 25	Chi	5	NY	4	Clausen, WP	Baldwin, LP
September 26	Chi	9	NY	5	McGill, WP	Rusie, LP
September 27	Chi	7	NY	2	Clausen, WP	German, LP

THE 1894 SEASON

>> Baltimore's Orioles, with John McGraw at third, Hughie Jennings at shortstop, an OF with Famers Keeler and Kelley, and Wilbert Robinson behind the plate, won the pennant, hogging baseball's headlines. But the real story was at the Polo Grounds, where the Giants under manager Monte Ward kept the pressure on the O's all summer long before winding up in second place, having won twice as many games as they lost, and humiliating the Ansonmen in the season series with 10 wins in 12 tries.

>> Two Chicagoans, pitcher Clark Griffith, who registered the first of his six straight 20-win seasons, and shortstop Bill Dahlen, who put together hitting streaks of 42 and 28 games (he had a hit in 72 out of 73 games during those streaks) came of age in Hall of Fame careers. In the midst of his second streak, his four-hit game at the Polo Grounds on August 21 was highlighted by a triple and two doubles (see the box score of the Giants' 13 to 11 victory).

>> On May 24, Fred Pfeffer accepted a record 21 chances in an 11 inning game against St. Louis at Chicago's West Side Park.

>> Versatile George Decker, who played every OF and INF position, boomed a tape measure blast of some 500 feet in Chicago's 24 to 6 rout of Pittsburgh on July 25.

>> The Giants swept the Orioles in the Temple Cup series 4 games to none, Amos Rusie and Jouett Meekin each winning two, to pace the Giants as they had done during the regular season, when Rusie won 36 and Meekin, 33 games.

>> The 1894 Colts-Giants, Dahlen highlight game of August 21. Box
    score:

Chicago	R	H	PO	A		New York	R	H	PO	A
Ryan, rf	2	3	2	0		Burke, lf	2	2	2	0
Dahlen, ss	3	4	6	4		Tiernan, rf	0	0	2	0
Wilmot, lf	1	1	2	0		Davis, 3b	2	1	1	1
Decker, 1b	1	0	7	0		Doyle, 1b	1	2	11	0
Lange, cf	0	1	5	0		Ward, 2b	2	1	3	4
Irwin, 3b	1	1	2	1		Van Haltren, cf	1	0	4	1
Parrott, 2b	0	1	2	2		Fuller, ss	2	1	0	6
Schriver, c	1	2	1	3		Wilson, c	1	1	4	0
Hutchison, p	2	2	0	1		German, p	2	3	0	1
Stratton, p	0	0	0	2						
Totals	11	15	27	13		Totals	13	11	27	13

Line Score: New York   000 332 410   13–11–5
               Chicago   320 300 003   11–15–1

2BH—German, Dahlen 2
3BH—Burke, Ryan, Dahlen, Irwin
HR—Burke, Hutchison
SH—Wilmot, Ward
SB—Ward, Fuller, Wilmot, Decker
LOB—New York 6; Chicago 7
HPB—Decker
PB—Schriver
WP—German 2; Hutchison
Umpire—Mr. McQuaid

The 1894 Season Series

June 7	NY	8	Chi	7	Westervelt, WP	Terry, LP
June 8	NY	3	Chi	0	Rusie, WP	McGill, LP
June 9	Chi	10	NY	9	Griffith, WP	Meekin, LP
June 28	NY	6	Chi	5	Rusie, WP	Terry, LP
June 29	NY	14	Chi	8	Meekin, WP	Hutchison, LP
August 18	Chi	6	NY	4	Stratton, WP	German, LP
August 20	NY	1	Chi	3	Rusie, WP	Griffith, LP
August 21	NY	13	Chi	11	German, LP	Hutchison. LP
September 17	NY	5	Chi	4	Meekin, WP	Hutchison, LP
September 18	NY	4	Chi	3	Rusie, WP	Terry, LP
September 18	NY	9	Chi	6	Clarke, WP	Griffith, LP
September 19	NY	4	Chi	3	Meekin, WP	Hutchison, LP

Season Standings: 1895–1901

Year	Team	Pos.	Won	Lost	Pct.
1895	Baltimore	1	87	43	.669
	Chicago	4	72	58	.554
	New York	9	66	65	.504
1896	Baltimore	1	90	39	.698
	Chicago	5	71	57	.555
	New York	7	64	67	.489
1897	Boston	1	93	39	.705
	New York	3	83	48	.634
	Chicago	9	59	73	.447
1898	Boston	1	102	47	.685
	Chicago	4	85	65	.567
	New York	7	77	73	.513
1899	Brooklyn	1	101	47	.682
	Chicago	8	75	73	.507
	New York	10	60	90	.400
1900	Brooklyn	1	82	54	.603
	Chicago	5(t)	65	75	.464
	New York	8	60	78	.435
1901	Pittsburgh	1	90	49	.647
	Chicago	6	53	68	.381
	New York	7	52	85	.380

The turbulence of the '90s stretched into the turn of a new century, a decade plus, accented by powerful forces and movements that not only stirred America, but nations abroad, as well. The more discerning in foreign capitals sensed major trouble ahead even though a deceiving surface calm prevailed. The situation in Organized Baseball was no less volatile despite a failed 1890 revolution that gave rise, and a quick demise, to the Players League. Even so, the issues embedded in that revolt simply refused to go away, and by the end of the era, with the advent of another new league, there was no alternative in the minds of baseball's mighty but all out warfare—once again.

Although the New Yorks and Chicagos escaped the embarrassment of complete failure or franchise dissolution, they floundered through the last years of the century, fielding teams that were but shadows of their former greatness. New York's third place finish in 1897 and Chicago's fourth place finishes in 1895 and '98 were about all that either could manage. And as for the Chicago-New York rivalry, there was only one season during which the Giants placed ahead of Chicago, 1897, when its final third place position far outdistanced Cap Anson's last team, which was unceremoniously dumped into ninth place, its miserable 59–73 record a sad coda for the 19th century's greatest diamond figure. Aside from that momentary spark of first division vigor, the Giants' ineptitude, much to the humiliating chagrin of the New York faithful, put the ball club on a oneway ride headed for the basement of the league. That's where they finally landed in 1902 even as John McGraw, recently employed in July of that same year, came to New York to try his hand at restoring at least a semblance of order among the ranks of a thoroughly disoriented and lackluster ball club. My-Way-Or-the-Highway McGraw would waste not a moment in setting about his task.

The 1895 and 1896 Seasons

1895

>>   .300 hitters were a dime a dozen in the mid–'90s. Both Chicago and New York had three heavy duty hitters: New York with Mike Tiernan (.347), George Davis (.343) and George Van Haltren (.340). Chicago's Cap Anson, who had hit .388 the season before (at age 42), hit .335, rookie Bill Everitt (.358), Bill "Little Eva" Lange (.389) and Jimmy Ryan (.317). The league averaged .296.

>>   Clark Griffith (26–15) led Chicago's paper-thin pitching staff, while "The Hoosier Thunderbolt," Amos Rusie, could muster only a break-even 23–23 record for New York's woebegone ninth place team.

>>   More than controversial, Andrew Freedman took over the Giants franchise in January, alienating one and all from fellow owners to players, to managers, to the press, and even to crusty Tammany Hall officials. Steinbrenner-like, he hired and fired incessantly, using up three managers his first season at the helm.

Clark Griffith, a foxy, tough pitcher in the clutch, who beat the Giants four times without a setback in 1898. That season he won a career-high 26 games.

>> On July 6th Amos Rusie and "Wild Bill" Hutchison met for the last time, as Rusie "Chicagoed" Anson's charges, 8 to 0. During the course of their rivalry the two famous 19th century hurlers posted the following records:

1890	Rusie, 1–5	Hutchison, 5–1
1891	Rusie, 5–2	Hutchison, 2–5
1892	Rusie, 1–3	Hutchison, 3–1
1895	Rusie, 1–0	Hutchison, 0–1
Totals	Rusie, 8–10	Hutchison, 10–8

Rusie vs. Chicago, 1890 to 1898:	W30; L20
Hutchison vs. New York, 1889 to 1895:	W17; L20

>> On June 23 the entire Chicago ball club was arrested because on that Sunday Rev. W. W. Clark, head of the "Sunday Observance League" notified Cleveland police that a game was to take place. Chicago owner James A. Hart posted bond, the game went on (10,000 were on hand), and Chicago beat Cleveland 13 to 4 behind Clark Griffith.

The 1895 Season Series

May 14	NY	14	Chi	1	Rusie, WP	Terry, LP
May 15	NY	9	Chi	1	Meekin, WP	Hutchison, LP
May 30	NY	7	Chi	6	Meekin, WP	Hutchison, LP
May 30	Chi	3	NY	2	Terry, WP	Rusie, LP
May 31	NY	11	Chi	4	Clarke, WP	Hutchison, LP
June 10	NY	5	Chi	4	Clarke, WP	Griffith, LP
July 6	NY	8	Chi	0	Rusie, WP	Hutchison, LP
July 8	Chi	5	NY	4	Terry, WP	Clarke, WP
July 9	NY	1	Chi	0	Rusie, WP	Griffith, LP
September 3	NY	6	Chi	3	Meekin, WP	Hutchison, LP
September 10	Chi	13	NY	2	Friend, WP	Rusie, LP
September 10	Chi	8	NY	6	Parker, WP	Meekin, LP

1896

>> The biggest 1896 off-the-field battle occurred in the front office of the Giants where Mr. Freedman, who had leveled a $200 fine on popular star Amos Rusie, soon found that his ace pitcher would not sign his 1896 contract. It precipitated not only a sabbatical for Rusie, who didn't throw a single pitch that season, but a series of events pivoting once again on players' rights that stretched over several seasons of legal posturing and, finally, another acrimonious battle over the

league's presidency, its management, and its confrontations with the insurgent forces that aligned themselves with a new league bearing the "presumptuous" title, the American League.

>> In 1892 the National League averaged .245. When the move to a 60'6" distance from the plate to a new 12"×4" pitching mound was made in 1893, the league average soared to .280. In 1894 it moved upward to .309, in 1895 back to .295, and dropped still farther in 1896 to .290, still high, but on a downward trend. Pitchers like Cy Young, Kid Nichols, Nig Cuppy and Billy Rhines had come on to tame the hitting beast somewhat. The trend would continue until during the new century's first decade, when the .300 hitter would become a rarity. The era of trick pitches, crafty moundsmen, defensive piracy and intimidating, scuffling ball players was right around the bend. As a matter of plain fact, the Baltimores and Pittsburghs and Clevelands were already "into it."

>> Handyman George Decker, who occasionally spelled Anson, but whose regular patrol was in the OF, ran together a 26-game hitting streak, but Bill Dahlen, Jimmy Ryan, Anson, now 44 and still capable of a strong .331 with 90 ribbies, Bill Everitt and Bill Lange all hit better than .300 to lead the Colts to a fifth place finish at 71 and 57.

Scrappy Bill Dahlen, Chicago shortstop from 1891 to 1898. He hit .357 and stole 42 bases in 1894.

>> The Giants' top foursome of Van Haltren, newly acquired 2nd-baseman Kid Gleason, old reliable Mike Tiernan and George Davis hit .335 between them and Jouett Meekin had a 26–14 year, but there was little help elsewhere and three managers could coax no more than a 64–67 record out of Freedman's seventh place finishers.

>> On July 12 at Chicago's West Side Park digs, "Big Ed" Delehanty entered the record books with baseball's second, four-dinger game, although

his Phillies lost to the homestanding Colts by the margin of a home run, 9 to 8.

The 1896 Season Series

May 18	Chi	15	NY	3	Terry, WP	Seymour, LP
May 19	NY	7	Chi	0	Clarke, WP	Friend, LP
May 20	NY	19	Chi	4	Meekin, WP	Parker, LP
June 1	NY	10	Chi	3	Doheny, WP	Friend, LP
June 2	NY	8	Chi	5	Meekin, WP	Griffith, LP
June 3	Chi	14	NY	8	Friend, WP	Clarke, LP
July 9	Chi	9	NY	1	Terry, WP	Sullivan, LP
July 10	Chi	11	NY	5	Griffith, WP	Clarke, LP
July 11	Chi	3	NY	2	Friend, WP	Meekin, LP
August 19	NY	8	Chi	5	Clarke, WP	Terry, WP
August 20	NY	9	Chi	5	Meekin, WP	Griffith, LP
August 21	NY	8	Chi	6	Clarke, WP	Friend, LP

1897: The Captain Says Goodbye

Adrian Constatine Anson, for 27 seasons a professional ball player *par excellence,* played his last game in St. Louis on October 3, 1897, setting records and playing all-out to the very end. In the first game of two played in the Mound City that day he became the oldest player ever to hit for the circuit. He was 45, and it was time to bid adieu to the game he loved, the team he captained and managed for so many years, and to the many people in baseball who, though they might not have appreciated or liked his style, respected him as they did few others. He had been a colossus astride the world of baseball, there from the very beginning of the professional game in 1871, and still a force to be reckoned with 27 seasons later.

In the best of all baseball worlds Chicago would have been a National League champion in 1897, sending The Captain off with one last triumphant

The one and only Adrian "Cap" Anson, bicycle handle mustache and all.

hurrah, but Anson's last ball club was not cut from that kind of cloth. Boston, under Frank Selee, soon to be tapped for a major reconstruction job of the Orphans,[8] was the 1897 champ, chased doggedly by Baltimore. The third place team in the '97 race was the Giants, managed by the kind of a scrapper Anson could relate to, Bill Joyce, who shook the New Yorkers out of their second division swoon long enough to hoist them into momentary respectability.

Finishing ninth, some 34 games out of the running, Anson's last ball club had but two players, Jimmy Ryan and Fred Pfeffer, back in Chicago for one last season in The Bigs, who had been part of the mid–'80s champions. New York's Giants, on the other hand, won 83 ball games with a veteran lineup that sported solid pitching (Rusie, Meekin and lefty Cy Seymour who would later tear the league apart with a league-leading .377 in 1905 as a Cincinnati Redleg), and five .300 hitters. The difference in their 19-game leap from 64 wins the year before was hustle. It was to be their last brush with respectability until McGraw, at the time busily engaged with Baltimore's perennial contenders, would come along.

In an otherwise dismal season there was one last explosion reminiscent of the old White Stockings power. On June 29 the Colts pummeled Louisville's Colonels, racking up 36 runs, scoring in every inning, as each player registered at least one hit and scored at least one run. It was the third time a Chicago team had scored 30 runs or more in a nine inning ball game. The others: Chicago 30, Louisville 7, July 22, 1876; Chicago 35, Cleveland 4, July 24, 1882; Chicago 31, Buffalo 7, July 3, 1883. The box score of the June 29, 1897 game follows.

Chicago	AB	R	H	PO	Louisville	AB	R	H	PO
Everitt, 3b	7	3	2	0	Clarke, lf	4	0	3	2
McCormick, ss	8	5	6	4	McCreery, rf	4	1	0	0
Lange, cf	7	4	4	4	Pickering, cf	5	1	2	1
Anson, 1b	4	4	1	10	Stafford, ss	5	1	0	3
Ryan, rf	6	5	2	0	Werden, 1b	5	1	3	14
Decker, lf	4	2	3	0	Dexter, 3b	5	0	4	3
Connor, 2b	6	4	4	2	Butler, c	5	0	0	3
Callahan, p	7	4	5	1	Johnson, 2b	0	0	0	0
Donahue, c	6	3	3	5	Fraser, p	0	0	0	0
Thornton, lf	2	2	2	1	Jones, p	3	2	1	0
					Delehanty, 2b	3	1	1	1
Totals	57	36	32	27	Totals	39	7	14	27

Line Score: Chicago   357 121 278   36–32–1
             Louisville   001 050 100   7–14–9

2BH—Callahan 2, Werden 2, Dexter 2, Everitt, Ryan, Decker, Jones, Donahue,
    Delehanty
3BH—Lange, McCormick, Connor
HR—Ryan, McCormick
SH—Everitt, McCreery
SB—McCormick 2, Lange 2, Connor, Callahan, Donahue
LP—Fraser
Umpire—John Sheridan
Time—2:15

The 1897 Season Series

May 24	NY	4	Chi	1	Sullivan, WP	Griffith, LP
May 25	NY	8	Chi	0	Rusie, WP	Denzer, LP
May 26	Chi	6	NY	2	Griffith, WP	Doheny, LP
June 5	Chi	10	NY	4	Griffith, WP	Rusie, LP
June 6	NY	10	Chi	6	Sullivan, WP	Griffith, LP
July 22	Chi	4	NY	3	Griffith, WP	Rusie, LP
July 23	Chi	14	NY	3	Friend, WP	Clarke, LP
July 24	NY	7	Chi	3	Meekin, WP	Friend, LP
August 26	NY	19	Chi	6	Rusie, WP	Griffith, LP
August 27	NY	9	Chi	3	Meekin, WP	Friend, LP
August 27	NY	6	Chi	3	Sullivan, WP	Briggs, LP
August 30	Chi	7	NY	5	Griffith, WP	Seymour, LP

From 1898 To Nowhere

The era titled "Losing It and Putting It Back Together" came to an end with a portentous brace of four years, from 1898 through 1901, that spelled big trouble, and not only for the New York and Chicago franchises. The National League was no less vulnerable to the fierce winds of change howling at its doorstep. By the time it was all over a new century had dawned, Andrew Freedman, seemingly bent on bringing down both his own franchise and the league with it, would be on the way out, and a new league, side-stepping existing conventions and power structures, audaciously calling itself "major," would debut right under the noses of National League cities. The mass upheaval carried with it untold numbers of strange twists and turns for players, managers, fans, and frantic owners around the league.

One of the stranger of those twists and turns involved no less than the recently retired Cap Anson, who was put back into a uniform, that of the Giants, at that, as manager of the faltering New York forces in mid–June of 1898. Anson's enthusiasm for the job quickly waned, however, in the face of the meddling, abrasive Andrew Freedman, who was soon informed, in the usual brusque, Ansonesque manner, that hizzoner would need a new manager, better suited to the "yes, sir" role than The Captain. For Freedman, accepting Anson's resignation was just another thing to do on a long list for another day. The Giants' managerial reins promptly fell back into the hands of Bill Joyce, who had started the season as New York's skipper. Freeman saw the whole sordid mess as business *de rigueuer*.

In Anson's last farewell to the game the Giants had played at a sub-.500 clip, winning but 9 of the 24 games he managed. Even the one bright spot, Cap's return to Chicago for a two-game set at the end of June, for which over 9,000 turned out to watch the venerable warrior receive a huge floral piece before the game, was marred by two straight losses to his former Chicago charges, although it would have been understandable if some inner alarm bell had gone off, prying loose a run or two for the old White Stockings.

In 1898

>> Silent Mike Tiernan hit for the cycle on August 25.

>> Frank Chance debuted as Chicago's catcher on April 29 in a game against Louisville with Clark Griffith on the mound. The Orphans beat the Colonels 16 to 2. The "next Anson" crossed paths with Chicago's erstwhile major domo during Anson's brief managerial stint in New York.

>> Tommy Burns led the Orphans to an 85 and 65 record, but after a 75 and 73, 1899 season he was released in favor of the veteran manager Tom Loftus.

>> Talented George Van Haltren, by '98 into his 12th ML season, became the first Giant to garner 200 hits in a single season, with 204. His 654 ABs led the N.L..

The 1898 Season Series

June 7	Chi	3	NY	0	Griffith, WP	Seymour, LP
June 8	Chi	9	NY	1	Callahan, WP	Rusie, LP
June 9	Chi	10	NY	8	Kilroy, WP	Doheny, LP
June 10	Chi	7	NY	6	Griffith, WP	Meekin, LP
June 29	Chi	12	NY	4	Callahan, WP	Meekin, LP
June 30	Chi	7	NY	5	Isbell, WP	Seymour, LP
July 1	NY	8	Chi	4	Rusie, WP	Thornton, WP
July 2	NY	8	Chi	6	Meekin, WP	Callahan, LP

August 12	NY	4	Chi	3	Rusie, WP	Callahan, LP
August 13	NY	9	Chi	2	Meekin, WP	Woods, LP
August 27	Chi	10	NY	3	Griffith, WP	Seymour, LP
August 28	Chi	12	NY	7	Callahan, WP	Doheny, LP
August 29	NY	2	Chi	1	Rusie, WP	Thornton, WP
August 30	Chi	1	NY	0	Griffith, WP	Meekin, LP

1899 and "Syndicate Baseball"

Baseball's world at the close of the 19th century, per its 1890s habits, teetered at the edge of self-destruction. "Syndicate Baseball," a management ploy that enabled owners like Chicago's Al Spalding and New York's John Brush to hold stock in more than one franchise (Spalding, interestingly, owned stock in the New York Giants), as well as renewed interest in the formation of another major league, had the magnates uneasy. By the end of a season that produced a Brooklyn championship in the 12-team N.L., but no playoff winner of any kind for the first time since 1883, there was common consent at least on one thing: 12 teams in one league were four too many. The weaker among them had to go. That item of business was finally settled in March of 1900 when Louisville, Washington, Cleveland and Baltimore were pared from the senior circuit's vine.

On the field of play the New York and Chicago entries, suffering under the distraction of management whose heads were clearly elsewhere, played out the season, "Orphaned" in Chicago not only by Adrian Anson, but by the front office as well, and in New York by Andrew Freedman, whose interests were, as usual, *not* primarily out there on the diamond. The two teams staggered to a 7 to 6 season series, with Chicago finishing on top. Their .539 percentage in the annual New York-Chicago fracas matched their N.L. record, which wound up two games above the .500 level at 75 and 73. The Giants, inept to the very end, wound up their season losing to a career one-gamer, Billy Ging of Frank Selee's Boston Beaneaters, 2 to 1 at the Polo Grounds. *Sporting Life*'s correspondent reported:

> The Giants could do nothing with Ging of New London, and barely avoided a shutout [*Sporting Life*, November, 1899].

Had it not been for the four teams that were soon to be jettisoned from the league, the Chicagos and the New Yorks would have wound up in the last two spots in the standings, a morose state of affairs as the century wound down to its last hours. Despite that there were some redeeming moments afield. 24-year-old Bill Carrick, who lost 27 but still managed to be the Giants' ace with 16 wins and a league league-leading 40 complete games, shut out the Orphans and Jack Taylor 3 to 0 at Coogan's Bluff, and three double plays helped Taylor get revenge later in the season when he scattered nine hits in a tight, 3 to 2 win at West Side Park. Carrick soon dropped out of sight, but more would soon be heard from "The Brakeman," and for several interesting reasons.

To close out this 19th century review of Chicago and New York baseball heroes, we present a listing of the teams' top hurlers and how they fared in New York and Chicago games:

Name	Years	Won	Lost	Pct.
Jim McCormick, Chicago	1885–86	11	3	.786
Larry Corcoran, Chicago	1883–85	13	10	.611
Amos Rusie, New York	1890–98	30	20	.600
Clark Griffith, Chicago	1893–00	16	12	.571
Bobby Mathews, New York	1874–76	13	10	.565
John Clarkson, Chicago	1884–87	12	10	.545
Jouett Meekin, New York	1894–99	13	9	.542
Mickey Welch, New York	1883–90	33	28	.541
Tim Keefe, New York	1885–89	16	18	.471
Bill Hutchison, Chicago	1890–95	17	20	.459
George Zettlein, Chicago	1871, '74–'75	7	12	.368

The 1899 Season Series

June 18	Chi	3	NY	2	J. Taylor, WP	Meekin, LP
June 29	Chi	17	NY	9	Griffith, WP	Doheny, LP
July 1	Chi	10	NY	9	Phyle, WP	Meekin, LP
July 18	Chi	7	NY	6	Griffith, WP	Meekin, LP
July 19	NY	3	Chi	0	Carrick, WP	J. Taylor, LP
July 20	NY	4	Chi	1	Seymour, WP	Garvin, LP
August 28	NY	6	Chi	4	Seymour, WP	Griffith, LP
August 28	Chi	11	NY	3	Cogan, WP	Gettig, LP
August 29	NY	6	Chi	2	Gettig, WP	Garvin, LP
August 30	Chi	3	NY	2	J. Taylor, WP	Doheny, LP
September 12	NY	6	Chi	5	Gettig, WP	Griffith, LP
September 13	NY	13	Chi	2	Seymour, WP	Malarkey, LP

1900—1901: Nowhere To Go But Up

The restlessness in Organized Baseball continued apace as a new century dawned. Before the first season of the 1900s began, the new eight-team circuit was rechristened with its former title, The National League. That replaced the former "League Association," a name as awkward sounding as the 12-team "union" that came into existence when the older National League literally swallowed up its American Association competitors. The renamed circuit's schedule called for each team to play the others in the league 20 times in a trimmed-down, 140-game season.

The 20 game, Giants-Orphans season series wound up with the Giants on the losing end 12 times. Their .400 "winning" percentage was just about as abysmal as their eighth place wind up in the league standings, marking a first in New York's history: a dead last finish in the league standings. In 1901 they escaped the cellar, but not by much. Cincinnati outdid them in the race for the basement by a game as New York lost two less than the Reds. That year they tied Chicago for 6th place by virtue of winning 52 and losing 85 while the Orphans tallied 53 wins and 86 losses, the ineptitude of the two teams having been separated by a mere percentage point, .381 (Chicago) to .380 (New York). After a season like that both teams had no place to go but up.

But there were at least some signs of life during the final two years of the era, although the indications were infrequent and feeble in both New York and Chicago. For example, Pittsburgh, beneficiaries of Louisville's players via syndicate transfer, and Brooklyn, which fell heir to Baltimore stars Hughie Jennings, Joe McGinnity, Harry Howell and Gene DeMontreville, became prohibitive favorites to win the N.L.'s first 20th century championship. And yes, they finished 1–2, with Brooklyn winning out over the Pirates by 4½ games. In the longer run, however, it was Pittsburgh, with the incomparable Honus Wagner, "Tommy the Wee" Leach, Fred Clarke, Jack Chesbro and Deacon Phillippe, all inherited from the defunct Louisville franchise, that would forge a mini-dynasty of its own, winning three straight flags from 1901–'03 before the Giants and Cubs began to dominate the National League in the early years of the century.

The story unraveling in St. Louis, however, was not only as interesting as the pennant race, but far more intriguing. On the banks of the Mississippi the newly named Cardinals had already acquired, indeed by the same syndicate transfer of players that benefited the Brooklyn Superbas (later known as the Dodgers) and the Pirates, the best of the Cleveland players, including Lave Cross, Bobby Wallace, and the one and only Cy Young. As for intrigue, the Cardinals managed somehow to pry loose three of the former championship Baltimore team's heroes, Uncle Wilbert Robinson, their sturdy catcher, second baseman Billy Keister and third baseman John McGraw. Defying the syndicate "rules of the game," St. Louis purchased the contracts of the three for $15,000, got away with it, and raised the level of its championship hopes by several notches.

The signing of John McGraw and the totally out-of-character circumstances surrounding his contract negotiations with St. Louis, and later with Freedman and the New York Giants, was probably the single most symbolic event in the beginning of the end of management's stranglehold on the game. It was John McGraw, the banty rooster known as "Muggsy," from tiny Olean, New York, whose relentless determination as a player and manager, and whose I-won't-stand-for-it defiance, enabled him to look The Establishment squarely in the eye, not suggesting, but demanding, "We're going to do this the way I want it done." And between his Baltimore departure and his July, 1902, signing with New York, here, very briefly, is the way it was done:[9] 1) McGraw first swam upstream by staying behind in Baltimore for the 1899 season while most of his teammates (good friend Wilbert Robinson also remained with the O's) were moved to Brooklyn. Only 26 at the time, he was, significantly,

Don't let that faint smile fool you. The intense, adversarial John McGraw was a battler who had no room for losers. He meant business—always.

tapped for the managerial post. 2) St. Louis purchased the contracts of Robinson, Keister and McGraw, but McGraw's and Robinson's contracts, negotiated chiefly by John J. himself, were to contain no reserve clause, leaving both of them free to negotiate on their own for the 1900 season. In a world of ruthless, two-fisted ownership, where the owner was Lord and Master over all, that was an astounding, if not unbelievable turn of events. Not even Curt Flood, a 1960s Cardinal, who played at a time when legal assistance and sentiment were overwhelmingly behind him, could pull that that off, though his efforts were largely responsible for precipitating the final demise of baseball's air-tight control and say-so over the rights and welfare of the players. 3) For John McGraw, and for that matter, for Wilbert Robinson and Cy Young, each one a Hall of Famer in the making, St. Louis was to be no abiding city. McGraw, in particular, had New York in the back of his mind from the very start. Consequently, the next round of negotiations took place between 1900 and the ultimate 1902 contract signing with the Giants. In each step along the way, whether in the freshly coined American League, or with the league offices, or with the Baltimore or New York Giant franchises, McGraw got what he wanted. That there was mutual interest, or hatred, as in the case of the American League's prexy, Ban Johnson, or benefit was secondary to the determination of the man in the driver's seat—and that was Mr. McGraw. Thus, a new chapter in New York baseball was opened even as the Giants and the Orphans, with their own unique recovery program about to materialize, limped through the first three seasons of the new century. Some of the Chicago–New York highlights from the otherwise ho-hum 1900 season follow:

>>   On May 14 Ned Garvin, who had pitched a 13-hit shutout against Boston in 1899 (that's right—13), blanked the Giants at Chicago, beating Bill Carrick, who, in turn, whitewashed the Orphans on June 12, 2 to 0.

>>   Keeping the shutout theme going, Emerson "Pink" Hawley shut down Chicago on the very next day, the 13th, beating Clark Griffith, 5 to 0. Griffith came back on August 16 to return the shutout favor, 2 to 0, scattering four singles in besting New York's Win Mercer.

>>   At Brooklyn, Christy Mathewson debuted against the pennant-winning Superbas, losing in relief to Joe McGinnity on July 17. The two "Big M's" would soon be linked, however, leading the Giants to consecutive pennants in 1904 and 1905. "Big Six," a name that would become synonymous with Mathewson and the championship Giants very soon, made his first appearance in a Chicago–New York tilt on September 13, when he was charged with the Giants' 6 to 5 loss.

>>   Buck Ewing, who started the season as the Giants' manager, was released on July 11. It was his last appearance in a New York uniform, and one of the final disengagements with the championship Giants teams of yore.

The 1900 Season Series

May 12	Chi	13	NY	3	Callahan, WP	Doheny, LP
May 13	Chi	10	NY	9	Griffith, WP	Hawley, LP
May 14	Chi	4	NY	0	Garvin, WP	Carrick, LP

May 15	Chi	10	NY	8	J. Taylor, WP	Seymour, LP
June 12	NY	4	Chi	0	Carrick, WP	Callahan, LP
June 13	NY	5	Chi	0	Hawley, WP	Griffith, LP
July 8	Chi	11	NY	3	Cunningham, WP	Carrick, LP
July 9	Chi	3	NY	2	J. Taylor, WP	Mercer, LP
July 10	Chi	5	NY	2	Griffith, WP	Doheny, LP
July 31	NY	9	Chi	4	Mercer, WP	Garvin, LP
August 1	NY	8	Chi	5	Carrick, WP	J. Taylor, LP
August 2	Chi	7	NY	6	Griffith, WP	Mercer, LP
August 16	Chi	2	NY	0	Griffith, WP	Mercer, LP
August 18	NY	5	Chi	2	Hawley, WP	J. Taylor, LP
August 19	Chi	2	NY	1	Garvin, WP	Carrick, LP
September 11	NY	14	Chi	3	Hawley, WP	Callahan, LP
September 12	Chi	9	NY	1	Menefee, WP	Mercer, LP
September 12	NY	7	Chi	6	L. Taylor, WP	J. Taylor, LP
September 13	Chi	6	NY	5	Cunningham, WP	Mathewson, LP
September 14	NY	5	Chi	1	Hawley, WP	Garvin, LP

1901: Looking Up

John T. Brush, a native Hoosier, and Byron Bancroft Johnson, better known as "Ban," a pair of hard-bitten boardroom warriors, were prime movers in the baseball world for almost 40 years. Their far-ranging influence at the turn of the 20th century extended all the way from franchise ownership to contractual negotiations between players, teams and leagues, and on to the rearrangement of the baseball map. They first crossed swords in Cincinnati over the movement of players from league to league and franchise to franchise, discovering that the only thing they shared in common was a bitter hatred of one another.

By 1901, having gone their separate ways, Brush was in New York about to succeed Andrew Freedman, the Giants' CEO at the time, and Johnson was soon to begin a 27 year reign as president of an upstart "major" league that had, by stealth, piracy and devious dealings, shouldered its way into the very *sanctum sanctorum* of Organized Baseball (that was the way N.L. magnates saw it, in any case), declaring that its status was equal to that of the National League. That kind of competitive insolence didn't do much for the Johnson-Brush relationship, at all. In fact, right then and there the intense disdain of the National League for what was called the "Junior Circuit" was born, and no one was more outspoken, or seethed more over every player lost, every dollar spent on the new National League-American League rivalry, than the Giants' Mr. Brush.

That kind of scorn was also a part of John McGraw's makeup and surfaced regularly in years to come after Johnson had landed hard on McGraw's antics in Baltimore both on and off the field of play. And when Andrew Freedman, still the principal owner of the Giants at the time, brought McGraw to New York to manage the Giants, the new field leader found a ready-made ally in John Brush. Without getting into the ultimate Brush-McGraw, National League put-down in 1904 of refusing to play in the World Series, it should be pointed out that the relationship established between John McGraw and John Brush, born in 1901 and lasting through Brush's, New York presidency from 1903 through the 1912 pennant winners, endured principally because they not only liked one another, but because John McGraw was to become the major force in the organization through a financial stake in the very ownership of the club, and through player control. Thus, right from the start, the man who directed every last move on the field of play was also the man who assumed the role of what would today be known, in effect, as the general manager.

While all this was going on, in Chicago, a hotbed of activity what with a pennant winner in the new American League's first year, it was evident that Tom Loftus was not the answer for the Anson-less west side ball club. A 53–86 record convinced President Hart that he needed to seek managerial help. Fast.

Enter Frank Selee, the sharp-eyed wizard of Beantown's success during the 1890s. Though already in what must have been the early stages of the tuberculosis that ultimately took his life in 1909, and caused his resignation as manager in 1905, he agreed to make the move from Boston in order to undertake the rebuilding job so badly needed in Chicago. Consequently, even while the 1901 season was another nightmare afield, the course had been charted for a fresh start.

Among the few New York and Chicago bright spots in 1901, these stand out:

>> In the opening season series of four games at the Polo Grounds, New York and Chicago pitchers threw three shutouts: New York's John Menefee, a 3–0 winner; Mathewson (see below); and Malcolm "Kid" Eason, a 4–0 winner over the Giants.

>> Christy Mathewson picked off two base-runners, scattered nine hits, and shut out Chicago at the Polo Grounds On May 15, 4 to 0. It was his third straight whitewash of the season. On July 15 he threw a no-hitter at the Cardinals, winning 5 to 0.

>> On June 9 the Giants came up with a team record 31 basehits in a slugfest with Cincinnati. They beat the Reds, 25 to 13.

>> Rube Waddell, in an Orphans uniform, bested Christy Mathewson on June 15, 9 to 2.

>> Between May 18 and September 20 the Orphans ran a streak of 106 straight games without being shut out, a still standing club record.

>> Chicago, in winning two more games in the season series than New York did, also edged the Giants in the final standings—by one percentage point.

Right: The one and only Rube Waddell, 14 and 14 for the 53 and 86, 1901 Cubs. He struck out 6 batters a game. That number would rise to 8.39/game two years later, his career high.

The 1901 Season Series

May 14	NY	3	Chi	0	Menefee, WP	Denzer, LP
May 15	NY	4	Chi	0	Mathewson, WP	J. Taylor, LP
May 16	Chi	11	NY	3	Waddell, WP	L. Taylor, LP
May 17	Chi	4	NY	0	Eason, WP	L. Taylor, LP
June 13	NY	9	Chi	7	Doheny, WP	J. Taylor, LP
June 14	NY	4	Chi	1	L. Taylor, WP	Menefee, LP
June 15	Chi	9	NY	2	Waddell, WP	Mathewson, LP
June 29	NY	14	Chi	1	Mathewson, WP	Waddell, LP
July 1	NY	6	Chi	4	L. Taylor, WP	J. Taylor, LP
July 2	NY	6	Chi	3	Phyle, WP	Hughes, LP
July 17	Chi	7	NY	4	Waddell, WP	Mills, LP
July 18	Chi	6	NY	5	Eason, WP	L. Taylor, LP
July 19	Chi	5	NY	2	J. Taylor, WP	Mathewson, LP
July 20	Chi	7	NY	2	Waddell, WP	Phyle, LP
July 21	Chi	5	NY	2	Eason, WP	L. Taylor, LP
September 2	NY	6	Chi	1	L. Taylor, WP	Hughes, LP
September 2	Chi	3	NY	1	Eason, WP	Hickman, LP
September 3	Chi	10	NY	6	Menefee, WP	Maul, LP
September 26	NY	5	Chi	1	L. Taylor, WP	J. Taylor, LP
September 28	Chi	5	NY	2	Menefee, WP	Phyle, LP

V

CHAMPIONS EAST
AND WEST

The winter of discontent in New York and Chicago was about to give way to a springtime of high expectations. Still smarting from a rockbottom finish to open the 20th century and a disastrous 1901 campaign, it was time for drastic changes in the Big Apple. That's just what New York got when, on July 9, 1902, McGraw signed a contract that he made certain was to *his* liking. Back in March Frank Selee had taken the Orphans to their spring training base at the University of Illinois in Champaign with strict instructions to do whatever was necessary to shake up a moribund conglomeration of wannabes and has-beens.

Neither Selee, who started several months earlier than McGraw, nor the slight, wiry infielder they would soon be calling "Little Napoleon" wasted any time. Heads rolled and lineups changed. Immediately. And so did expectations that demanded a new style of play, completely and radically revolutionizing both ballclubs. The move from the bottom of the ladder was underway and the ultimate, top-end perch, was closer than anyone dared believe.

A strong case could be made for contending that even more influential or important than style and managerial fire, especially in McGraw's case, was the extraordinary ability of both managers to spot major league talent in players often turned aside by others who were less perceptive or perhaps less patient. Both knew what they wanted and what to do with it, and both insisted that their players had to fit into the scheme of things according to the their own plan, or else, though Selee and McGraw were light years apart in the way they went about accomplishing their desired goals.

By 1902 the game had undergone a radical revolution. Playing rules, players, the game's very structure and administration—all of it—would have been barely recognizable to A. G. Spalding, John Day, William Hulbert, the pioneering players and those "cranks" of days gone by. And yet the passing years, actually amounting to only a quarter century, did not dim the early rivalries or the keen, inter-metropolitan competition, especially between the citadels of power in the East and Midwest, New York and Chicago. Nowhere was that more evident than on the field of play, an evolving laboratory of playing sophistication that had risen to unheard-of levels of excellence during the first 15 years of the new century. So enamored were fans, as well as players and managers, of the style of play during those years, especially by the Giants and Cubs, that many could not, and furthermore would not adjust to a "new look" and a whole "new game" personified by The Bambino," Babe Ruth, when it came along in the '20s. For John McGraw, despite later successes, and for Johnny Evers, Frank Chance, Buck Herzog, Roger Bresnahan and a host of other Cub and Giant deadball era players, there would always and ever be but "one game," the rough and tumble, intimidating, grit and hustle, and "scientific" game they knew. It was that very scenario that provided the stage for the dramatic and oft-times savage rivalry that would heat to fever pitch in the years directly ahead.

By 1903, with their respective houses in far better order and the failures of the past behind them, McGraw and Selee expected to, and did indeed wind up among the first division teams of the National League. Between 1901 and 1903 Chicago had risen from 6th to just a game and a half behind New York's second place finish. Wholesale changes in personnel and deft changes in lineups and positions, each suited to the strategies of their managers, had their desired effect. A look at the difference between the New York and Chicago lineups of August, 1902, and those of one year later, best illustrates the radical surgery performed by the two managers. For the August 14, 1901, New York encounter with Boston, manager George Davis's lineup card read: Van Haltren, cf; Davis, ss; McBride, rf; Selbach, lf; Hickman, 2b; Strang, 3b; Ganzel, 1b; and the catcher, Warner, batting eighth.

On August 17, 1901, Chicago manager Tom Loftus used this lineup against the St. Louis Cardinals: Hartsell, lf; Green, cf; Dexter, rf; Doyle, 1b; Raymer, 3b; Childs, 2b; McCormick, ss; and catcher Kahoe batting eighth. Check those lineups against those that New York and Chicago used in John McGraw's first game as a playing-manager with the Giants at the Polo Grounds on August 7, 1902.

New York	R	H	PO	A		Chicago	R	H	PO	A
Browne, lf	0	3	3	0		Jones, rf	0	1	1	0
McGraw, ss	0	0	2	2		Slagle, lf	1	1	2	0
Bresnahan, c	1	0	10	3		Chance, 1b	0	0	18	1

New York	R	H	PO	A		Chicago	R	H	PO	A
McGann, 1b	0	3	11	1		Dobbs, cf	0	11	0	0
Brodie, cf	0	1	5	0		Tinker, ss	0	0	2	6
Wall, rf	1	1	1	0		Lowe, 2b	0	0	4	4
Lauder, 3b	1	1	2	5		Kling, c	1	2	8	5
Smith, 2b	0	1	4	3		Schaefer, 3b	1	0	3	3
Cronin, p	0	0	0	1		Williams, p	0	1	1	1
Bowerman, ph	0	0	0	0						
McGinnity, p	0	0	1	1						
Totals	3	10	39	16		Totals	3	6	39	20

Line Score: Chicago   100 000 200 000 0   3–6–0
             New York 000 001 002 000 0   3–10–3[10]

2BH—McGann, Browne
SB—Slagle 2, Brodie
SH—Schaefer, Brodie
LOB—Chicago 5; New York 11
DP—Kling and Schaefer; Lauder and McGann
PB—Bresnahan
K—Cronin 5, Williams 6, McGin'ty 4
BB—Cronin, 2, Williams 7, McGin'ty, 1
Umpire—Mr. Emslie
Time—2:35
Attendance—12,100

A New Ball Game for a New Century

The winds of change, revealed dramatically in the August 1901 and 1902 New York and Chicago lineups (above), were indicative of the national pastime's transformation during the first decade of the new century. There to seize the moment were the old rivals, readying themselves to do battle, and not merely for bragging rights in New York or Chicago. This time subduing the arch rival would be the last big step to the ultimate reward: pennant gold. And that would call for the ultimate effort each and every pitch, each and every out, each and every game. For John McGraw it could be no other way, and while it might be said with some truth that the Chicago challenge was no different for him than that of any other team in the league (there was no single enemy—they were *all* hated foes), it was Frank Selee and his warriors who, with the passing of one bitterly fought battle after another, became the "Most Wanted," thus raising the New York-Chicago confrontation several notches above all the others. That, precisely, is what made them both the championship forces they were, and further, what prompted the bitter exchanges, both verbal and physical, between them.

Their dislike and disdain for one another was best expressed by the Cubs' taciturn shortstop, Joe Tinker. His oft-quoted line:

> If you didn't honestly and furiously hate the Giants, you weren't a real Cub [From Anderson, David: *More Than Merkle*, Nebraska Univ. Press, Lincoln, NE, 2000, p. xvii.].

Predictably, the Giants and the Cubs, though tested sternly by the Pittsburgh Pirates over the course of the 1902 to 1913 era, were at one another's throats from that August 7, 1902, 3 to 3 tie forward when, under McGraw, the Giants first encountered the Cubs. During that time Chicago wrested 131 victories from the Giants, while the latter captured 120. Four times the season series wound up in a tie, each team winning 11 of the 22 scheduled tilts.

Pittsburgh, whose three straight pennants welcomed the 20th century, soon discovered that the Cubs and Giants, even though in the midst of rebuilding, would not be pushovers. In 1902 and '03 the Cubs won 19 times from the Pirates while losing 21, and the 1903 Giants broke even at 11 and 11. And although the era opened in 1902 with both clubs in the second division (the Giants wound up dead last at 48 and 88) their remarkable recovery in 1903 put them within reach of pennant contention. They had both served notice on the league that they had arrived.

The 1902 and 1903 Season Standings

	Team	Pos	Won	Lost	Pct.
1902	Pittsburgh	1	103	36	.741
	Chicago	5	68	69	.496
	New York	8	48	88	.353
1903	Pittsburgh	1	91	49	.650
	New York	2	84	55	.604
	Chicago	3	82	56	.594

Here are some of the more interesting jottings from the 1902 and 1903 Notebooks:

1902

>> "Brakeman Jack" Taylor, enjoying his finest major league season (22 wins, a 1.33 ERA and 7 shutouts), beat Pittsburgh's "Deacon" Phillippe 3 to 2 in a 19 inning pitching masterpiece on June 22. Veteran Bobby Lowe, Cub captain and a Selee favorite, who was baseball's

first player to hit four homers in one game, singled home the winning run. Remarkably, both hurlers went the route.

Taylor, who tossed 33 complete games, finishing everything he started, would continue completing every game he started until he was finally lifted at the Polo Grounds in 1907, having set a record with 189 consecutive complete games. It would become one of those records in the Joe DiMaggio 56 straight, or the Giants' 26 consecutive win class that will probably endure indefinitely.

Jack Taylor, the irascible, flinty Cub righthander who set an unbreakable ML mark: 187 (count 'em!) *consecutive* complete games. In his career he completed 278 out of 287 games started, an incredible completion rate of .9686 percent! (George Brace photograph)

>> July 9, 16 and 19: Culminating with John McGraw's first game as the Giants' manager on July 19, the New York front office went through a fortnight of negotiations with other teams and McGraw brought Iron Man McGinnity and the versatile Roger Bresnahan to the Polo Grounds (July 16). On July 9, McGraw finally inked his pact, a four-year deal at $11,000 per annum, plus virtual control over player personnel and a $6000 share of the franchise stock.

>> In Chicago Frank Selee was busy rearranging his ball club, switching Frank Chance to first base, Joe Tinker from third base to shortstop and Johnny Evers from shortstop to second base, the most significant of many such position changes. The famed Tinker to Evers to Chance combination played together for the first time on September 13. Two days later they would turn their first double play at the expense of the Cincinnati Reds as Selee's revamped lineup, behind another newcomer, "The Iceman" Carl Lundgren, won in Chicago before a "crowd" estimated at less than 275. That, too, would soon change.

>> Christy Mathewson, at 14 and 17, led the league with eight shutouts. Newly acquired teammate McGinnity logged an 8–8, New York record (dating from July 16).

239 wins and 48 saves grace Mordecai Brown's Hall of Fame statistics. Three Finger, a rugged, superbly conditioned athlete, was the mainstay of those brilliant, early 1900s Cubs pitching staffs.

1903

>> Except for two games in the season series, when the Cubs won by scores of 10 to 6 and 16 to 9, the losing team managed no more than four runs, signalling the arrival of the low-scoring, defensive game that characterized the deadball era. In 10 of the 22 games the losing team scored two or less runs.

>> Rookie Mordecai Brown opened the season against Chicago with a one-hit victory on April 19 for the Cardinals. He so impressed manager Frank Selee, that he insisted the Cubs acquire him. Brown became a Cub in a post-season trade for "Brakeman Jack" Taylor.

>> On May 16, 31,500 jammed the Polo Grounds to see their Giants, then in first place, take the measure of the Pirates. The attendance total established a new major league record.

>> In August Iron Man McGinnity won three doubleheaders for the Giants against Brooklyn, Boston and Philadelphia. He combined with Christy Mathewson for 61 of New York's 84 victories (58%).

>> Leon "Red" Ames debuted for the Giants on September 14 with a five-inning no-hitter, defeating St. Louis in the second game of a double header, called by darkness. He would go on to a 12 year, 108 victory career in a Giants' uniform.

>> Southpaw Jacob Weimer, dubbed "Tornado Jake," was the first of five Chicago hurlers to become rookie 20-game winners during the early years of the deadball era. The others were "Big Ed" Reulbach in 1905, Jack Pfiester, 1906, Leonard "King" Cole, 1910 and Larry Cheney, 1913.

The 1902 and 1903 Season Series

1902

May 9[11]	Chi	5	NY	0	St. Vrain, WP	Evans, LP
May 25	Chi	3	NY	1	St. Vrain, WP	Dunn, LP
June 3	Chi	12	NY	4	J. Taylor, WP	L. Taylor, LP
June 4	NY	4	Chi	3	Evans, WP	W. Williams, LP
June 5	NY	4	Chi	3	Sparks, WP	Menefee, LP
July 8	NY	1	Chi	0	Mathewson, WP	Rhoades, LP
July 8	Chi	2	NY	0	Lundgren, WP	L. Taylor, LP
July 13	Chi	5	NY	1	Lundgren, WP	L. Taylor, LP
July 13	Chi	4	NY	0	Rhoades, WP	Evans, LP
August 8	Chi	6	NY	0	Menefee, WP	Miller, LP
August 9	Chi	8	NY	2	J. Taylor, WP	Mathewson, LP
August 9	NY	9	Chi	3	McGinnity, WP	Lundgren, LP
August 16	NY	6	Chi	3	L. Taylor	Lundgren, LP
August 17	NY	3	Chi	2	McGinnity, WP	Menefee, LP
August 17	NY	3	Chi	1	Cronin, WP	W. Williams, LP
August 18	NY	5	Chi	0	Mathewson, WP	Rhoades, LP
September 10	Chi	4	NY	3	W. Williams, WP	L. Taylor, LP
September 10	NY	6	Chi	0	Mathewson, WP	Rhoades, LP
September 11	NY	3	Chi	2	Miller, WP	Lundgren, LP
September 11	Chi	7	NY	2	Morrissey, WP	McGinnity, LP

1903

May 26	NY	4	Chi	3	Mathewson, WP	J. Taylor
May 27	NY	5	Chi	4	McGinnity, WP	Weimer
May 28	Chi	7	NY	1	J. Taylor, WP	L. Taylor
June 4	NY	9	Chi	1	Mathewson, WP	Lundgren, LP
June 5	NY	5	Chi	2	McGinnity, WP	J. Taylor, WP
June 6	NY	7	Chi	4	L. Taylor, WP	Weimer, LP
June 7	NY	9	Chi	4	McGinnity, WP	Menefee, LP
June 18	Chi	1	NY	0	Weimer, WP	Mathewson, LP
June 22	NY	5	Chi	4	McGinnity, WP	J. Taylor, LP
June 22	Chi	10	NY	6	Menefee, WP	Mathewson, LP
July 4	Chi	16	NY	9	Weimer, WP	L. Taylor, LP
July 5	NY	7	Chi	1	McGinnity, WP	J. Taylor, LP
July 6	NY	5	Chi	1	Mathewson, WP	Menefee, LP
August 22	Chi	8	NY	3	Weimer, WP	Miller, LP
August 24	Chi	7	NY	3	J. Taylor, WP	McGinnity, LP
August 24	NY	8	Chi	1	Mathewson, WP	Menefee, LP
September 19	Chi	3	NY	0	Weimer, WP	Mathewson. LP
September 20	NY	6	Chi	2	McGinnity, WP	J. Taylor, LP
September 21	NY	8	Chi	3	Mathewson, WP	Currie, LP
September 22	Chi	6	NY	1	Weimer, WP	McGinnity, LP

The fellow they called "Laughing Larry," Giant second baseman Larry Doyle, a quintessential Giant player under McGraw. He was the N.L.'s MVP for the 1912, N.L. champion Giants.

The Pennant Express

During the deadball years the Giants and Cubs amassed 11 pennants within a span of 15 seasons from 1904 to 1918. Frank Chance, Chicago's "Peerless Leader," and New York's new hero, John Joseph McGraw, saw to it that the pennant express visited their respective stations with clockwork regularity. Larry Doyle, a Giant standby during that time, put it this way: "It's great to be young and a Giant!" Over in Chicago, Cub players might have said the same thing about their team. Finishing up there in the money year in and year out, those 1904 to 1918 New York teams wound up lower than third place but three times and Chicago's not at all.

The express was 'round the bend and heading for the station already in 1903, when both the Giants and Cubs finished right behind Pittsburgh's champions. After the frenetic wheeling and dealing of the previous year, both clubs had pretty much settled on the core of their championship lineups. Magnificent pitching, heady defensive ballplayers, and team smarts were club trademarks. So when 1904 rolled around the word was already out: Look out! These guys mean business. By the time the season was over McGraw & Co. had dusted all comers aside, Chicago by 13 games and the rest of the league by much, much more. As different as the new light bulb age was to the gas light era, when the New Yorks first won a world's championship with those grand 1888 and 1889 teams, so was the difference between those ballclubs and McGraw's 1904 Giants. Times had changed and so had ballclubs and the style of play, but as to a championship? Well, now, a championship is a championship is a championship!!

The 1904 and 1905 Season Standings

	Team	Pos	Won	Lost	Pct.
1904	New York	1	106	47	.693
	Chicago	2	93	60	.608
	Cincinnati	3	88	65	.575
1905	New York	1	105	48	.686
	Pittsburgh	2	96	57	.627
	Chicago	3	92	61	.601

Winning 10 of its first 12 games, the Giants took command of the 1904 pennant race right from the start and never looked back. Chicago, clearly the best of the rest, was the only club to break even with the McGrawmen in the annual 22 game season series between the league's teams. When the final inning had been played it was evident that Selee and McGraw had become helmsmen for ballclubs that would bring major headaches to those with pennant ambitions for years to come, such was the youthful, yet finely honed ballclubs both fielded. And so it was to be.

In the season series between the top two contenders there were 10 games in which either Chicago or New York was held without a run, and in no less than 15 of the 22 games the losing team could muster no more than two runs. Given that miniscule margin for error, there was bound to be contention on every close call, real or imagined. Frank Chance, just as mentally, and indeed physically as tough as his famed predecessor, Cap Anson, was already the leader on the field of play, heading up a gritty, hustling club that would fight to the last out for every advantage and every run it could get its hands on. That made both "The Peerless Leader," and his Chicago teammates prime targets for the likes of a McGraw team. And so the battle, as they say, was engaged.

But in 1904, the first championship year since 1889, New York celebrated a pennant. The Giants, though not to McGraw's complete satisfaction (there was *always* something missing or wrong or bungled in McGraw's mind), had outplayed and outdone their opposition in numerous categories of play. In the space of 2½ seasons of play under him, the team had swept from last to first, and in 1904 paced the league in these significant team categories:

1) Runs scored (744) and run differential (268, or 1.7/game)
2) Hits (1347), 2BH (202) and BB (434)
3) Team BA (.262), SA (.344), and Batting Runs (87)
4) Stolen Bases (283)
5) Strikeouts (707) and Fewest Hits/game (7.4)

"The Peerless Leader," Frank Chance, whose rookie season, 1898, came the year after Cap Anson retired, thus establishing an 1876–1912 Chicago continuity in baseball prominence. Chance, elected to the Hall of Fame in 1946, seven years after Anson, was every bit as tough and talented as the original "Papa Cub."

    6) Pitching Staff ERA (2.17)
    7) Shutouts (21) and Saves (15)
    8) Fielding Average (.956) and Double Plays(t) (93)

    Those sparkling team achievements and individual heroics aside, the most interesting matchup between the Giants and Cubs during the summer of 1904 was on June 11, when the Giants were stopped cold by the righthanded slants of Bob Wicker, who whitewashed them, 1 to 0 in a 12-inning duel with Joe McGinnity at the Polo Grounds. Wicker had held the Giants hitless through the first 10⅓ innings before outfielder Sam Mertes singled sharply to center. It was the only hit the Giants could come up with against the Cubs' 17-game winner who had won 20 for Chicago in 1903. Here is the box score:

Chicago	AB	R	H	PO		New York	AB	R	H	PO
Slagle, lf	5	0	0	2		Bresnahan, cf	5	0	0	4
Casey, 3b	5	0	2	1		Browne, rf	5	0	0	1
Chance, 1b	5	1	3	15		Devlin, 3b	5	0	0	0

Chicago	AB	R	H	PO	New York	AB	R	H	PO
Kling, c	5	0	0	10	McGann, 1b	4	0	0	18
Jones, rf	5	0	2	2	Mertes, lf	4	0	1	4
Evers, 2b	3	0	2	3	Dahlen, ss	4	0	0	4
Tinker, ss	4	0	1	0	Gilbert, 2b	4	0	0	2
Williams, cf	4	0	0	1	Warner, c	3	0	0	3
Wicker, p	4	0	0	2	McGinnity, p	4	0	0	0
Totals	40	1	10	36	Totals	38	0	1	36

Line Score	Chicago	000 000 000 001	1–10–2
	New York	000 000 000 000	0–1–0

2BH—Evers SH Evers 2
SB—Browne, Devlin, Tinker
LOB—Chicago 5, New York 3
DP—Gilbert, Dahlen, McGann
K—Wicker 10, McGinnity 2
BB—Wicker 1, McGinnity 0
Umpires—Emslie and O'Day
Time—2:15
Attendance—28,805

There were other Giants-Cubs headlines in 1904, starting with the infamous and unfortunate World Series brouhaha that shut down the post-season classic. That petty incident had to be an all time low not only for baseball, but especially for John Brush and manager McGraw whose fit of peevishness deprived New Yorkers and Bostonians of a Pilgrims-Giants world's championship clash. But there were other and far more positive highlights:

>> Joe McGinnity set a National League record with 434 innings pitched. His 35 wins, plus Mathewson's 33, along with Luther Taylor's 21, accounted for 89 of New York's 106 wins. The "Iron Man's" streak of 14 straight wins was broken in the 12-inning Wicker masterpiece. McGinnity's 9 shutouts led the N.L., as did his W% (.814) and 1.61 ERA. It was his best season.

>> Between June 6 and July 5 the Giants won 18 straight games, finally losing to the Phils, 6 to 5 in 10 innings in a game that infuriated McGraw for the misplays and errors that gave the game away.

>> Frank Chance was hit five times in a Chicago-Cincinnati twin bill on May 30 by Redleg pitchers, one of which felled him with a concussion. He played on, nonetheless.

>> Just two weeks later, on June 13, Chance missed hitting for the cycle

when he homered, tripled and doubled in four times up in a 3 to 2 victory over Christy Mathewson at the Polo Grounds. The only other hit the Cubs had that day was a single by Johnny Evers in one of the classic Three Finger Brown-Mathewson duels.

>>   "The Orator," Jim O'Rourke, Giants' Famer of the 1888-89 championship teams came back for a hero's return to the 1904 lineup on September 22 to help the Giants win their 100th game of the season. Serving as Joe McGinnity's battery mate, he came up with a single in four trips to the plate, caught nine innings, and celebrated the 7 to 5 win over Cincinnati—at age 42!

Hall of Famer, the gritty old warrior Joe McGinnity the "Iron Man" was still pitching in Organized Baseball for Dubuque of the Mississippi Valley League in 1925, at age 54. He pitched *two* ML games in one day, *five* times.

>>   On October 3, "The Big Six" K'd 16 batters to set the franchise record, still unsurpassed.

>>   The very next day, October 4, Sam Mertes hit for the cycle with a homer, triple, double and single, in that order, on the last day of the season at the Polo Grounds.

The 1904 Season Series

May 20	Chi	3	NY	2	Weimer, WP	Mathewson, LP
May 21	NY	3	Chi	0	McGinnity, WP	Corridon, LP
May 22	Chi	3	NY	1	Brown, WP	L. Taylor, LP
June 10	NY	5	Chi	0	Mathewson, WP	Weimer, LP
June 11	Chi	1	NY	0	Wicker, WP	McGinnity, LP
June 13	Chi	3	NY	2	Brown, WP	Mathewson, LP
July 21	NY	4	Chi	3	Mathewson, WP	Weimer, LP
July 22	Chi	6	NY	3	Briggs, WP	L. Taylor, LP
July 23	NY	5	Chi	1	Mathewson, WP	Brown, LP
July 24	NY	6	Chi	4	McGinnity, WP	Weimer, LP
August 3	NY	4	Chi	3	Mathewson, WP	Wicker, LP
August 4	Chi	3	NY	2	Weimer, WP	McGinnity, LP

August 4	NY	3	Chi	0	L. Taylor, WP	Brown, LP
August 24	NY	3	Chi	0	Mathewson, WP	Briggs, LP
August 25	NY	4	Chi	1	McGinnity, WP	Wicker, LP
August 25	NY	12	Chi	1	Wiltse, WP	Wicker, LP
August 26	Chi	5	NY	0	Brown, WP	Elliott, LP
September 27	NY	5	Chi	2	Ames, WP	Lundgren, LP
September 28	Chi	7	NY	2	Briggs, WP	Wiltse, LP
September 29	Chi	7	NY	3	Wicker, WP	Mathewson, LP
September 30	Chi	12	NY	9	Weimer, WP	McGinnity, LP
September 30	Chi	5	NY	3	Lundgren, WP	L. Taylor, LP

Atop Baseball's Summit

Outside of New York, where he could do no wrong, John McGraw didn't have many friends, especially after frustrating the baseball world with his refusal to play in the October, 1904 world's championship. Further, his incessant baiting and brawling in every ballpark and over every last little baseball iota added fuel to the fires of outright hatred raging

around the league. But all of that didn't seem to bother him in the least. His ball club was better than any other, at least in his own mind, and if anything else mattered more, he couldn't think what that might be. Championships, no matter how they were won, were clearly more important to John McGraw than social graces or public relations.

And yet, 1905 would be different. Although they successfully repeated as National League champions, the Giants were fully aware that out there in the hinterlands Frank Selee had patiently and adroitly put together a ball club capable of giving them the comeuppance everyone so fervently hoped for. That old New York wariness crept back into consciousness, the same worried eye cast westward as it had been from the very beginning of baseball time in the 1870s. That only sharpened, to a lethal edge,

The incomparable Christy Mathewson, John McGraw's Prince Valiant, whose Hall of Fame career extended through two of the Giants' championship eras.

The 1905 New York Giants, arguably John McGraw's best team among the 30 he managed: Standing: Roger Bresnahan, George "Hooks" Wiltse, Luther "Dummy" Taylor, Geroge Browne, Art Devlin, John Dunn, Harry McCormick, Claude Elliott. Kneeling and Seated: Sandy Mertes, Joe McGinnity, Dan McGann, John Warner, William Marshall, Manager John J. McGraw, Leon "Red" Ames, Christy Mathewson, Bill Dahlen, Frank Bowerman. Missing when the picture was taken: Billy Gilbert, Mike Donlin and Sammy Strang.

each confrontation, whether at the Polo Grounds or at West Side Park, where overflow crowds strained the restraining ropes around the perimeters of the outfield and foul lines. The days of everything-on-the-line ball games between the two behemoths of the league were at hand.

1905 would also be different in that the New Yorkers agreed to meeting the American League champion in October, thus renewing the interrupted world championship series between the leagues. And this, without a peep of contention. No wrangling, no bickering, no bitter sarcasm. The abrupt about-face by the Giants begs answers for questions like: what was so different in 1905 that made Connie Mack's champions more worthy of a chance to compete with the contemptuous Giants than the Cy Young-led 1904 Boston Pilgrims? Or, did the clamor over New York's refusal to play in 1904 "get to" Messr's. John Brush and John McGraw? Or, were there back-room pressures from above that were either persuasive or powerful enough to shut down the two New York hotheads? A full accounting would make for a fascinating story, now wouldn't it?

As far as the action afield was concerned, however, there was in both leagues stiff contention for pennants that were won in the nation's two largest cities, Philadelphia, where Connie Mack's A's beat out the Chicago White Sox by two games, and New York, whose Giants, though nine games up on the league at season's end, had a struggle on their hands through much of the season. Typical of the heat generated in those races was the *guerre à mort* staged at the New York and Chicago ballparks. And the mighty armies assembled to wage that warfare were beyond doubt among baseball's premier teams up that point in time. McGraw himself considered the 1904-'05 Giants his very best. Just how good they were will be put to the test shortly, but for now, it is sufficient to acknowledge the surpassing talent of a Mathewson, a McGinnity, a Dahlen or a Bresnahan on display at Coogan's Bluff, or the fiery genius of the Cubs' Tinker, Evers and Chance, who, along with Mordecai Brown. Ed Reulbach, Fred Schulte, et al., would very soon take to the summit of the National League themselves. Thus primed, the two met 22 times, New York emerging victorious just enough to better the Cubs 12 to 10 in the season series.

During the 22 game set the New Yorkers won via the shutout route six times and Chicago four. In 19 of the 22 games the Cubs averaged but three runs per game, though they managed to defeat the great McGinnity four times, three of which were Chicago shutouts. The "Iron Man's" Hall of Fame partner, Christy Mathewson, faced the Chicagoans five times, allowing them one or no runs in four of those games, his only Cubs loss during the season coming on July 12, when Three Finger Brown beat him 14 to 1 on a day when he just didn't have it. It was one of his nine losses as against 31 victories. Just a month earlier he had beaten Brown in another of their celebrated duels, firing a no-hitter at the Cubs in Chicago on June 13. The box score follows:

New York	R	H	PO		A	Chicago	R	H	PO	A
Donlin, cf	0	1	3		0	Slagle, cf	0	0	3	0
Browne, rf	0	1	1		1	Schulte, lf	0	0	1	0
McGann, 1b	1	1	14		0	Maloney, rf	0	0	5	0
Mertes, lf	0	1	3		0	Chance, 1b	0	0	8	0
Dahlen, ss	0	1	2		3	Tinker, ss	0	0	3	4
Devlin, 3b	0	0	0		1	Evers, 2b	0	0	2	2
Gilbert, 2b	0	0	1		5	Casey, 3b	0	0	1	2
Bowerman, c	0	0	3		0	Kling, c	0	0	4	2
Mathewson, p	0	0	0		4	Brown, p	0	0	0	0
Totals	1	5	27		14	Totals	0	0	27	10

Line Score	New York	000 000 001	1–5–2
	Chicago	000 000 000	0–0–2

SB—Schulte, Dahlen
LOB—Chicago 1, New York 4
DP—Browne and McGann
K—Brown 3, Mathewson 2

BB—Brown 2, Mathewson 0
Balk—Brown
Umpires—Messrs, Bauserwine and
    Emslie
Time—1:25
Attendance—9,000

The combination of Christy Mathewson's famed slider, known during his day as a "fadeaway," and his pinpoint control put him in command of Cub hitters all the way. His mastery was challenged, however, by the impressive artistry of Mordecai Brown, who held the Giants hitless through 7⅓ innings, finally surrendering the game's lone tally in the ninth. It was far and away the best pitched game of the season.

At the time Cubs manager Frank Selee was already wondering just how long he could hang on, caught as he was in the lingering and evermore serious throes of tuberculosis. Within another six weeks there would be no more conjecture. Under his physician's orders he resigned,

Mordecai Centennial "Three Finger" Brown, aka "Miner," illustrious Hall of Famer, the ace of the Chicago pitching staff of Frank Chance's 1904–12 juggernaut.

turning over the reins to "Big Husk," Frank Chance, the Cubs' acknowledged team leader. It was, of course, a heartbreaking loss, lamented widely. The 46-year-old manager, who had painstakingly put together another pennant contending powerhouse, lived only four more years, just long enough to share from afar the Cubs' 1906, '07, and '08 successes. By midseason of 1909, July 5, he had passed away.

Under Frank Chance the Cubs picked up the pieces and moved on, though unsuccessful in their attempts to chase down the fast-moving McGraw machine that outdistanced the Cubs by nine lengths. The McGrawmen had won their second straight flag and New York was the center of the baseball universe. It was time to put that universe in order by whipping the upstarts of the American League. That was accomplished in short order when, led by Christy Mathewson's amazing shutout trifecta, the McGrawmen swept to a 4 to 1 World Series conquest over Philadelphia's Athletics. The victor's spoils included specially designed uniforms with WORLD CHAMPIONS emblazoned across the chest. Imagine how that played in Peoria—or Chicago! 1906 would be another matter...

Right: Stern visaged but perceptive Frank Selee, who patiently laid the foundation for Chicago's early 1900s powerhouse. He was a 1999 Hall of Fame selection. (George Brace photograph)

The 1905 Season Series

May 13	NY	1	Chi	0	L. Taylor, WP	Lundgren, LP
May 15	NY	4	Chi	0	McGinnity, WP	Brown, LP
May 16	NY	4	Chi	0	Ames, WP	Reulbach, WP
May 17	NY	4	Chi	2	Wiltse, WP	Lundgren, LP
June 11	Chi	4	NY	0	Reulbach, WP	McGinnity, LP
June 12	Chi	5	NY	4	Weimer, WP	Ames, LP
June 13	NY	1	Chi	0	Mathewson, WP	Brown, LP
June 14	Chi	1	NY	0	Wicker, WP	McGinnity, LP
July 14	NY	3	Chi	2	Wiltse, WP	Reulbach, LP
August 7	Chi	4	NY	0	Reulbach, WP	McGinnity, LP
August 8	NY	4	Chi	3	L. Taylor, WP	Weimer, LP
August 9	Chi	7	NY	2	Wicker, WP	Ames, LP
August 10	NY	1	Chi	0	Mathewson, WP	Reulbach, LP
August 17	NY	3	Chi	0	Mathewson, WP	Weimer, LP
August 18	NY	5	Chi	4	McGinnity, WP	Weimer, LP
August 19	Chi	8	NY	2	Reulbach, WP	Wiltse, LP
September 22	Chi	7	NY	4	Reulbach, WP	L. Taylor, LP
September 23	Chi	1	NY	0	Lundgren, WP	Mathewson, LP
September 24	Chi	10	NY	5	Wicker, WP	McGinnity, LP

Was McGraw's 1905 Team His Greatest?

The question was previously raised as to whether John McGraw's 1905 team was his greatest, as he contended in later years. The answer to that question will be found in the Great Teams listings that follow. The first of these arranges not only the Giants and Cubs teams, but National and American League teams from 1876 forward. The sorting in this first list is done on the basis of one overriding factor, Run Differential, because the run is the most basic unit in the game, the coinage of the realm, as it were. The contention is that the difference in the number of runs scored in a season will be the major, if not *the* primary comparison factor. While there are other factors the experts consider, the Run Differential factor sorts out the team's greater overall efficiency and productivity as none other can. The listing follows.

The Great Teams in Major League History: List I

Rank	Team/Lg/Yr	GP	Runs	Opp. R.	R.Differential
1)	New York, A.L., 1939	152	967	556	411
2)	New York, A.L., 1927	155	975	599	376
3)	Chicago, N.L., 1876	66	624	257	367
4)	Chicago, N.L., 1885	113	834	470	364
5)	Baltimore, N.L., 1895	132	1009	646	363
6)	Boston, N.L., 1897	135	1025	665	360
7)	Baltimore, N.L., 1894	129	1171	819	352
8)	Chicago, N.L., 1886	126	900	555	345
9)	Pittsburgh, N.L., 1902	142	775	440	335
10)	New York, A.L., 1936	155	1065	731	334
11)	Baltimore, N.L., 1896	132	995	662	333
12)	Chicago, N.L., 1906	155	705	381	324
13)	Baltimore, N.L., 1898	154	933	623	310
14)	New York, A.L., 1998	162	965	656	309
15)	New York, A.L., 1937	157	979	671	308
16)	New York, A.L., 1942	154	801	507	294
17)	Baltimore, N.L., 1897	136	964	674	290
18)	Philadelphia, A.L., 1929	151	901	615	286
19)	St. Louis, N.L., 1942	157	772	490	282
20)	New York, A.L., 1932	156	1002	724	278
21)	*New York, N.L., 1905*	*155*	*780*	*505*	*275*
22)	St. Louis, N.L., 1944	156	755	482	273
23)	*New York, N.L., 1904*	*158*	*744*	*476*	*268*
24)	Brooklyn, N.L., 1953	155	955	689	266
25)	Baltimore, A.L., 1969	162	779	517	262

Note the 1904 and 1905 McGraw teams which rank among the top 25 from the standpoint of Run Differential. If the list were extended, the

Giants' 1912 team, often listed among the top 20 to 25 teams in the game's history, would rank in a 31st place tie with the 1909 Pittsburgh Pirates.

To give you a comparison point, here is a much shorter list that pulls together several experts on the subject as they rate the best teams, all time. The legend for this listing:

N   Rob Neyer, ESPN baseball analyst and sabermetrician.

E   Eddie Epstein, who with Rob Neyer co-authored *Baseball Dynasties*, W.W. Norton, NY, 2000, a thorough study of baseball's great teams.

A   Paul Adomites and Saul Wisnia, who wrote *Best of Baseball*, Publications International, Lincolnwood, IL, 1997, which discusses baseball's ten best teams in chronological order.

R   Lowell Reidenbaugh, baseball analyst for *The Sporting News*. Note: 15 of the 25 teams listed for TSN's *Baseball's 25 Greatest Teams*, 1988, are presented here.

The Great Teams in Major League History: List II

Rank	N List	E List	R List	A List (Chronological)
1)	1939 Yankees	1939 Yankees	1927 Yankees	1885–88 St.L.Browns
2)	1970 B.Orioles	1927 Yankees	1961 Yankees	1902 Pirates
3)	1998 Yankees	1970 B. Orioles	1929–31 A's	1904–05 Giants
4)	1975 Cinc.Reds	1998 Yankees	1906–08 Cubs	1906–08 Cubs
5)	1906 Cubs	1906 Cubs	1955 Br.Dodgers	1927 Yankees
6)	1927 Yankees	1975 Cinc.Reds	1975–76 Reds	1929–31 Phl. A's
7)	1929 Phl.A's	1974 Oak.A's	1972–74 Oak.A's	1936–39 Yankees
8)	1986 NY Mets	1961 Yankees	1954 Cl.Indians	1949–53 Yankees
9)	1942 St.L.Cards	1953 Yankees	1969–71 Orioles	1954 Cl.Indians
10)	1961 Yankees	1986 NY Mets	1936 Yankees	1975–76 Cinc.Reds
11)	1911 Phl. A's	1942 St.L.Cards	1904–05 Giants	
12)	1974 Oak. A's	1929 Phl. A's	1957–58 Mil.Braves	
13)	1912 Giants	1911 Phl. A's	1953 Yankees	
14)	1955 Brk.Dodgers	1955 Brk.Dodgers	1911–13 Giants	
15)	1953 Yankees	1912 Giants	1902 Pitt.Pirates	

The Great Teams in Major League History: The Wilbert Top Ten

Rank	Team	Comment
1)	1939 Yankees	That whopping 411 Run Differential shows Domination. Baseball's very best ballclub, even without Gehrig, plus great pitching.

2)   1927 Yankees   With Gehrig and Ruth, Inc., they put together a monster season, just a tiny tad behind DiMaggio's '39 Yanks.

3)   1906 Cubs   A gritty, accomplished ballclub that knew how to win and scored more than 300 runs than its opponents. Deserves top-3 billing.

4)   1929 Athletics Connie Mack's best ball club, a powerhouse without a weak link—anywhere. Tough in the clutch and a 286 Run Differential.

5)   1970 Orioles   Canny Earl Weaver knew what he wanted and his awesome front line pitching gave it to him. And— *two* Robinsons, to boot!

6)   1975 Reds   Sparky Anderson didn't run a red machine, it was in fact a destroyer. Stingy defense, power hitting and Bench. Need one say more?

7)   1885 Whites   Cap Anson's juggernaut was the best 19th century ballclub. And the White Stockings scored 364 more runs than their opponents.

8)   1905 Giants   The consensus backs McGraw's choice of his best ballclub. Timely hitting, unbending determination, Mathewson and McGinnity. Ouch! This outfit also happens to be is one of baseball's greatest over-achieving ball clubs—to be expected from a McGraw team.

9)   1998 Yankees   They were a brilliant combination of perseverance, power, potent pitching with other-worldly relieving, and not least, knew how to cut down big innings. Result? A straight A, 300 plus Run Diff.

10)   1955 Dodgers   Walt Alston's Boys of Summer. Strong armed, clutch hitting, never-say-die warriors who won a World Series in Flatbush. From Jackie to Duke to Oisk, a colorful, gifted bunch of classy winners.

Another Threepeat for Chicago

West Baden, Indiana, located just a mile or two north of one of the better known American spas, French Lick, was the site of the Cubs' 1906–'08 spring training base. During the three seasons following their spring drills in Hoosierland, the Cubs, now under the virile management of Frank

Chance, displaced McGraw's Giants as the National League's reigning royalty with one of the best lineups in the game's history. They simply trampled their senior circuit rivals underfoot, outthinking, out-hustling and out-playing them at every turn.

In 1909 the Cubs headed south, training at Shreveport, Louisiana. That year the Pirates won the pennant. Guess where the Bruins trained in 1910? Right. West Baden, Indiana. They promptly won their fourth flag in five tries. For the superstitious among us there might have been a connection between the waters at the spa or something else connected with the heart of Hoosierland and those championships, but the facts of the matter suggest otherwise.

To begin with, the Cubs sliced up their New York nemesis 14 times in their 22 meetings in 1906. In 1907, their first World Series championship year, the tally was even better, 16 and 6, and in 1908, though dropping to an 11–11 tie, they won when they had to, winning the pennant amid one of those rare, unbelievable scenarios that might just as well have come out of one of the fictional pulp magazine stories popular at the time. That one, of course, was the famous, or infamous depending on one's vantage point, "Merkle Game."

But before getting into some of the more interesting details of the Cubs' dynastic hegemony between 1906 and 1910, the season standings:

	Team	Pos	Won	Lost	Pct.
1906	Chicago	1	116	36	.763
	New York	2	96	56	.632
	Pittsburgh	3	93	60	.608
1907	Chicago	1	107	45	.704
	Pittsburgh	2	91	63	.591
	New York	4	82	71	.536
1908	Chicago	1	99	55	.643
	New York	2(t)	98	56	.636
	Pittsburgh	2(t)	98	56	.636
1909	Pittsburgh	1	110	42	.724
	Chicago	2	104	49	.680
	New York	3	92	61	.601
1910	Chicago	1	104	50	.675
	New York	2	91	63	.591
	Pittsburgh	3	86	67	.562

Between 1906 and 1910 the Cubs went on a 529 game winning tear, *averaging* 106 victories per season, an absolutely awesome achievement. Their .692 winning percentage bordered on a seven out of ten pace over

One of the best teams in baseball history, the 1906 Cubs. Standing: Mordecai Brown, John Pfiester, Art Hofman, Mr. C. Williams, Orv Overall, Ed Reulbach, John Kling. Seated: Harry Gessler, Jack Taylor, Harry "Steinie" Steinfeldt, Jim McCormick, Manager Frank Chance, Jim Sheckhard, Pat Moran, Fred Schulte. Seated, front row: Carl Lundgren, Tom Walsh, Johnny Evers, Jimmy Slagle, Joe Tinker. Missing when picture was taken: Bob Wicker and Fred Beebe. (George Brace photograph)

the five season span, starting with a record-setting 116 victories in 1906, garnered by a pitching staff that excelled even the great corps of moundsmen assembled by Connie Mack (Philadelphia A's), and Fred Clarke (Pittsburgh Pirates), and at very least equaling Chicago's White Sox and McGraw's Giants. If the low-hit, low-run ballgame was to be the national pastime's prime staple, then Chicago was the place to see it happen. Nowhere else in 1906 would that rare combination of superb pitching and brainy defense be displayed so consistently and with such artistic flair. In a word, the Cubs out–McGrawed McGraw. The most important New York and Chicago pitching staff numbers bear this out:

Category	NY Staff/Lg. Rank	Chi Staff/Lg.Rank
ERA	2.49/3	1.75/1 (ML record)
Hits per Game	8.1/3	6.6/1
Shutouts	19/5	30/1
Strike Outs	639/2	702/1
Fewest Walks	394/2	446/5
Lowest Opp. B.A.	.249/3	.207/1
Pitching Runs	20/3	135/1

Category	NY Staff/Lg. Rank	Chi Staff/Lg.Rank
Saves	18/1	10/3
Complete Games	105/8	125/3

Afield the Cubs also held the upper hand, placing first in fielding average (.969), first with the fewest errors (194) and third in double plays. New York was third in fielding average, third in fewest errors with 233, and sixth in double plays with 84. With that kind of fielding to back up its extraordinary pitching, the Cubs could well afford to score but 4.59 runs per game (they allowed only 2.46 per game on average). Yet, their offense led the league in quite a number of categories, as well. All of this helps to explain not only balance, but superiority that enabled them to play the game at orbital levels. Net result? 116 victories and a pennant cinching date of September 19. But not without a trouble spot or two. Not with John McGraw's Giants around to make life interesting.

Throughout McGraw's tenure as the Giants' major domo, starting with his very first game at the Giants' helm, there was always the threat of some incident or full blown conflagration in the air. That was especially so when the Cubs were in town, either in New York or in Chicago. Beginning already in the earliest series of games back in 1903, special details of New York's or Chicago's Finest were dispatched to patrol the grounds. By 1906, tensions between the two relentless antagonists charged every play. The Giants weren't about to give up their championship without a last ditch struggle.

On August 4 the Cubs opened a four game series at the Polo Grounds leading the Giants by 5½ games. At that point it was not beyond the realm of possibility for the Giants to overtake Chicago's North Siders, and to make certain things got off on the right foot they sent Mathewson to face Jack Taylor, recently reacquired from St. Louis. With over 25,000 on hand, Matty beat the Cubs 7 to 4. Then came a day off, and on the 6th Frank Chance sent out "Brownie" to duel Joe McGinnity. Chicago won that one, 3 to 1, but evening out the series was almost beside the point compared to the bizarre nature of the post-game "festivities," which featured a near riot as umpire Jim Johnson was accosted leaving the playing field. Disgruntled fans vented their frustrations on one of the National League's better arbiters (Cubs' fans at West Side Park were just as testy and equally hard-nosed), threatening him with everything, including the kitchen sink. It turned out that Johnson hadn't made much of a hit with John McGraw, either, and so he left orders to shut the door in the umpire's face when game time rolled around the next day. Who on the planet save John McGraw would have dared a move like that! The ploy drew the inevitable furor—and the league's wrath, something that had befallen McGraw more than once before. This time the incident cost him a ball game via the forfeit route because umpires Emslie and Johnson did not work the game and in fact declared it a forfeit to Chicago.

Chicago, now up, two games to one in the series, readied to play the final game of the series on August 8. Umpires Johnson and Emslie were also ready, accompanied to the Polo Grounds by N.L. prexy Harry Pulliam. Consequently, there was no choice for the Giants but to take the field, though without manager McGraw, who had been suspended. In the game that followed the Cubs won again, this time behind "Big Ed" Reulbach, relieved by the tireless Brown, enabling them to leave town well in command of the pennant race. As things turned out, John McGraw had ironically given them a big boost toward the 1906 flag. And for New Yorkers the thought of losing to the Cubs was a tragedy beyond description. William Kirk, the *New York American's* "Baseball Poet Laureate," also thought so, but he did have words to describe the impending disaster:

If Chicago Should Win Two Pennants

In Chicago, where the gentle stockyard zephyrs
Sweep across the shrinking city night and day
Where some cows that in the misty past were heifers
Through the Jungle make their uncomplaining way;
In Chicago, where the veteran Charles Comiskey
And the new rich Charley Murphy get their stake,
Many a wild-eyed rooter brags that a brace of big league flags
Will be waving in the city by the lake.

The Athletics under Con McGillicuddy
Still maintain that they can beat the White Sox out,
And McGraw is spending all his time in study,
Planning how the Cubs may yet be put to rout.
But the fans who swarm in windy old Chicago—
Not the stingiest concession will they make—
Hear them boast, without fatigue, that in neither major league
Will the pennant miss the city by the lake.

We are hoping that their clubs are overrated,
We are praying there will be no such mishap;
If they get it all a wind will be created
That will blow the game of baseball off the map.
So let us pray that some more cultured centre
Will divide with them the pennant rake.
Spare us, god of baseball hosts, from the never ending boasts
Of the wheexy, breezy city by the lake!

Precisely, what was feared most, happened. But what was to transpire next was absolutely beyond anyone's imagination. That, of course, was the mighty Cub dreadnaught's collapse in the World Series, something that must have given John McGraw the most exquisite bittersweet moment of his life as he saw Chicago's North Siders go down, but to an American League team, of all things, and in the world's championship series, at that!

And so there was a pox on both houses. In Chicago and in New York it would be a long winter...

The 1906 Season Series

May 20	Chi	10	NY	4	Lundgren, WP	Ames, LP
May 21	NY	6	Chi	4	Wiltse, WP	Reulbach, LP
May 22	NY	8	Chi	2	McGinnity, WP	Wicker, LP
May 24	NY	6	Chi	5	Mathewson, WP	Lundgren, LP
June 5	Chi	5	NY	0	Brown, WP	McGinnity, LP
June 6	Chi	11	NY	3	Overall, WP	L. Taylor, LP
June 7	Chi	19	NY	0	Pfiester, WP	Mathewson, LP
June 8	NY	7	Chi	3	Wiltse, WP	Brown, LP
July 17	Chi	6	NY	2	Brown, WP	Mathewson, LP
July 19	NY	5	Chi	2	McGinnity, WP	Reulbach, LP
July 20	Chi	6	NY	3	J. Taylor, WP	Mathewson, LP
August 4	NY	7	Chi	4	Mathewson, WP	J. Taylor, LP
August 6	Chi	3	NY	1	Brown, WP	McGinnity, LP
August 7	Forfeit to Chicago, 9 to 0					
August 8	Chi	3	NY	2	Reulbach, WP	Ames, LP
August 18	Chi	6	NY	2	Brown, WP	Mathewson, LP
August 19	NY	7	Chi	0	Wiltse, WP	J. Taylor, LP
August 20	Chi	3	NY	0	Pfiester, WP	McGinnity, LP
August 21	Chi	4	NY	2	Brown, WP	Ames, LP
September 21	Chi	6	NY	2	Lundgren, WP	Wiltse, LP
September 24	Chi	10	NY	5	Reulbach, WP	Mathewson, LP

Taming The Tiger: 1907-1908

For the Cubs there was one only one difference between 1906 and 1907 that really mattered, and it was huge. In 1907 they emerged from the World Series as baseball champions of the world, and although it took a year of waiting, their conquest of Detroit's Tigers brought with it the lifting of the burden of their 1906 ignominy at the hands of Fielder Jones's White Sox. That they had blitzkrieged the National League, winning the pennant by 17 games over Pittsburgh, would have meant next to nothing had they not brought home the big trophy. Additionally, it restored the mastery of the senior circuit over an American League that was no longer taken lightly, and was, as a matter of fact, a dangerous threat to the N.L.'s superior ranking among baseball's professionals. The World Series had become *the* showcase for annual validation of that very supremacy. And the A.L.'s Tigers? Why, they found themselves in exactly the same predicament as the Cubs a year prior to their four game sweep of the Hughie Jennings led Detroiters. Their chant was the same: "Wait till next year!"

Frank Chance took virtually the same lineup to the 1907 battlegrounds that he did in 1906, as the Cubs thrashed their closest competitors 42 out of 66 games, beating second place Pittsburgh 12 times, an improved Phillies club 14 times, and the fourth place Giants 16 times in 22 tries. The race was already leaning Chicago's way in July, when Christy Mathewson momentarily stalled the Cub pennant dash with a three-hitter, edging Carl Lundgren, who gave up but four hits himself, in a four-star pitching duel, 1 to 0. The standings after that game read:

	Won	Lost	Pct.	GB
Chicago	51	21	.744	—
New York	48	30	.615	6
Pittsburgh	48	31	.608	6½
Philadelphia	46	34	.558	9

By August 17, after Johnny Kling had homered in the 12th stanza to beat "The Big Six," 3 to 2, in a game that went to "Jack the Giant Killer" Pfiester in relief of Cub ace Brown, the Cubs had upped their lead to 14½ games over Pittsburgh and the race was, for all intents and purposes, over. The box score:

Chicago	R	H	PO	A	New York	R	H	PO	A
Hofman, cf	1	2	2	1	Shannon, rf	2	3	3	0
Sheckard, lf	0	1	1	0	Browne, rf	0	0	0	0
Schulte, rf	1	2	4	0	Devlin, 3b	0	0	2	1
Chance, 1b	0	1	20	0	Seymour, cf	0	1	6	0
Steinfeldt, 3b	0	0	0	2	Bresnahan, c	0	1	11	1
Tinker, ss	0	1	1	5	Bowerman, 1b	0	1	11	0
Evers, 2b	0	0	6	2	Shay, ss	0	2	0	2
Kling, c	1	1	2	3	Doyle, 2b	0	0	3	2
Brown, p	0	0	0	7	Strang, ph	0	0	0	0
Moran, ph	0	0	0	0	Mathewson, p	0	0	0	3
Pfiester, p	0	0	0	2					
Totals	3	8	36	22	Totals	2	8	36	9

Line Score New York 101 000 000 000 2–8–1
Chicago 000 000 002 001 3–8–4

2BH—Schulte, Chance, Tinker
HR—Kling
SH—Browne 2, Bowerman, Seymour, Sheckard
SB—Bresnahan
LOB—New York 4, Chicago 5
DP—Hofman and Kling
K—Mathewson 10, Brown 1
BB—Mathewson 1
Umpires—Rigler and Emslie
Time—2:20
Attendance—20,105

In contrast to Chicago's October climax, New York hit its zenith early in the season. When the two teams first met, McGraw's Giants had already strung together a 17 game winning streak, and when Joe McGinnity avenged the Cubs season series opening victory with a 7 to 1 win on May 22 the McGrawmen found themselves atop the league with a scorching 25 and 5 record. That put them a full game ahead of the Chicagoans. But as the season wore on the Giants fell steadily behind, dropping finally to fourth for their lowest finish since 1902.

Some things hadn't changed, however. One was the brilliance of the pitching staff, which kept firing away on a par with Frank Chance's hurlers. Another was the irascible McGraw, in and out of one scrape after another. The log on McGraw misdemeanors was growing year by year. Donald Dewey and Nick Alcocella summed the more glaring incidents this way:

> Field fights (Ed: at the ballpark) were incessant, and as often as not involved fans jumping down from the stands to join in. As for McGraw himself, he was blamed for inciting two riots of Polo Grounds fans against umpires in 1907; arrested for fomenting a riot in Boston in 1908; (and) arrested for joining umpire Cy Rigler in a brawl against some Cuban fans in a Havana bar in 1911... In addition to all these personal incidents, there was never any doubt in the N.L. office that the manager's temperament was the catalyst for the regular series of fracases involving New York players [In *The Biographical History of Baseball*, Carroll & Graf Pub., NY, 1995, p. 307].

But despite the constant swirl of buzzing bees that accompanied every day and every game, the man tended to the business of managing his ball club like few others before or since. Say what you will about his impossible behavior, but grant him the brilliance of his Hall of Fame credentials as one of the game's finest field generals, remembering, too, that his players asked only, "How high?"

As to the pitching brilliance that was a New York hallmark throughout the deadball segment of the McGraw years, the following listing presents some rather persuasive evidence of its lofty status in the pitching fraternity. The minimal level listed for games won is 20, and for ERA, 3.00.

Year	Games Won/ERA
1903	McGinnity, 31; 2.43 ERA; Mathewson, 30; 2.26 ERA
1904	McGinnity, 35; 1.61 ERA; Mathewson, 33; 2.03 ERA; L. Taylor, 21; 2.34 ERA; Wiltse, 13; 2.84 ERA
1905	Mathewson, 32; 1.27 ERA; McGinnity, 22; 2.87 ERA; Ames, 22; 2.74 ERA; Wiltse, 14; 2.47 ERA
1906	McGinnity, 27; 2.25 ERA; Mathewson, 22; 2.97 ERA; L. Taylor, 2.20; Wiltse, 2.28 ERA
1907	Mathewson, 24; 2.00 ERA; Wiltse, 2.18 ERA
1908	Mathewson, 37; 1.43 ERA; Wiltse, 23; 2.24 ERA
1909	Mathewson, 25; 1.14 ERA Wiltse, 20, 2.01 ERA; Raymond, 2.47 ERA
1910	Mathewson, 27; 1.90 ERA; Crandall, 17; 2.55 ERA; Wiltse, 2.72 ERA
1911	Mathewson, 26; 1.99 ERA; Marquard, 24; 2.49 ERA; Crandall, 2.63 ERA
1912	Mathewson, 23; 2.12 ERA; Marquard, 26; 2.57 ERA; Tesreau, 22; 2.17 ERA
1913	Mathewson, 25; 2.06 ERA; Marquard, 23; 2.50 ERA; Tesreau, 1.96 ERA; Ames, 2.46 ERA
1914	Tesreau, 26; 2.38 ERA; Mathewson, 24
1915	Tesreau, 2.19 ERA
1917	Schupp, 21; 1.95 ERA; Sallee, 2.17 ERA; Perritt, 1.88 ERA
1919	Barnes, 25; 2.40 ERA; Toney, 1.84 ERA
1920	Toney, 21; 2.65 ERA; Barnes, 20; 2.65 ERA; Nehf, 21

The 1907 season series between two legendary pitching staffs was loaded with masterpieces. Notice first that with the exception of the last meeting between these two clubs on October 2, the winning team held the losing team to four runs or less in every game. In those losing efforts the average number of runs scored was 1.57. The winners in those 21 games averaged 4.48 runs, resulting in a 5 to 2 score, on a typical 1907 summer's day at either West Side Park or the Polo Grounds. 10 games were decided by one run, and there were 17 times (out of 22, mind you) when the fans saw the winning pitcher give up two runs or less. The pitcher's heyday was on—full swing!

The 1907 Season Series

May 21	Chi	3	NY	2	Brown, WP	Mathewson, LP
May 22	NY	7	Chi	1	McGinnity, WP	Overall, LP

May 23	Chi	5	NY	2	Lundgren, WP	Wiltse, LP
June 5	Chi	8	NY	2	Brown, WP	Mathewson, LP
June 6	Chi	3	NY	2	J. Taylor, WP	McGinnity, LP
June 8	Chi	4	NY	3	Brown, WP	Ames, LP
July 19	Chi	12	NY	3	Brown, WP	McGinnity, LP
July 20	NY	1	Chi	0	Mathewson, WP	Lundgren, LP
July 22	Chi	2	NY	0	Reulbach, WP	Wiltse, LP
July 23	NY	1	Chi	0	Ames, WP	Brown, LP
August 2	Chi	5	NY	1	Brown, WP	Mathewson, LP
August 3	Chi	3	NY	2	Overall, WP	Wiltse, LP
August 4	Chi	2	NY	1	Reulbach, WP	McGinnity, LP
August 5	NY	5	Chi	4	Ames, WP	J. Taylor, LP
August 6	Chi	2	NY	0	Brown, WP	L. Taylor, LP
August 17	Chi	3	NY	2	Pfiester, WP	Mathewson, LP
August 19	NY	2	Chi	1	Lynch, WP	Lundgren, LP
August 20	Chi	6	NY	2	Pfiester, WP	McGinnity, LP
August 21	NY	12	Chi	4	Ames, WP	J. Taylor, LP
September 30	Chi	6	NY	0	Reulbach, WP	Wiltse, LP
October 1	Chi	2	NY	1	Lundgren, WP	Mathewson, LP
October 2	Chi	13	NY	7	Brown, WP	L. Taylor, LP

Merkle and More

On some days it seems as though the world stands still, so earth-shaking are the events that fill their short span of hours. Historians mark them, carefully pointing out their momentous significance. July 4, 1776, November 11, 1918, and June 6, 1944, are but three of them.

For baseball buffs September 23, 1908, is one of those dates, the day of the oft chronicled "Fred Merkle Game." Whatever else happened during the season of 1908, and there was plenty in an action-packed year, pales in the face of the one play on which a championship turned. In *Total Baseball: The Official Encyclopedia of Major League Baseball*,[12] the "Merkle Game" is referred to as "the most controversial game ever played." Everything about that game, what led up to it, its consequences, and the famed playoff game it necessitated has been covered with excruciating care, including interviews with virtually every player on both teams, the umpires, sportswriters and league officials. And still, the mere mention of it stirs our curiosity.

In this review of the Giants-Cubs history during the years it dominated both the National League and baseball's headlines, there is hardly room to cover that spectacular series of events. Instead, one of the more telling statements coming out of that whole affair, attributed to Christy Mathewson, captures the very essence of the aura that surrounded the make-up game, made even more trenchant simply because it involved the Cubs and Giants. Mathewson said:

> If this game goes to Chicago by any trick or argument, you can take it from me that if we lose the pennant thereby, I will never play professional baseball again."13

Every last ounce of calculated, contentious sentiment that surrounded Cubs-Giants ballgames, and especially this one, seems to have been crammed into that one short Mathewson warning. Of course, the game was played, the Giants lost, and Christy Mathewson, despite his ominous declaration, moved on in his Hall of Fame career.

Box scores of the two pivotal games of that exceptional 1908 season have appeared in countless numbers of publications. Rather than either of these games, however, one of equal portent appears here, having been played as the second game of the previous day's doubleheader which, at a point in the race that was as tight as wet rope, involving the Cubs and Giants, as well as Pittsburgh, featured "Miner" Brown, who vanquished the Giants on a sparkling six-hitter, 3 to 1. This is the September 22, 1908, box score of the second game, which completed the twin-killing, thus enabling the Cubs to stay at the heels of the league-leading Giants. After play that day the standings read: (The box score follows.)

	Won	Lost	Pct.
New York	87	50	.635
Chicago	90	53	.629
Pittsburgh	88	54	.619

New York	AB	R	H	PO	Chicago	AB	R	H	PO
Tenney, 1b	4	0	0	17	Hayden, rf	5	0	2	2
Herzog, 2b	4	1	2	0	Evers, 2b	4	1	2	3
Bresnahan, c	4	0	2	4	Schulte, lf	4	0	0	0
Donlin, rf	3	0	1	0	Chance, 1b	3	1	2	13
Seymour, cf	4	0	1	4	Steinfeldt, 3b	4	0	1	2
Devlin, 3b	4	0	0	0	Hofman, cf	3	0	0	4
McCormick, lf	3	0	0	2	Tinker, ss	4	0	1	0
Bridwell, ss	2	0	0	0	Kling, c	3	1	1	3
Crandall, p	2	0	0	0	Brown, p	4	0	0	0
Merkle, ph	1	0	0	0					
McGinnity, p	0	0	0	0					
Totals	30	1	6	27	Totals	34	3	9	27

Line Score	Chicago	000 002 001	3–9–0
	New York	000 100 000	1–6–0

This threesome of vintage super stars, Art Devlin of the Giants, shown here with Frank Chance and the Cubs' crack third baseman, Harry "Steinie" Steinfeldt, played prominent roles in the success of arch-enemies New York and Chicago.

2BH—Herzog, Bresnahan 2, Hayden, Chance, Steinfeldt
3BH—Herzog
SB—Chance, Donlin
SH—Hofman, Donlin
LOB—Chicago 5, New York 8
DP—Evers and Steinfeldt
K—Brown 3, Crandall 2, McGinnity
1 BB—Brown 2, Crandall 3, McGinnity 0
WP—Brown
Umpires—O'Day and Emslie
Time—1:35
Attendance—30,009

You will certainly have noticed in the box score above that Fred Merkle's name appears, this time as a pinch-hitter for pitcher James "Doc" Crandall in the seventh inning. The circumstances and Merkle's at-bat are explained by the clever *New York Times* sportswriter W. W. Aulick in the *Times'* September 23 edition, *the same day* as the celebrated "Merkle Boner" game.

> Three men on bases... Come on, Merkle, if they won't let Crandall bat. We trust in you, Merkle, darlin'. You'd never throw us down now, would you, with three men on bases, a single to tie, and a chance to win out on the inning? Of course, you wouldn't. Step up there, good man, and play base

ball. Phaw! Why did you hit at that first one? Why didn't you wait? It wasn't worth your effort. Pick out a bonny one, and strike for the freedom of your sires, and a little bit more. Not that one, not that, Merkle. Didn't we give you waiting orders? Never mind, there is one chance left. Use it wisely. Get a firm hold on your bat, and slash away over yonder along third-base line. If you are not in a position make it the right field, up as near the grandstand as you can get without fouling. Or, if you think you can pull it off, a Texas leaguer will demoralize them. Or you might—Mr. Merkle has struck out, gentlemen. Donlin, Devlin, Bridwell, what of them? Were you ever at a reception where the lion of the hour and day came over to your corner, shook hands with the neighbor on your right, and the neighbor on your left, and then—looked coldly past you and walked on, leaving you with your dexter fork extended in the air and feeling foolish all over? That's how Messrs. Donlin, Devlin and Bridwell felt when Mr. Merkle passed them up. Let's all go home. And they call themselves Cubs!

It seems that Mr. Merkle, only 19 at the time, was not without a practice swing or two before his "big moment" came only 24 hours later. Among the limited possibilities inherent in that instant, he chose, unfortunately, the one that negated at least a momentary spot in the dazzling sunlight of glory. While Al Bridwell's base hit might not have won the pennant, it would indeed have won the game, thus solidifying a much stronger hold on first place—had the young fellow, who had singled crisply to become another Giant baserunner, only touched second base instead of heading for the clubhouse. But the baseball gods had decreed otherwise, and, given a second chance, Evers, Tinker, Brown, Reulbach, Steinfeldt, and the rest of those persistent Cubs made the most of it.

As tight as the National League race was, the American League pennant drill was even tighter. Its race came down to the last weekend of the season with four teams sharing championship hopes. Detroit finally survived, despite a legitimate

Fred Merkle, who played well for both the Giants and the Cubs during his fine, 16-year major league career.

concern regarding the number of games it had played, thus putting its right to the flag in question. But again, those baseball gods, wherever they might have been, had apparently decreed a second straight, Cobb-led pennant for the Detroiters. The Tigers, who had waited a full year to get back at the Cubs, now had their chance, but the Bruins, now under full sail, would have nothing to do with anything less than the victor's spoils, dispatching them in four out of five games, to win their second straight world's championship. The Frank Chance Cubbies settled in as Chicago's "toast of the town," worthy heirs of Anson's titans, their 1906 World Series failure by now exorcised.

Inside the confines of the major leagues' two ultra-exciting pennant chases there was no lack of season highlights. Here are some of them.

>> Mordecai Brown led Cub pitchers with a career best 26 and 6 mark. One of those losses was to the Giants' Leon "Red" Ames, 1 to 0. The 20-gamer was in the midst of a six-straight run of 20-game seasons. On July 4 he logged his fourth consecutive shutout against the Pirates.

>> Another July 4 firecracker was thrown by the Giants' George "Hooks" Wiltse, who pitched a 10-inning no-hitter at the Polo Grounds, beating the Phils, 1–0.

Southpaw George "Hooks" Wiltse, who won in double figures for the Giants from 1904 to 1911. He made several game-saving plays as a first baseman to help Christy Mathewson win game two of the 1913 world series.

>> Christy Mathewson registered the last of his four, 30-game seasons with an eye-popping 37 victories. He also led the league in ERA (1.43), K's (259), shutouts (12), innings pitched (391) and complete games (34).

>> Tinker, Evers and Chance, at the height of their magical infield play, are immortalized in the poetry of Franklin P. Adams. The last four lines: Ruthlessly pricking our gonfalon bubble, Making a Giant hit into a double, Words that are weighty with nothing but trouble; Tinker to Evers to Chance.

>> On October 1, "Big Ed" Reulbach duplicated Three Finger Brown's four consecutive shutout feat earlier in the season by whitewashing Cincinnati, 6 to 0 at Chicago's West Side Grounds. On September

Left and below: "Big Ed" Reulbach, Cub Mainstay throughout the mighty Cub pennant era, 1906–1910. Despite bad eye-sight, which prompted Cub catchers to paint their gloves white, he pitched the first world series one-hitter against the White Sox in the 1906 world series.

26 he had shut out Brooklyn in both ends of a doubleheader, 5 to 0 and 3 to 0. He was a 24 game winner with a 2.03 ERA in 1908.

>> The Giants, with the best Run Differential in the league, 196, paced most of the offensive statistics, leading the league in hits with 69 more than closest rival, Chicago, and made a clean sweep of the BA, OB% and SA stats.

>> On October 14 big, burly Orval Overall whiffed 10 and shut out the Tigers to close out the World Series. Only 6,210 were on hand to witness Detroit's, and especially Ty Cobb's final humiliation.

Left: Orv Overall, big righthander, who came to the Cubs in a trade with Cincinnati early in 1906 and justified Frank Chances insistence on adding him to the Chicago roster. His sparkling 12–3 log and a 1.88 ERA capped a sensational Chicago debut. (George Brace photograph)

The 1908 Season Series

May 24	NY	6	Chi	4	McGinnity, WP	Fraser, LP
May 25	Chi	8	NY	7	Brown, WP	Wiltse, LP
May 26	NY	7	Chi	4	Crandall, WP	Reulbach, LP
May 27	NY	1	Chi	0	Wiltse, WP	Pfiester, LP
June 18	Chi	7	NY	5	Reulbach,WP	Wiltse, LP
June 19	NY	6	Chi	3	Crandall, WP	Pfiester, LP
June 20	NY	4	Chi	0	Mathewson, WP	Fraser, LP
June 22	NY	7	Chi	1	Wiltse, WP	Lundgren, LP
July 15	NY	11	Chi	0	Wiltse, WP	Brown, LP
July 16	NY	4	Chi	3	Crandall, WP	Reulbach, LP
July 17	Chi	1	NY	0	Brown, WP	Mathewson, LP
July 18	Chi	5	NY	4	Pfiester, WP	Wiltse, LP
August 8	NY	4	Chi	1	Wiltse, WP	Brown, LP
August 10	NY	3	Chi	2	Mathewson, WP	Overall, LP
August 11	Chi	4	NY	0	Pfiester, WP	Wiltse, LP
August 27	Chi	5	NY	4	Pfiester, WP	Wiltse, LP
August 29	Chi	3	NY	2	Brown, WP	Mathewson, LP
August 30	Chi	2	NY	1	Pfiester, WP	McGinnity, LP
September 22	Chi	4	NY	3	Overall, WP	Ames, LP
September 22	Chi	3	NY	1	Brown, WP	Crandall, LP
September 23	"Merkle Game," 1–1 tie, replayed on October 8					
September 24	NY	5	Chi	4	Wiltse, WP	Brown, LP
October 8	Chi	4	NY	2	Brown, WP	Mathewson, LP

One More Time

Between 1903 and 1912, New York, Chicago and Pittsburgh finished 1-2-3 in the National League's composite standings. Never before had three teams so controlled the championship end of the standings, nor would such three-team domination ever happen again. The Pirates, always dangerous and sometimes successful at winning it all, won the N.L. crown in 1909, thus providing the inimitable Honus Wagner and his Pittsburgh teammates with one last hurrah, and even though Frank Chance's Cubs won 104 games, setting a record for a second place team, the Pirates' 110 victories were more than enough to bring the crown back to Pittsburgh after years of frustrating second and third place finishes. The Giants, winding up nearly 20 games off the Pirates' blistering pace, were nonetheless in the thick of the race a good part of the season.

Although they would come back to win the pennant in 1910 with another year of 100-plus wins, the Cubs would not win a fourth straight pennant, and, in fact, had already entered what can only be called an eon of time during which a world's championship would elude them. Pennants? Yes, extending through the 1945 season. But in seven successive World Series attempts after their 1908 victory over the Tigers they would come up empty. And to this very day legions of Cub fans everywhere are still waiting.

The Giants and Cubs broke even in the season series, their two pitching staffs running up still more glitter, as the Mathewsons, Browns, Reulbachs, Pfiesters and Ameses kept right on throwing low-hit games at one another. One of the better Giant-Cub tussles occurred on Chicago's President's Day, September 16, when William H. Taft, a baseball nut of the first order, attended a game at the West Side Grounds. The 1910 Spalding Guide included a two-page review in its annual baseball publication for this special occasion, reporting:

> Though a special box had been provided for him, the President preferred that he might join the real "rooters," and, among them and one of them, he enjoyed one of the brilliant games of the year in company with more than 30,000 other enthusiasts, who witnessed the defeat of the Chicago team by New York by the score of 2 to 1 [Spalding's Baseball Guide, 1910 edition, American Sports Publishing Co., NY, 1910, p.51].

The defeat of the Cubs that day was administered by the great Mathewson, who victimized his old rival Three Finger Brown in a game that was over, from the standpoint of the final score, in the second inning, when the Cubs answered two Giant opening stanza tallies with a run in the bottom

The old West Side Grounds, Wrigley Field predecessor, scene of those thrilling Giant and Cub skirmishes between 1893 and 1915. This action shot was taken down the left field line in 1906.

half of the second inning. The box score of that game on September 16 follows:

New York	AB	R	H	PO	Chicago	AB	R	H	PO
Doyle, 2b	4	0	2	2	Evers, 2b	4	0	1	3
Seymour, cf	3	0	0	1	Sheckard, lf	4	0	0	3
McCormick, lf	4	1	0	1	Schulte, rf	4	0	2	1
Murray, rf	4	1	2	2	Chance, 1b	4	0	0	9
Devlin, 3b	4	0	1	2	Steinfeldt, 3b	4	0	1	2
Bridwell, ss	4	0	0	4	Hofman, cf	4	0	0	2
Tenney, 1b	3	0	1	11	Tinker, ss	3	1	1	3
Meyers, c	3	0	0	4	Archer, c	3	0	1	3
Mathewson, p	3	0	1	0	Brown, p	3	0	1	1
Totals	32	2	7	27	Totals	33	1	7	27

Line Score			
New York	200 000 000	2–7–0
Chicago	010 000 000	1–7–0

2 BH—Doyle, Tinker
SH—Seymour
SB—Murray, Devlin, Hofman, Schulte
LOB—New York 4, Chicago 5
DP—Doyle, Bridwell and Tenney
K—Mathewson 4, Brown 2
BB—None
Umpires—Johnstone and Rigler
Time—1:35
Attendance—30,000

From the 1909 Scrapbook

>> The Pirates won 14 straight games between May 30 and June 15, moving into a commanding league lead.

>> In Brooklyn on August 10, Ed Reulbach won his 14th straight game, finishing up the season with 19 wins and a 1.42 ERA, a mark that was only good enough for third place among N.L. pitchers. Mathewson, with a 1.14 and Brown, with a 1.31, bettered "Big Ed."

>> Two tragic deaths occurred in July: Frank Selee died on the 5th and N.L. President Harry Pulliam took his own life on the 28th, depressed over the New York franchise's constant friction (Brush, McGraw and other Giants were not the only troublemakers in the league) and contention in league matters.

>> On April 15, Leon "Red" Ames, entering his seventh season as a Giant starter, tossed a no-hitter for nine innings against Brooklyn's Superbas,

Leon "Red" Ames, New York Giant righthander. He was the strong, "third man" on those Mathewson-McGinnity and Mathewson-Marquard pitching staffs of McGraw's pennant-winning teams.

only to lose the game in the 13th inning, 3 to 0. On September 18 he beat Orv Overall 2 to 0, after having lost a game by the same score to Jack Pfiester in 11 innings on August 30.

>> The Cubs helped the Pirates inaugurate Forbes Field on June 30, before 30, 338 fans, but ruined Pittsburgh's big day by beating them 3 to 2.

>> The season series between the Braves and Cubs was a disaster for Boston. They won only once in the 22 game series. Chicago's 21 for 22 record against Cincinnati in 1945 tied the franchise record established in 1909.

>> The top four spots among pitchers for fewest walks per game went to the top three teams in the league, with Mathewson of the Giants at 1.18, first; Brown of the Cubs second at 1.39; Wiltse, NY, 1.70, third; and Nick Maddox, 13 and 8 for Pittsburgh, fourth at 1.73.

>> Legendary Hans Wagner won his fourth straight batting title with a

.339. There were only two other .300 hitters with enough plate appearances to qualify for the batting crown. Both were Redlegs: Mike Mitchell, at .310, and Richard "Doc" Hoblitzel, .308.

>> Note that in the season series (following) the Cubs' pitching staff held the Giants to *two* runs or less in nine of their 11 1909 victories. In 14 of the 22 games in the series, the losing team scored *one or no runs at all.*

The 1909 Season Series

May 11	Chi	4	NY	3	Brown, WP	Wiltse, LP
May 12	NY	3	Chi	2	Marquard, WP	Overall, LP
May 13	NY	4	Chi	1	Mathewson, WP	Kroh, LP
May 14	Chi	6	NY	0	Pfiester, WP	Raymond, LP
June 8	NY	3	Chi	2	Mathewson, WP	Brown, LP
June 10	Chi	5	NY	0	Pfiester, WP	Marquard, LP
July 22	Chi	3	NY	1	Reulbach, WP	Wiltse, LP
July 24	Chi	4	NY	1	Brown, WP	Raymond, LP
August 12	NY	5	Chi	2	Wiltse, WP	Brown, LP
August 12	NY	3	Chi	0	Mathewson, WP	Pfiester, LP
August 13	NY	6	Chi	2	Raymond, WP	Kroh, LP
August 14	NY	5	Chi	2	Ames, WP	Reulbach, LP
August 15	Chi	9	NY	0	Brown, WP	Crandall, LP
August 27	Chi	8	NY	6	Higginbotham, WP	Raymond, LP
August 28	Chi	6	NY	1	Brown, WP	Mathewson, LP
August 30	Chi	2	NY	0	Pfiester, WP	Ames, LP
August 30	NY	5	Chi	0	Mathewson, WP	Reulbach, LP
August 31	Chi	2	NY	0	Brown, WP	Wiltse, LP
September 16	NY	2	Chi	1	Mathewson, WP	Brown, LP
September 17	NY	4	Chi	1	Wiltse, WP	Pfiester, LP
September 18	NY	2	Chi	0	Ames, WP	Overall, LP
September 20	Chi	3	NY	2	Pfiester, WP	Marquard, LP

One Last Curtain Call

The beginning of the end of the Cubs' towering championship run during the 20th century's first decade came during their last series of the season at Cincinnati when Johnny Evers suffered a compound fracture sliding into home plate. That put him on crutches and out of the World Series. Even as the Cubs clinched the pennant during that series, there were signs, at least for those who chose to see them, that the Chicago juggernaut was not quite what it had been, despite rolling up 104 wins during the season. They had once again brushed aside the hated Giants and the pestering

Pirates, but Evers, who was as usual at the very edge of a breakdown on any given day, and the "Peerless Leader," Frank Chance, in and out of the lineup because he was slowing up and knew it, and Miner Brown, just a tiny morsel slower to home plate, were three of the mainstays, among others, who had just entered that painful stage during a player's career when playing, and especially winning, was just plain everyday harder.

During the 1910 World Series the Bruins ran into the same Connie Mack buzzsaw that would tear the Giants apart in 1911 and 1913, falling to the Athletics four games out of five. McGraw's legions could do no better, losing to Philadelphia by the same four to one margin in 1913 after a four to two setback in 1911. Both of the feared N.L. dynamos, it seems, ran out of steam at about the same time. A retooling was in order.

They called him "The Crab." About him, Ogden Nash wrote: E is for Evers, his jaw in advance; Never afraid to tinker with Chance. (Dennis Colgin photograph)

But there were those days during the 1910 season when Giants and Cubs of old were spectacularly on display. On June 28, for example, Joe Tinker became the first major leaguer to steal home twice in one game as the Cubs beat Cincinnati at Chicago, 11 to 1, behind Mordecai Brown, who was magnificently on target all day

Steady and Brainy, far-ranging Joe Tinker (Hall of Fame, 1946) He was just as much a part of the Bruin braintrust as were the more heralded John Evers and Frank Chance. Tinker was the Cubs' 1916 manager.

long. On August 25 Leonard "King" Cole, Chicago's sensational freshman righthander, who in 1910 would set a rookie record for winning percentage at .833 (he won 20 and lost only four), pairing with Brown to amass 45 of Chicago's 104 wins. Just two days later Christy Mathewson and Co. put on a hitting clinic to down the Cubs in Chicago, embarrassing them by an 18 to 9 count. The August 25 box score follows:

New York	AB	R	H	PO	Chicago	AB	R	H	PO
Devore, lf	5	1	4	1	Evers, 2b	3	2	2	4
Doyle, 2b	6	4	5	3	Kane, 2b	0	1	0	0
Snodgrass, cf	3	3	2	4	Sheckard, lf	5	2	3	0
Murray, rf	6	0	1	1	Hofman, cf, 3b	5	2	2	1
Bridwell, ss	5	1	1	0	Archer, 1b	5	0	2	11
Devlin, 3b	6	1	2	0	Zimmerman, 3b	4	1	1	2
Merkle, 1b	5	1	2	12	Overall, rf	0	0	0	0
Meyers, c	6	2	2	4	Schulte, rf, cf	5	0	1	1
Mathewson, p	4	2	2	0	Tinker, ss	5	1	3	4
Keeler, lf	1	2	1	2	Needham, c	2	0	0	2
Dickson, p	0	0	0	0	Kling, c	3	0	1	2
Wiltse, p	1	1	1	0	Reulbach, p	0	0	0	0
					Richie, p	1	0	0	0
					Foxen, p	1	0	0	0
					Beaumont, ph	1	0	0	0
					Steinfeldt, ph	1	0	0	0
					Pfeffer, p	0	0	0	0
					McIntire, ph	1	0	0	0
					Cole, ph	1	0	0	0
Totals	48	18	23	27	Totals	43	9	15	27

Line Score	New York	410 222 304	18–23–2
	Chicago	200 020 500	9–15–6

2BH—Mathewson, Devore, Kling, Devlin, Evers, Doyle, Snodgrass, Sheckard, Hofman, Zimmerman, Tinker 2, Archer 2
SH—Merkle
SB—Tinker
LOB—New York 7, Chicago 7
DP—Bridwell, Doyle, Merkle
TP—Evers and Zimmerman
WP—Foxen
Balk—Foxen
Time—2:30
Umpires—Rigler and Emslie

An item on the Giants lineup in this game is in order. Note that three

Fred Snodgrass, who with Fred Merkle and "Heinie" Zimmerman, formed an unfortunate threesome, each involved in misplays that were, at best, incidents of shared blame. Snodgrass was important enough in the McGraw scheme of things to play for the Giants from 1908 to 1915.

names, all prominent in the Giants' history book as perpetrators of unforgivable misplays in games with a championship on the line, appear here. The first two are Merkle, of 1908 "boner" fame, and fiery Fred Snodgrass, who was to commit the $30,000 muff on a fly ball in the 1912 World Series. The third is Heinie Zimmerman, in this game playing as a Cub third baseman, but later with McGraw's Giants, who would chase Eddie Collins of the White Sox across home plate in the 1917 World Series. And lest we forget, John McGraw always stood by his players, defending each of the three, and in fact giving Snodgrass a raise for the 1913 season.

There always seemed to be something about that New York-Chicago matchup that brought about some kind of wizardry, or alchemy, or some kind of heroic miracle, or even outright baseball disaster when the two clashed during those magic days of National League preeminence. 1910 was no exception. Here are a few samples:

>>   The old "Giant Killer," Jack Pfiester, won only six games all year long, but three of those were against the Giants, and by convincing 2 to 0, 3 to 0, and 5 to 1 scores.

>>   On August 2, Floyd "Rube" Kroh, whose only victories in 1910 were against the Giants, made the mistake of beating Christy Mathewson, 5 to 4. The next time they met, on August 5 in the concluding game of the series, Matty dusted off the Cubs and Kroh, 10 to 1.

>>   Although he was a 25-game winner in 1910, Three Finger Brown was roughed up with a four-run outburst in the first inning of the July 9 game which the Giants won 7 to 3. That chased the Cub mainstay as he took the loss, one of two during the season to New York, while beating them three times. He did not face off against Mathewson during the 1910 season.

The 1910 Season Series

May 9	Chi	2	NY	0	Pfiester, WP	Raymond, LP
May 10	Chi	9	NY	5	Overall, WP	Mathewson, LP
May 11	Chi	4	NY	3	Kroh, WP	Marquard, LP
May 12	NY	9	Chi	1	Wiltse, WP	McIntire, LP
June 10	Chi	6	NY	5	Richie, WP	Mathewson, LP
June 13	Chi	6	NY	2	Brown, WP	Ames, LP
June 14	Chi	9	NY	4	Kroh, WP	Wiltse, LP
July 9	NY	7	Chi	3	Wiltse, WP	Brown, LP
July 10	NY	10	Chi	9	Crandall, WP	Brown, LP
July 11	Chi	4	NY	2	Richie, WP	Crandall, LP
August 2	Chi	5	NY	4	Kroh, WP	Mathewson, LP
August 3	Chi	3	NY	0	Pfiester, WP	Wiltse, LP
August 4	Chi	5	NY	1	Brown, WP	Ames, LP
August 5	NY	10	Chi	1	Mathewson, WP	Kroh, LP
August 25	Chi	6	NY	1	Cole, WP	Wiltse, LP
August 26	Chi	3	NY	1	Brown, WP	Drucke, LP
August 27	NY	18	Chi	9	Mathewson, WP	Reulbach, LP
August 28	Chi	10	NY	2	Reulbach, WP	Ames, LP
September 22	Chi	5	NY	1	Pfiester, WP	Drucke, LP
September 22	NY	5	Chi	1	Wiltse, WP	Reulbach, LP
September 23	NY	6	Chi	4	Crandall, WP	Cole, LP
September 24	NY	6	Chi	5	Mathewson, WP	Weaver, LP

Back on Top the Season Standings: 1911–1913

	Team	Pos	Won	Lost	Pct.
1911	New York	1	99	54	.647
	Chicago	2	92	62	.597
	Pittsburgh	3	85	69	.552
1912	New York	1	103	48	.682
	Pittsburgh	2	93	58	.616
	Chicago	3	91	59	.606
1913	New York	1	101	48	.664
	Philadelphia	2	88	63	.583
	Chicago	3	88	65	.575

It was as though McGraw & Co. had said, "Enough already," promptly reeling off three pennants in a row between 1911 and 1913 to match Chicago's 1906 to 1908 triad. So it was, that the New Yorkers fought and slashed and out-defensed their N.L. rivals just as they had done back in those glory days of 1904 and 1905. As suddenly as they had been swept aside then, just as suddenly did they reappear in 1911. Interestingly, the three flags didn't

John McGraw was always fired up for a ball game despite his rather calm pregame appearance here.

come at Chicago's expense inasmuch as the season series' outcome during that three year span wound up with New York victorious over the Cubs in games played by a narrow 34 to 32 margin. But while New York's return to the top, accomplished by dint of masterful managing, shrewd manipulation of talent, and just the right mixture of veteran and younger players, marked the Manhattanites, once again, as the N.L.'s team to beat, the story in Chicago was far less encouraging. The Cubs, in fact, were headed in another direction despite five successive first division finishes after their 1910 pennant. The edge was gone, however, and they begun an era of drifting mediocrity that produced but one championship between 1910 and 1929, which came in 1918. Frank Chance, Johnny Evers, who during the 1911 season actually did fall victim to a nervous breakdown, and Harry Steinfeldt were no longer the infield stalwarts of pennant years past, replaced by Vic Saier at first, Jack Doyle at third, and Heinie Zimmerman at the pivot. The pitching staff finally began to show the wear and tear of past pennant strains, and the replacements for the old warriors were good, but not great.

On the other hand, John McGraw went about his business at the Polo Grounds with renewed determination, spurred by an inner fire that always flared in the face of continued frustration or defeat. Digging deep into the hearts and psyche of his players, he drove them relentlessly, without favor for any one player over another, except perhaps for his ace, the peerless Mathewson. The defense behind the Giants' masterful pitching was refurbished, and the offense returned to its run-at-a-time attack, stealing, using the hit-and-run and the run-and-hit, and all the old tricks out of Baltimore's 1890s play book (refined by McGraw to suit a new day) that constantly had their opponents on edge. And it produced. Big Time. The Giants cut down runners, choking off more runs each season. In 1912 they permitted 25 fewer runners to cross home plate than in 1911, their first championship season in six years. That may not seem like much, but the 1911 team allowed only 567 runs as it was. Their 542 total in 1912, in company with a staff ERA of 2.58 and 125 twin killings resulted in one of the better Run Differential performances, 214, in the game's history. And, oh, how they stole bases: 347, amounting to better than two per game. Although there is much to be said for the 1904-05 Giant powerhouses as McGraw's best, these 1911–13 New York teams, if not quite as good, didn't miss by much, at all.

Still, the Giants were unable to take home a World Series championship during the last of the great Mathewson years. And the demon of World Series defeat must surely have eaten at John McGraw, more so by far than any of the players who endured one agonizing, freakish misplay after another during their encounters with the Athletics in 1911 and 1913, and particularly with the Boston Red Sox in 1912. Such is the game, however. Ask Bobby Cox's Atlanta Braves of the 1990s.

In 1913 the Cubs fell to third place behind a Philadelphia team that was soon to win a pennant of its own behind "the second Mathewson," Pete Alexander, and the Pirates, who for more than a decade had shadowed both Chicago and New York, fell from contention. It would not be until 1929 that the three would hook up in another 1-2-3 race to the wire, the flag on that occasion returning to Chicago after an absence of 11 seasons.

1911: A Pennant for the Polo Grounds

Sturdy defense, brash base running, timely hitting, and above all, superb pitching, time-tested McGraw hallmarks, produced champions during the dead ball era. McGraw's 1911 ballclub was no exception. The Giants returned to the National League's summit with more than enough of each to finish the race 7½ games ahead of the Bruins, 14½ ahead of the Pirates and miles ahead of everyone else. McGraw's starting rotation, Mathewson (26 and 13), Richard "Rube" Marquard, who finally emerged as a premier frontliner (24 and 7), James "Doc" Crandall (15 and 5 with 5 saves), and Red Ames (11 and 10), was easily the best in the league, continuing a long-standing tradition of well nigh invincible pitching. That standard of pitching excellence, paralleled, but not excelled by the great Selee-Chance pitching corps of the Cubs, is underscored by the following table, complied by the respected baseball historian Bill Deane.[14]

Hypothetical Cy Young Award Winners, 1902–1913

1902	J. Taylor, Cubs	1908	Mathewson, Giants
1903	Mathewson, Giants	1909	Mathewson, Giants
1904	McGinnity, Giants	1910	Mathewson, Giants

1905	Mathewson, Giants	1911	Mathewson, Giants
1906	M. Brown, Cubs	1912	Marquard, Giants
1907	Mathewson, Giants	1913	Mathewson, Giants

You will not fail to notice that the list is dominated by Christy Mathewson, and further, that only Cubs and Giants were named award winners. The years coincide almost exactly with their magnificent era of National League dominance.

Another significant award, inaugurated in 1911 by the president of the Chalmers Motor Company, baseball aficionado Hugh Chalmers, honored one player in each league with what is today recognized as the Most Valuable Player award. The 1911 award winner was Frank Schulte, Chicago's hard-hitting outfielder (1904–16), whose career year matched his pet horse's name, "Wildfire." The choices for a Schulte sobriquet were, naturally, limited to one, Wildfire, and that is what his gaudy 1911 figures amounted to: 21 roundtrippers, 107 RBIs, a .534 SA, and 40 Batting Runs, all league-leading figures. Although Schulte out-pointed Mathewson for the league's award, the hypothetical Cy Young award winner went to the World Series while the husky Kentuckian and his Cub teammates had to content themselves with a Chicago City Series—which they lost in a humbling, 4-zip set to the White Sox.

The Giants' big year was also one of unbelievable superstition that wrapped itself around John McGraw's good-luck charm, Victory Faust, whose apt last name will always be associated with Giant success during 1911. The story, fully detailed in a number of baseball histories,[15] was a lesser headline along the way to the pennant, but nonetheless as real as it was pure fantasy. Faust, who even appeared in twp games managed to provide an otherwise taut, intense Giant dugout with a much-needed moment or two of levity,

Wildfire Schulte, whose stellar 1911 season resulted in the first N.L. MVP award.

also made a road trip with the New Yorkers, an indication of the serious nature of McGraw's entrancement.

Highlights from the Giants' 1911 Pennant Year:

>> The McGrawmen won 20 of their last 24 games, and when lean, Rube Marquard shut out the Cubs in Chicago on October 1, the Giants put the race beyond the reach of Frank Chance's charges.

>> Between the Giants' victorious season opener on April 14 and their scheduled game the next day, fire consumed the Polo Grounds, forcing the New Yorkers to play their home games at the Yanks' Hilltop Park until their new facility, the horseshoe-shaped Polo Grounds III was ready for its June 28 opening.

>> With four hits and two sensational fielding gems, Joe Tinker almost single-handedly beat the Giants and Mathewson on August 7 by an 8 to 6 score. The old Mathewson nemesis doubled and tripled, stole a base, and initiated a double play with an unbelievable stop of a hard smash into the hole. Another old Mathewson rival, Miner Brown, was the winning pitcher.

>> With 347 stolen bases the Giants established a still-standing major league record. Outfielders Josh Devore (67) and Fred Snodgrass (51) led the team.

>> One June 3, MVP winner Wildfire Schulte hit a monstrous grand slam that beat the Giants. It was the first of four in 1911, his only career grand slammers.

>> Pittsburgh's 13 game winning streak between July 20 and August 1 enabled manager Fred Clarke's Pirates to move from fifth place to third, and into a challenging position in the pennant race. Honus Wagner's .334 won his eighth and final N.L. batting championship in 1911.

>> Doc Crandall, one of baseball's first relief aces, finished the 1911 season with eight consecutive victories. His five saves were the N.L.'s second best. Mordecai Brown's 13 led both major leagues.

The 1911 Season Series

May 9	NY	5	Chi	3	Mathewson, WP	Brown, LP
May 10	NY	11	Chi	1	Wiltse, WP	Pfiester, LP
May 11	Chi	6	NY	3	Richie, WP	Ames, LP
May 12	Chi	9	NY	3	McIntire, WP	Crandall, LP

June 2	NY	7	Chi	6	Ames, WP	Cole, LP
June 3	Chi	8	NY	4	Reulbach, WP	Marquard, LP
June 4	Chi	6	NY	5	McIntire, WP	Ames, LP
June 5	NY	7	Chi	1	Mathewson, WP	McIntire, LP
July 6	Chi	6	NY	2	Richie, WP	Crandall, LP
July 7	NY	5	Chi	0	Ames, WP	Reulbach, LP
July 8	NY	5	Chi	2	Marquard, WP	Brown, LP
August 7	Chi	8	NY	6	Brown, WP	Mathewson, LP
August 8	Chi	3	NY	1	Richie, WP	Wiltse, LP
August 9	NY	16	Chi	5	Marquard, WP	Reulbach, LP
August 21	NY	3	Chi	2	Marquard, WP	Richie, LP
August 22	NY	6	Chi	5	Crandall, WP	Brown, LP
September 27	Chi	8	NY	0	Richie, WP	Marquard, LP
September 28	Chi	2	NY	1	Cole, WP	Mathewson, LP
September 30	NY	3	Chi	1	Ames, WP	Brown, LP
October 1	NY	5	Chi	0	Marquard, WP	Richie, LP

Streaking to a
Second Straight Pennant

Christy Mathewson, well into his 32nd year but still at the top of his game, followed his 26 wins in 1911 with another 23, and over 300 innings pitched in 1912. That was enough to help put the Giants into the 1912 World Series, and to assist John McGraw's drive to a fourth New York flag since his 1903 arrival. Mathewson's sterling season was eclipsed, and by plenty, however, when New York's latest hero, a broad-shouldered, handsome southpaw who had hit his stride the year before, had the baseball world agog with a 19-game winning streak that began on opening day and was still intact on the fourth of July. His name was Rube Marquard, and he was slated to pitch again, in search of his 20th straight, on July 8. His opponent? Well now, it would be nice to be able to report that he would be opposing the Chicago Cubs. And as a matter of fact, it was, and in Chicago at

Richard "Rube" Marquard, who won 19 straight in 1912. The Hall of famer was also a vaudevillian, teaming with headliner Blossom Seeley, whom he married.

the old West Side Grounds. Young Jimmy Lavender, in his rookie season (his 16 and 13 record, along with another 16-game winner, Lew Richie and rookie phenom Larry Cheney, winner of 26, led the Cubs' moundsmen in 1912), challenged the Giants that day, and beat them 7 to 2, as the Cubs chased Marquard after six stanzas, bringing to a halt the New York lefty's magnificent streak, as well as New York's 14 game win skein, 1912's longest. That made Lavender's accomplishment doubly noteworthy, though it didn't do much more than lift the second place Cubs to within a "mere" 14 games of the streaking Giant express. The box score of the game on July 8 follows:

Chicago	AB	R	H	A		*New York*	AB	R	H	A
Sheckard, lf	4	0	0	0		Snodgrass, lf	2	1	1	0
Schulte, rf	4	0	1	1		Becker, cf	4	1	2	0
Tinker, ss	4	0	0	3		Merkle, 1b	4	0	1	1
Zimmerman, 3b	3	1	1	1		Murray, rf	4	0	1	0
Leach, cf	3	2	1	0		Herzog, 3b	3	0	0	3
Saier, 1b	4	3	3	0		Meyers, c	3	0	0	1
Evers, 2b	2	0	2	4		Wilson, c	1	0	0	0
Archer, c	3	1	1	3		Fletcher, ss	3	0	0	2
Lavender, p	4	0	1	2		Groh, 3b	3	0	0	3
						Marquard, p	2	0	0	1
						Devore, ph	1	0	0	0
						Tesreau, p	0	0	0	0
Totals	31	7	10	14		Totals	30	2	5	11

Line Score	New York	001 010 000	2–5–3
	Chicago	020 202 01x	7–10–0

2BH—Saier
3BH—Evers
SH—Evers 2
SF—Archer
HBP—Fletcher, Snodgrass, by Lavender
LOB—New York 5, Chicago 6
DP—Groh, Merkle
K—Marquard 5, Lavender 7, Tesreau 1
BB—Lavender 2, Marquard 3, Tesreau 0
WP—Marquard
Umpires—Klem and Bush
Time—2:05

The very next day, July 9, the final New York-Chicago chapter in the Mathewson-Brown saga was written as both hurlers went the route, with

Matty beating his arch-rival, 5 to 2. Thus after eight seasons (they would meet for the last time in 1916, each with 12 wins, and in that 25th confrontation, Ole Miner would be bested by Matty), the final, Giants-Cubs tally was: Brown, 11 wins; Mathewson, 5. 10 of Brown's Cub victories over the Giants came in a row after Matty's no-hit victory over Brown on June 13, 1905. For those interested in the final career record: Mathewson won 40 and lost 37 against the Cubs, and Brown won 32, losing but 15 times to the McGrawmen, for an outstanding .681 winning percentage against the National League's best.

During the 1912 campaign four of the top five hitters in the N.L. were Giants or Cubs, with Heinie Zimmerman leading the way at a blistering .372, to win the batting crown, followed by Giants' catcher Chief Meyers at .358, Johnny Evers, whose .341 and outstanding defensive season would have netted "Comeback Player of the Year," had it been given, and finally, that quintessential Giant, Larry Doyle, who hit .330 and was honored with the league's MVP award. Other significa from the 1912 notebook include:

>> Larry Cheney's 26 victories, nine of them in succession, established a Chicago rookie record. Grover Alexander holds the ML record at 28.

>> On June 13 "The Big Six" won his 300th game, defeating Cheney and the Cubs, 3 to 2.

>> Heinie Zimmerman hit in his 23rd straight game on May 14. He was hitting in the .430's at the time.

>> The Giants stole a major league record 11 bases on June 20 as they swamped the Braves, 21 to 12. Two days later they scored 17 and then 14 in a twinbill sweep of hapless Boston.

>> On September 6 spitballer Jeff Tesreau garnished his rookie season with a no-hitter over the Phillies in Philadelphia, 3 to 0. He was the league's ERA (1.96) leader, and fashioned the lowest Opponents' BA, at .204 while recording a 17 and 7 record for 1912.

>> Frank Chance, denounced by Cubs' CEO Charlie Murphy on September 28, was fired shortly thereafter when, during the ninth and final game of the Chicago City Series, the White Sox scored six, first inning runs. Incensed, he came to the Cubs' dugout from his box seat, fired Chance, and appointed Johnny Evers to succeed him right then and there. That ended the "Peerless Leader's" managerial reign over the Cubs' early 20th century dynasty.

The 1912 Season Series

May 10	NY	4	Chi	0	Ames, WP	Cheney, LP
May 11	NY	10	Chi	3	Marquard, WP	Richie, LP
June 10	Chi	9	NY	8	Lavender, WP	Crandall, LP
June 11	NY	8	Chi	3	Ames, WP	Lavender, LP
June 12	NY	3	Chi	2	Marquard, WP	Richie, LP
June 13	NY	3	Chi	2	Mathewson, WP	Cheney, LP
July 8	Chi	7	NY	2	Lavender, WP	Marquard, LP
July 9	NY	5	Chi	2	Mathewson, WP	Brown, LP
July 10	Chi	3	NY	0	Richie, WP	Ames, LP
July 11	Chi	11	NY	3	Cheney, WP	Crandall, LP
July 16	Chi	3	NY	1	Lavender, WP	Tesreau, LP
July 26	Chi	4	NY	3	Reulbach, WP	Mathewson, LP
July 27	Chi	7	NY	6	Lavender, WP	Marquard, LP
July 29	Chi	4	NY	3	Richie, WP	Tesreau, LP
July 30	NY	10	Chi	4	Mathewson, WP	Lavender, LP
August 15	Chi	5	NY	1	Richie, WP	Marquard, LP
August 16	NY	7	Chi	4	Tesreau, WP	Lavender, LP
August 17	Chi	6	NY	5	Richie, WP	Mathewson, LP
August 21	Chi	4	NY	0	Richie, WP	Tesreau, LP
September 14	NY	5	Chi	0	Tesreau, WP	Richie, LP
September 16	Chi	4	NY	3	Reulbach, WP	Mathewson, LP
September 17	Chi	5	NY	3	Cheney, WP	Marquard, LP

Matty's Last Stand

In two articles written for the *New York Times* prior to the 1913 World Series, John McGraw previewed the contenders and, as might have been expected, predicted that his Giants would beat the Philadelphia A's in the fall classic. In one sentence the little field general of the Giants, now 40, and fully convinced that his career had vindicated everything he knew and held dear about the game, summed the way he felt about the team he would soon meet. This is how John McGraw saw it:

> Taking the two contenders, team for team and man for man, I believe that my club is the better one [*New York Times*, October 6, 1913].

If a team-for-team, man-for-man comparison had turned out any other way, it would not, and could not have been written by John J. McGraw. There was simply no room in his life for second-best and it's quite possible that even when a team scored more runs than his team did, he was, in his own mind, still not beaten. With a lifetime won-loss record of 2,763–1,948, in a game where breaking even, after all the years and games have been counted, is better than a .500 record would seem to indicate, McGraw wound up on top three out of every five times his teams took the field. His teams won more games than any other manager in the game's history save Connie Mack, and Mack, it will be remembered, was around some 20 seasons more than "Little Napoleon."

And which National League team would beat the Giants in 1913? You know what McGraw would have said, and you know he would have been right. As July turned to August the McGrawmen were right up there atop the league standings, winning at a seven out of ten clip. The Phillies trailed by eight games, and the Cubs, in third, were 16 games in arrears, struggling to stay over the .500 mark under "New Management," i.e: under playing-manager Johnny Evers. And as October approached, the Giants, led by three 20-game winners (Marquard finished at 24 and 10, Mathewson, still winning in the 20s, at 25 and 11, and Tesreau, 22 and 13), readied for another crack at the talented Athletics with a pitching staff that turned in a league-low, 2.42 ERA and another airtight defense that permitted but 3.3 runs per game. The third straight New York pennant in 1913 was forged, as usual, on the familiar old McGraw anvil of timely hitting, offensive smarts, defensive grit, and masterful pitching.

Another of those patented Giant winning streaks enabled them to move from second place behind the Phils to a 6½ game lead on July 9, when Rube Marquard cut down the Cubs at the Polo Grounds. But the Cubs turned the tables the very next day knocking off Christy Mathewson in a tight one, 3 to 2, and in the process halting the Giants' winning streak at 14. It was one of but eight wins they were able to garner in the 1913 season series. One other is worth noting. It took place at the Polo Grounds when the teams met for their first encounter of the season on May 10. Not only did the occasion mark the start of another season's hostilities with the hated enemy from the Windy City, reason enough for New Yorkers to turn out in big numbers, but the game further provided an opportunity for the good citizens of Troy, New York, to honor their most famous son, John Joseph Evers, now the Chicago manager. After the usual gift and floral piece shower at home plate on such occasions, Evers personally led his Cubs to a 2 to 1 victory over New York, driving home the winning run himself. John McGraw took that defeat in better grace than any other loss at the hands of the Cubs because he respected John Evers, a player cut in his own image. Of course, two days later he had Mr. Mathewson out there to set the record straight with a 5–1 whipping of the Chicagoans. And, an interesting side note: on the very same day Frank Chance, at the time the New York Yankees' manager after having left the Cubs, led his team to a 10 to

9 conquest over the Tigers in Detroit. Meanwhile, Joe Tinker, at this point the manager of the Cincinnati Reds following an unpopular trade after the 1912 season, wound up on the short end of a 9 to 3 Brooklyn drubbing. 1913: Tinker to Evers to Chance; managers all.

For Christy Mathewson there was one last moment of World Series glory. That took place on October 8 when he shut out the Athletics, spacing eight hits in a 3 to 0, 10 inning thriller. It would appear that the victory used up the last ounce of the old Mathewson magic. Matty's next game in the series was his, and the Giants' last, losing to the A's, 3 to 1. In four World Series, he had broken even in ten decisions despite a superlative 1.15 ERA, having given up but 13 earned runs in 101 innings pitched. Remarkably, all but one of his ten World Series appearances resulted in a complete game, setting an enduring complete game record, yet another Hall of Fame credential for baseball's first idol.

The 1913 series also wrote *fini* to an unparalleled era in the history of the national pastime, during which no less than three ball clubs rode herd on a major league. Chicago, New York and Pittsburgh, each an annual pennant threat during the early 1900's, were the *real* story of the deadball era.

The 1913 Cubs-Giants Season Series

May 10	Chi	2	NY	1	Cheney, WP	Demaree, LP
May 12	NY	5	Chi	1	Mathewson, WP	Richie, LP
May 13	NY	8	Chi	2	Tesreau, WP	Toney, LP
May 14	NY	14	Chi	11	Marquard, WP	Lavender, LP
June 8	Chi	2	NY	1	C. Smith, WP	Tesreau, LP
June 9	NY	11	Chi	3	Mathewson, WP	Overall, LP
June 10	Chi	3	NY	2	Humphries, WP	Marquard, LP
June 11	NY	5	Chi	2	Fromme, WP	C. Smith, LP
July 8	NY	6	Chi	5	Tesreau, WP	Lavender, LP
July 9	NY	3	Chi	0	Marquard, WP	Cheney, LP
July 10	Chi	3	NY	2	C. Smith, WP	Mathewson, LP
July 11	NY	14	Chi	2	Fromme, WP	Lavender, LP
July 30	Chi	5	NY	0	Cheney, WP	Tesreau, LP
July 31	Chi	5	NY	4	Cheney, WP	Fromme, LP
August 1	NY	5	Chi	2	Mathewson, WP	Humphries, LP
August 2	NY	2	Chi	1	Tesreau, WP	Cheney, LP
August 21	NY	8	Chi	2	Mathewson, WP	Stack, LP
August 22	NY	8	Chi	1	Tesreau, WP	Cheney, LP
August 23	NY	3	Chi	2	Marquard, WP	C. Smith, LP
September 14	Chi	7	NY	0	Cheney, WP	Marquard, LP
September 15	NY	4	Chi	3	Tesreau, WP	Lavender, LP

VI

THE SABBATICAL YEARS

Sabbatical Leave: a period of absence with pay given every seven years. That is what the years 1914 to 1920 amounted to for both the Giants and the Cubs. During that span of seven seasons the greats of past championship teams gradually moved on, and even though both teams won pennants, New York in 1917 and Chicago in 1918, neither of those flag winners mustered the overall luster of their illustrious predecessors. Teams in the nation's two largest cities were in a period of transition. Not only were they challenged with successes by the Bostons, Brooklyns and Cincinnatis of the National League, they were sternly tested, as were all existing league franchises, by the newly organized Federal League. Beyond that, the fury and intensity of low-run games, pitching duels, and the slap-hitting, station-to-station baseball of the dead ball era, gradually gave way to a souped-up, home run bashing age that spiffed up the game even as the ragtime era of the '20s celebrated America's return from The Great War.

Accordingly, the "Champions East and West" era in the New York-Chicago rivalry between 1903 and 1913 was followed by a "sabbatical" during which the two franchises struggled mightily not only to overcome one another, but to bring under control the many transitional problems in ownership, rebuilding, and playing personnel brought on by the emergence of a third major league, World War I, and the loss of superstars the likes of Mordecai Brown, Joe Tinker, Ed Reulbach, Bill Dahlen and Christy Mathewson. No easy task. But even more difficult, at least for John McGraw, was the dawning realization that *his* game would no longer be *the* game. For him the retooling necessary to "wage war" in The Bigs meant that the Devlins, Herzogs, Doyles, Bresnahans and Devores, players he respected and honed to the sharpest possible slashing, fighting edge for every campaign, would no longer play a prominent part in the outcome of

134

those one-run ball games he so dearly loved. For McGraw the demise of the deadball game was the unkindest cut of all.

Nonetheless, the sabbatical years were not without their classic achievements. Among the more striking during that time, these are noteworthy:

>> Johnny Evers, traded to Boston's Braves (a story by itself), won the 1914 MVP award as Boston overcame both New York and Chicago, winning 34 of their last 44 games and the N.L. pennant, and then beat baseball's best team, Mack's A's, in a four game grand slam of the 1914 World Series.

>> Christy Mathewson was a 20-game winner for the last time in 1914, still setting ML records.

>> "Laughin' Larry" Doyle, Giant captain and second baseman, was crowned batting champion of the N.L. in 1915 with a .320 BA. He also led in hits, 189, and doubles, with 40.

>> The Giants ran up the most remarkable winning streak in the game's history, capturing 26 straight in 1916 between September 7 and 30, and yet could not move up in the standings, winding up fourth.

>> On May 2, 1917, Jim "Hippo" Vaughn of the Cubs threw a no-hitter at the Reds—for nine innings. He lost both the no-hitter and the game in the tenth frame to Fred Toney, whose no-hitter went the full ten innings.

>> Ferdie Schupp, the little Giant righthander who arrived in New York during the Giants' 1916, 26 game winning streak, beat the Cubs six times in seven tries en route to his 21–7 season during New York's pennant winning season of 1917.

>> During the Cubs' championship season of 1918 they beat the Giants 14 times out of their 20 scheduled games in the N.L.'s abbreviated, wartime slate.

>> On July 17, 1918, the Cubs and Phillies went at each other for 21 innings before the Cubs won 2 to 1 on out fielder Max Flack's fifth hit of the game. Both pitchers, George "Lefty" Tyler, who won it, and the Phils' John "Mule" Watson finished what they started in the longest errorless game in ML history.

>> In the 1919 season series between the Cubs and Giants, the Giants won 16 and lost only 6, allowing the Cubs three runs or less in 16 of that season's games.

>> The major league schedule was pared back to 140 games in 1919.

Consequently, there were only three 20-gamewinners in the N.L.: Slim Sallee of the pennant-winning Reds, a member of the Giants' 1917 championship staff, Hippo Vaughn of the Cubs with 21 and Jesse Barnes of the Giants, who led the league with 25.

>> Grover Cleveland Alexander dominated the 1920 pitching statistics with league-leading figures in wins, 27; complete games, 33; innings pitched, 363.1; K's, 173; ERA, 1.91; and Pitcher Runs, 49.5. The Cubs' star won four and lost two against McGraw's Giants.

>> In 1920 Jesse "Nubby" Barnes was a 20-game winner for the Giants, the second time in a row. On two occasions during the season he beat the Cubs 2 to 1, the first time on August 5, giving up two hits, and the second on September 11 when New York won on a ninth inning single by Frankie Frisch.

As for the record during these seven seasons of changing lineups, managers and fortunes, as the world of baseball endured yet another upheaval with the emergence and ultimate termination of a third major league, this time called the Federal League, a few notations on each year and the Cubs-Giants annual season series follow.

The 1914 to 1916 Season Standings

	Team	Pos	Won	Lost	Pct.
1914	Boston	1	94	59	.614
	New York	2	84	70	.545
	Chicago	4	78	76	.506
1915	Philadelphia	1	90	62	.592
	Chicago	4	73	80	.477
	New York	8	69	83	.454
1916	Brooklyn	1	94	60	.610
	New York	4	86	66	.566
	Chicago	5	67	86	.438

The 1914 Season

Some 30 games into the 1914 season the Giants, in second place, trailed the front-running Pirates by four games, the Cubs were in sixth, eight games off the pace, and Boston's Braves had nuzzled into the National League cellar, winners of but eight of their first 27 games. That caused manager George Stallings to lament, "I have 16 pitchers, all of them rotten."

In Chicago, Hank O'Day, successor to departed manager John Evers, who was in the process of goading some life into the moribund Braves, might well have been thinking the same thing. By the time the season was over, however, there was an immense difference between Boston and Chicago, something like 16 games and a world's championship. And there was no championship on the North Side. The South Siders saw to that, disgracing the Cubs in the Chicago City Series, as the White Sox once again won "their series" four games to three.

The baseball world had turned upside down in 1914, and not only in the N.L. standings. Not only did the Braves win the World Series in four straight over Philadelphia's A's, but in the process managed to break up the mighty Mack machine. And then there was the Federal League, which raised havoc with rosters, litigation and new franchises. In Chicago the tremors were sharp. Joe Tinker signed on as the manager of the Chicago Whales and Mordecai Brown picked up his curveball, went to St. Louis and signed a Federal League contract to manage the Terriers.

The 1914 pennant race was not, however, written solely by Boston. Despite significant shortcomings, both Chicago and New York, especially the latter, gave serious chase to the winner's circle. As late as September 6 the Giants were tied for the league lead with Boston, and Chicago, in third, was only two games behind the leaders. Then came a three game set in Boston over the Labor Day weekend and when it was over the Braves had usurped the lead from the Giants. The standings at that point read:

	Won	Lost	Pct.	GB
Boston	69	53	.566	
New York	68	54	.557	1
Chicago	69	59	.539	3

The Braves were never headed again, pulling away to a decisive pennant margin of 10½ games ahead of the second place Giants, while the Cubs dropped to fourth, a distant 16½ games behind Stallings, Evers & Co.

A pair of interesting New York victories involve the bellwethers of the Giant pitching staff, Mathewson and Marquard. On July 17 Marquard dueled the Pirates' Babe Adams in Pittsburgh, the Giants finally winning in the 21st inning. The game finally ended when Giants' center fielder Red Murray caught a fly ball as lightning struck Forbes Field. Unfortunately, the lightning struck Murray an instant after he had caught the ball, knocking him unconscious, though clinging to the ball for the final out. To the great relief of all in attendance, Murray recovered, and in fact was in the lineup the next day. Adams had not issued one base on balls during the game, setting an ML record for the longest non-walk game.

Of special interest in the Cubs-Giants battles, was a Christy Mathewson victory on August 29. It was his last victory over the Cubs, a 7 to 5 win, outlasting Bert Humphries to pick up his 40th lifetime victory over the Bruins.

As 1914 came to a close it was time to take the broom out of the kitchen closet in Chicago. The cleanup started at the top rung with the disposal of bothersome Charles Murphy, the cantankerous, bull-headed owner of the Cubs. *Sporting Life*'s Frank Adams responded with:

> Brought to the leash and smashed in the jaw,
>   Evers to Tener to Taft.
> Hounded and hustled outside of the law,
>   Evers to Tener to Taft.
> Torn from the Cubs and the glitter of gold,
> Stripped of the guerdons and glory untold,
> Kicked in the stomach and cut from the fold,
>   Evers to Tener to Taft.

Adams's tart poetry summed everything from Johnny Evers's departure, bitterly bemoaned in Chicago, to the National League front office (John Tener was the N.L. president at the time), to president Taft's involvement in the whole sordid affair. Between Murphy's firing and the advent of Bill Veeck, Sr., and the elder Wrigley, William, the ownership of the Cubs changed hands three times as the Cubs franchise floundered from top to bottom. And, as usual, the manager's head rolled. The new man in charge of the dugout was to be Roger Bresnahan, a fellow well known to Chicagoans, one of John McGraw's brighter pupils — and a Hall of Famer in the making.

Roger Bresnahan, the Duke of Tralee, a gifted athlete, who was John McGraw's captain and all around star. A fiery competition cast in the McGraw mold, he also managed the Cubs (1912–1915).

The 1914 Season Series

May 25	Chi	5	NY	1	Cheney, WP	Demaree, LP
May 26	NY	10	Chi	7	Mathewson, WP	Vaughn, LP
May 27	NY	3	Chi	1	Mathewson, WP	Zabel, LP
June 10	NY	4	Chi	1	Marquard, WP	Cheney, LP
June 11	Chi	7	NY	4	Vaughn, WP	Mathewson, LP
June 12	Chi	7	NY	6	Humphries, WP	Tesreau, LP
June 13	NY	8	Chi	4	Demaree, WP	Pearce, LP
July 12	NY	7	Chi	2	Tesreau, WP	Cheney, LP
July 13	Chi	4	NY	2	Vaughn, WP	Fromme, LP
July 14	NY	12	Chi	8	Mathewson, WP	Cheney, LP
July 15	Chi	5	NY	4	C. Smith, WP	Tesreau, LP
August 4	NY	4	Chi	1	Marquard, WP	Vaughn, LP
August 5	NY	3	Chi	0	Tesreau, WP	Lavender, LP
August 6	Chi	4	NY	3	Humphries, WP	Mathewson, LP
August 7	NY	8	Chi	4	Fromme, WP	Zabel, LP
August 27	NY	9	Chi	2	Tesreau, WP	C. Smith, LP
August 29	Chi	1	NY	0	Vaughn, WP	Marquard, LP
August 29	NY	7	Chi	5	Mathewson, WP	Humphries, LP
August 30	NY	8	Chi	1	Tesreau, WP	Cheney, LP
September 19	NY	5	Chi	4	Tesreau, WP	Hageman, LP
September 21	Chi	6	NY	0	Vaughn, WP	Marquard, LP
September 22	Chi	5	NY	0	Cheney, WP	Mathewson, LP

1915-1916: Back to the Drawing Board

Although only 3½ games separated Chicago, Pittsburgh and New York in 1915, the margin was not between the league's top contenders. It was, in fact, the difference between fifth place and the N.L.'s basement. This unaccustomed and discomfiting turn of events befell the three former frontrunners, who "only yesterday" ruled the roost, but now found themselves looking up at a new elite. Just how much the Giants' eighth place finish galled the proud Mr. McGraw will never be known, but one *can* guess with certainty that he would not take that kind of degradation lightly.

Another new manager in Chicago, Roger Bresnahan, unable to coax more than 73 wins out of an inconsistent, sputtering attack, and, worse yet, unable to bring the Chicago City Championship back to the North Side, joined the ranks of those who preceded him among the unemployed. The managerial roll call from 1912 forward shaped up like this: Frank Chance, 1912; Johnny Evers, 1913; Hank O'Day, 1914; Bresnahan, 1915; Joe Tinker, who was to follow in 1916; and, finally, Fred Mitchell, who would be around for an eternity, by comparison, from 1917 to 1920.

What was clear in all three ports of call, whether Pittsburgh, New York, or Chicago, was that it was time to get on with replacing the old heroes and the shopworn vestiges of those once-feared pennant-winning machines, which, in their time, were *nulli secondus.* Wagner, Mathewson and Brown notwithstanding, the baseball world was moving on.

One thing John McGraw must have enjoyed during the 1915 season, however, was the season series with the Cubs. Victorious in 14 of the 22 scheduled matches that season, the Giants put together 20 percent of their season's victory total at Chicago's expense. Even that, however was tempered by a no-hit loss to the Cubs, administered by Jimmy Lavender in the first game of a double header on August 31.

Once again, in 15 of the 22 games in the series, the losing team scored two runs or less, and only once during the summer did the winning team score in double figures, that coming with a 10 to 0 Marquard victory over George Washington "Zip" Zabel in the first meeting of the season on May 15. Three days later, in their second game of the year, another shutout, this one by the Cubs' Bert Humphries, the two teams settled down to the low-scoring style that was typical of their 1915 season series.

It was against Brooklyn, however, that the Cubs played the major league's most interesting game of the season. Both of the pitchers mentioned above, Humphries and Zabel, were involved in a 19 inning marathon at Chicago's West Side Grounds that was won on an error by the Dodger second baseman George Cutshaw, whose fielding average that season led the league. Ed Pfeffer went the route for the Dodgers and Zip Zabel pitched 18⅓ of the 19 innings, the other ⅔ of an inning going to Humphries, who was forced to retire in the first inning because a Zach Wheat sizzler split a finger on his pitching hand as he tried to field it. Zabel came on, and, without a warmup, relieved Humphries, going the rest of the way. Had the pennant chase ended after that game, the Cubs, who moved into first place as the result of the victory, would have won the flag. That was not to be. Wilbert Robinson's Dodgers went on to finish third, 7½ games ahead of the fourth place Cubs. The June 17 box score:

Brooklyn	AB	R	H	PO	A	*Chicago*	AB	R	H	PO	A
O'Mara, ss	8	1	1	7	2	Good, rf	9	1	1	1	0
Myers, cf	8	0	2	2	0	Fisher, ss	8	1	3	4	8
Daubert, 1b	8	1	0	18	1	Schulte, lf	8	1	3	7	0
Cutshaw, 2b	8	1	3	6	10	McLarry, 2b	7	0	0	6	6
Wheat, lf	8	0	2	5	0	Saier, 1b	6	1	1	20	1
Stengel, rf	6	0	1	4	1	Williams, cf	9	0	2	4	1
McCarty, c	4	0	1	5	1	Bresnahan, c	8	0	1	8	4

Brooklyn	AB	R	H	PO	A	Chicago	AB	R	H	PO	A
Miller, c	3	0	1	6	1	Phelan, 3b	5	0	3	5	7
Getz, 3b	6	0	0	2	3	Humphries, p	0	0	0	0	0
Pfeffer, p	7	0	0	1	4	Zabel, p	7	0	1	1	7
Totals	66	3	11	*56	23	Totals	66	4	11	*56	34

* Two out when winning run was scored.

Line Score	Brooklyn	100 000 010 000 001 000 0	3–11–3
	Chicago	200 000 000 000 001 000 1	4–11–4

2BH—Phelan, Bresnahan, Schulte, Myers, O'Mara
HR—Saier
SB–Williams, Getz
SH—Fisher, Zabel, Schulte, Getz
LOB–Brooklyn 8, Chicago 18
DP—Getz, Cutshaw, Daubert
BB–Zabel 1, Pfeffer, 8
K—Zabel 6, Pfeffer 6
Umpires —Rigler and Hart
Time—3:15

Two years after the 1913 New York N.L. championship, these changes had been made in the Giant and Cub lineups:

New York 1915: Snodgrass, cf; Lobert, 3b; Doyle, 2b; Burns, rf; Fletcher, ss; Robertson, lf; Merkle, 1b; Meyers, c; and pitching staff.

New York 1913: Burns, lf; Shafer, 3b; Fletcher, ss; Doyle, 2b; Merkle, 1b; Murray, rf; Meyers, c; Snodgrass, cf; and pitching staff.

Chicago 1915: (above, and pitching staff)

Chicago 1913: Leach, cf; Evers, 2b; Schulte, rf; Phelan, 3b; Saier, 1b; Mitchell, lf; Corriden, ss; Bresnahan, c; and pitching staff.

And the changes were only beginning. Between 1915 and 1920 both clubs, though winning pennants in 1917 (Giants) and 1918 (Cubs), shuffled lineups to meet changing times and circumstances. By the time another championship flag waved over the Polo Grounds in 1921, a new era, replete with fresh talent and new stars, had dawned. There was only one principal holdover: John J. McGraw.

The 1915 Season Series

May 15	NY	10	Chi	0	Marquard, WP	Zabel, LP
May 18	Chi	1	NY	0	Humphries, WP	Tesreau, LP
May 19	NY	5	Chi	1	Marquard, WP	Vaughn, LP
June 5	NY	3	Chi	0	Perritt, WP	Humphries, LP

June 6	Chi	8	NY	6	Vaughn, WP	Tesreau, LP
June 8	NY	9	Chi	3	Marquard, WP	Lavender, LP
July 13	NY	4	Chi	3	Ritter, WP	Humphries, LP
July 14	NY	6	Chi	5	Tesreau, WP	Adams, LP
July 14	Chi	8	NY	1	Cheney, WP	Tesreau, LP
July 15	Chi	5	NY	2	Lavender, WP	Perritt, LP
July 16	NY	2	Chi	0	Mathewson, WP	Zabel, LP
July 30	NY	3	Chi	2	Stroud, WP	Lavender, LP
July 30	Chi	4	NY	0	Humphries, WP	Perritt, LP
July 31	Chi	7	NY	5	Vaughn, WP	Mathewson, LP
July 31	NY	9	Chi	2	Tesreau, WP	Pearce, LP
August 28	NY	2	Chi	0	Tesreau, WP	Humphries, LP
August 31	Chi	2	NY	0	Lavender, WP	Schauer, LP
August 31	NY	7	Chi	1	Benton, WP	Vaughn, LP
September 19	NY	7	Chi	1	Stroud, WP	Humphries, LP
September 21	NY	5	Chi	4	Perritt, WP	Vaughn, LP
September 21	Chi	5	NY	3	Pearce, WP	Palmero, LP
September 22	NY	3	Chi	1	Benton, WP	Lavender, LP

1916: Minor Miracles, Matty and Miner

When the Cubs and Giants opened their 1916 season series in Chicago on May 15, McGraw's charges were four games into a 17-game winning streak. They proceeded to victimize the Cubs twice to extend their budding streak to six, but found themselves three games behind the seventh place Pirates with an 8 and 13 record. 11 of those losses were back to back, inflicted on the Giants before the season was 13 games old. Then, in an astounding about-face, the Manhattanites took 17 straight—*all of them on the road*. In the process, they had climbed to second place, only a game and a half behind the league-leading, and eventual pennant winners, Brooklyn's Dodgers. Winning 17 in a row on the road might easily have qualified as the most remarkable achievement of the 1916 season, a minor miracle, except...

The National League hadn't seen anything yet. Opening the season with a number of the defunct Federal League's players, most notably Benny Kauff, the "Ty Cobb of the Feds," John McGraw continued to sift, maneuver and rearrange his forces in the hope of finding a combination that would not only enable his Giants to overcome their disastrous 1915 campaign, but to return them to the ranks of legitimate contenders. But by midseason it was apparent that, while his ballclub had distanced itself from the worst of the also-rans, it was still not good enough to win a championship. What McGraw needed was a ballplayer or two who knew what it meant to be a Giant. Casting his eyes about the league, he saw Buck Herzog, one of his former favorites, who had been moved between New York and other N.L. teams on several occasions. Another McGraw-type, Heinie Zimmerman, and scrappy Mickey Doolan were added to the list, and soon all three were part of the Giants' latest makeover. With another six weeks remaining, McGraw reasoned that if winning the pennant was out of reach, the time could be well spent getting ready for 1917. That turned out to be exactly right, but not even John McGraw could have imagined what was to happen in September.

Beginning on September 7, the fourth place Giants took off on another victory parade. This one lasted through 26 consecutive conquests, a major league record that looks about as unbreakable as the DiMaggio 56 and Cal Ripken 2,632 numbers. Three of those wins, numbers 15, 16 and 17, came at the Polo Grounds in the final three game set of the season with the Cubs. Victory number 17, which tied the earlier season mark, was a seven-hit shutout by the elongated lefty, Slim Sallee. Checking the box score (below), the rapidfire lineup changeover on both clubs is apparent (compare especially the July 8, 1912, Giant-Cub lineups, page , with September 22, 1916, following).

Chicago	AB	R	H	PO	New York	AB	R	H	PO
Zeider, 3b	4	0	0	1	Burns, lf	4	2	2	2
Kelly, rf, cf	4	0	2	0	Herzog, 2b	3	1	1	1
Mann, lf	4	0	2	2	Robertson, rf	4	0	1	3
Saier, 1b	2	0	0	12	Zimmerman, 3b	4	1	2	1
Mollwitz, 1b	1	0	0	2	Fletcher, ss	3	0	0	3
Williams, cf	2	0	0	0	Kauff, cf	4	0	1	2
Flack, rf	0	0	0	0	Holke, 1b	3	1	1	11
Wilson, c	4	0	1	5	Rariden, c	2	0	1	3
Yerkes, 2b	3	0	0	0	Kocher, c	0	0	0	0
Wortman, ss	3	0	0	2	Sallee, p	3	0	1	1
Perry, p	2	0	1	0					
Knabe, ph	1	0	1	0					
Smith, ph	1	0	0	0					
Prendergrast, p	0	0	0	0					
Tinker, ph	1	0	0	0					
Totals	32	0	7	24	Totals	30	5	10	27

Line Score	Chicago	000 000 000	0–7–2
	New York	002 101 10x	5–10–0

2BH—Holke, Rariden
3BH—Robertson

SB—Zimmerman
SH—Fletcher, Holke, Herzog
LOB—Chicago 6; New York 5
DP—Fletcher, Herzog, Holke; Herzog, Fletcher, Holke
BB—Perry 1; Sallee 1
K—Sallee 3; Perry 3; Pendergrast 1
Umpires—Byron and Quigley
Time—1:36

The victory left the Giants in fourth place, and though they added another nine scalps to their winning streak, that's where they remained, in fourth place, a fate that was almost as implausible as their 26 in a row. When the dust had cleared from their momentous feat, they wound up exactly where they had started, still four plus games off Brooklyn's fron-trunning pace. This is the way the race ended in October:

1)	Brooklyn	94–60	
2)	Philadelphia	91–62	2½
3)	Boston	89–63	4
4)	New York	86–66	7
5)	Chicago	67–86	26½

Shortly before the Giants' victory streak began, a game of singular note took place at Chicago's Weeghman Park, the new home field of the Cubs that the first of the fast food kings, Charlie Weeghman, had built for his Chicago Whales of the Federal League. That game pitted Christy Mathewson, who was traded to Cincinnati in midseason to assume the managerial reins of the Reds, against Mordecai Brown in the last season of their luminous careers. Brown had been brought back by Joe Tinker for a few appearances after his Federal League years. On September 4 they met for one last time. On that much publicized day, which brought out a Standing Room Only crowd, Matty bested his old rival, 10 to 8, evening out the record of Brown and Mathewson at 12 and 12. A salute to their brilliance from the major league record book follows.

Major League Top 100 Career Records

	Brown	Mathewson
Wins/Rank	239/48	373/3 (t)
Winning %	.648/17	.665/8
Games Started	not in top 100	55½/3
Games Completed	271/58 (t)	434/13
Shutouts	55/14 (t)	79/3

	Brown	Mathewson
Hits/game	7.68/28	7.94/60
Ratio*	9.8/5 (t)	9.6/#3 (t)
ERA	2.06/3	2.13/5
Opp. BA	.233/37 (t)	.236/53 (t)
Opp. OB%	.278/17 (t)	.273/10 (t)
Wins Above Team#	29.0/49	64.9/4
TPI†	34.8/25	62.8/4

* Ratio:	Sabermetric Measure: Hits allowed plus BB allowed per nine innings pitched. A Ratio of 11–12 may be considered average. A career average of lower than 10 is exceptional.
# Wins Above Team	Indicates how many wins a pitcher earned beyond the number of an average pitcher on his team.
† TPI	Sabermetric Measure: The sum of a pitcher's Ranking Runs, taking his statistics both in pitching and fielding into consideration.

Note: Mordecai Brown's 1.04 ERA for the 1906 season ranks third all time, and Christy Mathewson's 1909 ERA, 1.14, ranks fifth. Mathewson's 1909, 7.45 Ratio ranks sixth; Brown's 1908, 7.72 Ratio ranks 12th.

The 1916 Season Series

May 14	NY	6	Chi	4	Tesreau, WP	McConnell, LP
May 15	NY	3	Chi	2	Perritt, WP	Vaughn, LP
June 10	NY	1	Chi	0	Perritt, WP	Lavender, LP
June 12	Chi	8	NY	2	Packard, WP	Anderson, LP
June 13	Chi	5	NY	2	Vaughn, WP	Stroud, LP
June 14	Chi	4	NY	0	Lavender, WP	Mathewson, LP*
July 19	NY	8	Chi	6	Benton, WP	Lavender, LP
July 20	Chi	1	NY	0	Hendrix, WP	Schupp, LP
July 21	NY	2	Chi	1	Tesreau, WP	Packard, LP
July 22	Chi	5	NY	2	Vaughn, WP	Perritt, LP
July 23	Chi	8	NY	3	Brown, WP	Benton, LP
August 3	NY	1	Chi	0	Perritt, WP	Vaughn, LP
August 4	Chi	6	NY	2	Lavender, WP	Tesreau, LP
August 5	NY	3	Chi	2	Sallee, WP	Hendrix, LP
August 7	NY	3	Chi	2	Schupp, WP	Lavender, LP
August 18	NY	6	Chi	1	Perritt, WP	Prendergrast, LP
August 18	Chi	8	NY	6	Carter, WP	Anderson, LP
August 19	Chi	3	NY	2	Brown, WP#	Tesreau, LP
September 20	NY	4	Chi	2	Schupp, WP	Lavender, LP
September 21	NY	4	Chi	0	Perritt, WP	Hendrix, LP
September 22	NY	5	Chi	0	Sallee, WP	Perry, LP

* The June 14 game, a one-hitter by Jimmy Lavender, marked the last appearance of Christy Mathewson against the Cubs in a Giants uniform.
# On August 19 Mordecai Brown appeared against the Giants for the last time, defeating them in relief of lefty Eugene Packard in 11 innings.

Perhaps Not Dominant—But Back On Top
The 1917 to 1920 Season Standings

	Team	Pos	Won	Lost	Pct.
1917	New York	1	98	56	.636
	Philadelphia	2	87	65	.572
	Chicago	5	74	80	.481
1918	Chicago	1	84	45	.651
	New York	2	71	53	.573
	Cincinnati	3	68	60	.531
1919	Cincinnati	1	96	44	.686
	New York	2	87	53	.621
	Chicago	3	76	65	.536
1920	Brooklyn	1	93	61	.604
	New York	2	86	68	.558
	Chicago	5 (t)	75	79	.487

That the Giants would come back from the miseries of a last place finish in 1915 to capture the N.L. flag in less time than it takes to say John McGraw was an achievement few would have considered even remotely possible. The "Little Napoleon" would have been one of the very few. Indeed, a strong case might be made that his 1917 champions were his very finest handiwork, the product of both extraordinary administration and managing. There were no superstars on this ballclub, no Mattys or McGinnitys or Bresnahans to call on. Team McGraw was *team* personified, an unselfish mix of veterans (Fletcher, Herzog, Sallee, Benton) and willing youngsters (Schupp, Holke, McCarty, Youngs) who played the game the way the boss said it should be played.

Although several clubs (the Cubs were in first place with a 20 and 9 record on May 16), including the Hornsby-powered Cardinals and Phillies, jockeyed with the Giants to gain an upper hand in the pennant race, the McGrawmen roared into first place to stay on the day the Giants' major domo returned from exile (the latest of his many suspensions was levied because of a direct hit that leveled Umpire Jim "Lord" Byron on June 8), perched along the third base coaching line, to lead his club to a 3 to 2 victory over the Braves on June 29. From that point forward they never relinquished the league's top slot, finally winning the flag by a very convincing 10 games. That was the good news.

The bad news for New York's faithful was delivered in Chicago—oh, that town again—where the White Sox, whose budding dynasty was just beginning to feel its oats, took the wind out of the Giants' sails, knocking them off in the World Series four games to two. Another of *"those incidents"* that the Giants seemed to have patent rights on, bubbled up in the fourth inning of what turned out to be the final game, when Heinie Zimmerman had no choice but to chase Eddie Collins across home plate because no one covered it. It was another of those Merkle-Snodgrass episodes that, like the plagues, bedeviled New York in almost every World Series effort, sending McGraw down to his fourth straight humiliation at the hands of the despised junior circuit.

Early in the 1917 season, on May 2, one of those rare baseball classics took place, also in Chicago, when the Cubs entertained the Reds in a game of utter futility for hitters on both teams. It was the day of the famed double-no-hitter[16], when two scratch hits, one by former Giant and Olympics hero Jim Thorpe, and a momentary lapse by Cub catcher Art Wilson cost Jim "Hippo" Vaughn his nohitter, shutout and the game by a 1 to 0 score in the tenth inning. Reds hurler Fred Toney finished the tenth without allowing a hit to seal *his* no-hitter and the Reds' victory.

In winning six out of seven decisions from the Cubs, Ferdie Schupp, en route to a sparkling 21 and 7 season and a 1.95 ERA, a righthanders with stuff aplenty, allowed the Cubs just a little more than two runs per game, shutting them out twice and permitting but a single run on two other occasions. Harry "Slim" Sallee, a junkball pitcher with edge-of-the-strike-zone control, won 18 and saved another five for the Giants to combine with another southpaw, the veteran Rube Benton (15 and 8) and righthanders Pol Perritt and Jeff Tesreau, winners of 17 and 13 respectively, giving the Giants a dependable and at times superb pitching corps that led the league with a staff ERA of 2.27. The Giants' team fielding average, a league-leading .968, was, as in former years, a part of the team's winning formula. The whole package had a familiar McGraw look, as a matter of fact. The results were predictable.

The 1917 Season Series

May 23	NY	5	Chi	3	Schupp, WP	Vaughn, LP
May 24	Chi	4	NY	3	Douglas, WP	Middleton, LP
May 25	Chi	6	NY	1	Demaree, WP	Perritt, LP
May 26	NY	4	Chi	1	Sallee, WP	Seaton, LP
June 9	NY	4	Chi	0	Schupp, WP	Demaree, LP
June 10	Chi	6	NY	5	Hendrix, WP	Tesreau, LP

June 11	NY	8	Chi	2	Benton, WP	Douglas, LP
June 12	NY	10	Chi	6	Schupp, WP	Seaton, LP
July 16	NY	4	Chi	2	Tesreau, WP	Vaughn, LP
July 17	NY	6	Chi	1	Schupp, WP	Demaree, LP
July 18	NY	4	Chi	2	Perritt, WP	Douglas, LP
July 26	Chi	7	NY	1	Vaughn, WP	Tesreau, LP
July 27	NY	3	Chi	1	Sallee, WP	Demaree, LP
July 28	Chi	6	NY	5	Douglas, WP	Schupp, LP
July 29	NY	6	Chi	5	Benton, WP	Vaughn, LP
August 24	NY	3	Chi	1	Perritt, WP	Douglas, LP
August 24	Chi	12	NY	2	Vaughn, WP	Demaree, LP
August 25	NY	6	Chi	1	Sallee, WP	Carter, LP
August 25	NY	2	Chi	1	Schupp, WP	Hendrix, LP
September 17	NY	5	Chi	0	Schupp, WP	Douglas, LP
September 18	NY	4	Chi	0	Benton, WP	Carter, LP
September 19	Chi	4	NY	3	Vaughn, WP	Sallee, LP

1918: A Pennant Flag for the Wrigley Mast

A significant number of players in the major leagues, as well as owners, lawyers, mobsters and betting agents, all involved at one time or another in the seamy side of life off the field of play, kept baseball's officialdom and attorneys busy at a time when the national pastime had its hands full keeping teams on the diamond and completing a season's schedule. That was especially true in 1918, when the American commitment to an all out war effort peaked. The combination of those extraordinary external pressures and the internal maneuvering surrounding the illegalities and corruption might well have decimated Organized Baseball had it not been for America's love affair with a game that had captured its heart. The prevailing sentiment was to "get it fixed" rather than ditching the whole sordid, outrageous affair. That is, of course, a chapter in the game's history that need not be reviewed here, except to reiterate its drastic effect on pennant races, teams and World Series play.

The effect was felt nowhere with more force than in baseball's twin epicenters, New York and Chicago. Especially in Chicago. As the 1918 season progressed John McGraw lost frontliners from his 1917 champions to military service, and more disturbing, it was becoming increasingly evident that some of his players were involved in betting on and throwing ball games. The net effect was predictable. Despite the genius of manager McGraw, second place would have to do for 1918, and even that was a major accomplishment considering the counter-productive forces at work in the board room and clubhouse.

New York had succeeded in taking the Cubs into camp ever since 1913, winning each season series, while piling up a huge 68–41 advantage in the won-loss column. But that came to a screeching halt in 1918.

The 1918 Cubs, with Dame Fortune looking over their shoulders, retained key players from their 1917 lineup, and, adding Fred Merkle and Larry Doyle, former Giants, catcher Bill Killefer, rookie shortstop Charlie Hollocher and one of the Braves' former aces, George "Lefty" Tyler, followed the lead of the National League's best pitcher, big Hippo Vaughn, to a ten game margin over the Giants for the "non-essential" season's championship. 14 of their 84 victories

Chicago's Hippo Vaughn, five-time 20-game winner, was the N.L.'s top pitcher in 1918.

were logged against the Giants in an abbreviated season that closed on September 2. Under manager Fred Mitchell they made the jump from 1917's fifth place finish to the league's top spot and into the World Series, played on the south side of Chicago at Comiskey Park so that more Cub fans could get in on the action. Unfortunately, neither huge crowds nor a World Series crown awaited the N.L. champs. The Red Sox lefty, Babe Ruth, almost single-handedly saw to it that the world's championship would find its way to Boston.

The 1919 *Spalding's Guide*[17] pegged the Chicago-New York game on July 7 as the pivotal game of the season. An excerpt follows:

> The turning point of the fight may have taken place in Chicago during a game which was played on the July trip of the New York team to the West. Demaree was the New York pitcher and Hippo Vaughn pitched for Chicago. It was the first game of the series in Chicago, and in some respects one of the most skillfully handled games in the history of Base Ball. Vaughn won it in the twelfth inning by the simplest kind of a ground hit to right field, which should have been handled by Holke, the New York first baseman. The latter, instead of playing for the ball—and he was the only possible fielder to get it—ran for the base and the ball bounded unmolested to the outfield, while Paskert scored the single run of the game...

It needed a victory like that to make the Chicago club "feel its oats." If prior to then Chicago had been doubtful as to what it had in reserve, or as to what it might accomplish with all steam on, it was not doubtful after what took place that memorable afternoon. The July 7, 1918, box score:

New York	AB	R	H	PO	Chicago	AB	R	H	PO
Burns, cf	5	0	1	2	Flack, rf	5	0	1	1
Youngs, rf	4	0	1	3	Hollocher, ss	4	0	0	1
Fletcher, ss	3	0	0	4	Mann, lf	4	0	2	1
Doyle, 2b	5	0	0	3	Merkle, 1b	4	0	0	19
Zimmerman, 3b	5	0	2	2	Paskert, cf	5	1	1	7
Thorpe, lf	5	0	1	5	Deal, 3b	5	0	1	0
Holke, 1b	5	0	1	14	Zeider, 3b	3	0	0	3
McCarty, c	4	0	0	1	Barber, ph	1	0	0	0
Demaree, p	4	0	0	1	Wortman, 2b	1	0	0	0
					Killefer, c	4	0	1	4
					Vaughn, p	5	0	2	0
Totals	40	0	6	35*	Totals	41	1	8	36

*Two out when winning run scored.

Line Score   New York   000 000 000 000   0–6–0
              Chicago   000 000 000 001   1–8–1

2BH—Mann, Killefer, Vaughn
SB—Thorpe, Mann, Killefer
LOB—New York 7; Chicago 9
DP—Zeider, Merkle; Fletcher, Doyle, Holke
BB—Vaughn 3, Demaree 4
K—Vaughn 2, Demaree 1

What took place thereafter (the victory was Vaughn's 15th against but four losses) was another pair of Chicago wins that upped its lead to six games over the second place Giants. That was also the finishing order.

The 1918 Season Series

May 25	Chi	7	NY	4	Tyler, WP	Demaree, LP
May 26	Chi	5	NY	1	Vaughn, WP	Sallee, LP
May 27	Chi	7	NY	3	Hendrix, WP	Perritt, LP
June 11	Chi	5	NY	3	Hendrix, WP	Tesreau, LP
June 12	NY	1	Chi	0	Perritt, WP	Tyler, LP
June 13	Chi	8	NY	4	Douglas, WP	Sallee, LP
June 14	NY	7	Chi	0	Demaree, WP	Vaughn, LP
July 6	Chi	1	NY	0	Vaughn, WP	Demaree, LP
July 7	Chi	6	NY	1	Douglas, WP	Perritt, LP

July 8	Chi	6	NY	3	Tyler, WP	Causey, LP
July 8	NY	3	Chi	1	Perritt, WP	Hendrix, LP
July 9	NY	7	Chi	6	Causey, WP	Douglas, LP
August 1	Chi	5	NY	0	Vaughn, WP	Toney, LP
August 2	Chi	11	NY	1	Tyler, WP	Perritt, LP
August 3	MY	4	Chi	2	Causey, WP	Douglas, LP
August 3	Chi	11	NY	6	Hendrix, WP	Perritt, LP
August 5	Chi	5	NY	3	Carter, WP	Toney, LP
August 21	Chi	9	NY	2	Tyler, WP	Perritt, LP
August 22	NY	4	Chi	2	Toney, WP	Vaughn, LP
August 22	Chi	3	NY	2	Martin, WP	Causey, LP

The End of an Era

The last two of those sabattical years during the post-domination era of 1914 to 1920 coincided with the end of the deadball era, as well, though there was no particular significance that might have linked the two. Chicago had simply run out of steam after its 1918 pennant, and the immediate future would call for another overhaul of its sputtering baseball machine. The record would show that between 1910 and 1929 only one pennant flag flew over Wrigley Field. 1919 was another of those years when the smart money was placed on either Chicago or New York, both having had very recent experience with pennant winners. But both were bettered by a Cincinnati ball club that was having nothing to do with the smart money. All they did was win. Accordingly, New York, too, was handed another humility pill in the form of the runnerup spot. But in the case of the McGrawmen, the pennant thirst would soon be slaked by a run of good fortune that set the Big Apple aflame with baseball prosperity four times hand-running from 1921 to 1924. That, however, gets us just a bit ahead of our story.

If the Giants could not dominate the rest of the league as they had done in days gone by, they could, and did bully up on the Cubs in both 1919 and 1920, when they beat the men of Wrigley 31 out of 44 times. Not that they beat them senseless. They just won and won by those old and familiar Giant margins of 2 to 1 and 3 to 2 and 1 to 0. Until it hurt. Check the 1919 season series below:

May 13	NY	3	Chi	2	Benton, WP	Alexander, LP
May 14	NY	3	Chi	2	Dubuc, WP	Vaughn, LP
May 15	NY	6	Chi	2	Causey, WP	Douglas, LP
May 16	NY	3	Chi	0	Barnes, WP	Tyler, LP
June 14	NY	1	Chi	0	Toney, WP	Vaughn, LP

June 15	NY	5	Chi	4	Benton, WP	Alexander, LP
June 16	NY	4	Chi	3	Barnes, WP	Douglas, LP
June 17	Chi	7	NY	2	Alexander, WP	Causey, LP
July 17	NY	2	Chi	1	Barnes, WP	Hendrix, LP
July 19	NY	3	Chi	2	Toney, WP	Vaughn, LP
August 8	Chi	3	NY	0	Hendrix, WP	Nehf, LP
August 9	Chi	3	NY	1	Vaughn, WP	Douglas, LP
August 10	Chi	2	NY	0	Alexander, WP	Benton, LP
August 16	NY	5	Chi	4	Nehf, WP	Vaughn, LP
August 19	Chi	4	NY	3	Alexander, WP	Douglas, LP
August 19	NY	5	Chi	1	Barnes, WP	Hendrix, LP
September 9	Chi	4	NY	1	Vaughn, WP	Barnes, LP
September 9	NY	7	Chi	1	Nehf, WP	Martin, LP
September 10	NY	7	Chi	2	Toney, WP	Hendrix, LP
September 11	NY	7	Chi	3	Benton, WP	Alexander, LP

Eight of the Giants' victories were one-run squeakers, and over the course of the season they held the Cubs to an average of 1.7 runs per game in the 14 games they won. A pair of rising stars, Frankie Frisch, only 20, and Ross Youngs, but 22, who were just beginning to warm to the challenges of Hall of Fame careers, helped a steady pitching staff, led by 20-game winners Slim Sallee and Hod Eller, get out in front and remain there into June, before finally bowing to the Reds' superior firepower. That 14 to 6 bulge in the season series with the Cubs, stoked by seven straight early season Cub conquests, was instrumental in building New York's early season lead.

The story of the year was not, however, written in Cincinnati, where an able crew of Red Legs ultimately won the 1919 pennant by nine games over the Giants (the Cubs wound up a weak third, 12 behind the Giants and 21 off the Reds' pace) and then went on to win the black-hued world series over Chicago's other team, the White Sox. There had been more than a rumor or two about betting and throwing ballgames all year long, and, finally, the whole baseball world exploded when the scandalous world's championship was played out, bet by bet, phone call by phone call, signal by signal, and game by game. Before another year was out that would bring disastrous ruin to the team on Chicago's South Side, as well as to the lives of many people.

The south side of town was not the only place where serious mischief was brewing. In the Cubs' camp, as well as in New York, a number of ballplayers had been in touch with not only players but booking and betting agents. To their credit, both William Wrigley and John McGraw got busy and rounded up those whose hands were in the wrong pockets, principally

Cubs hurler Claude Hendrix, the Giants' Heinie Zimmerman and Hal Chase, and banned them from future play. By the close of the decade no one involved in the game had escaped unscathed and there were only losers. The 1920s, just around the bend, would indeed be a most welcome sight, a time to get the game back on course and to ensure that the headlines were being made on the field of play rather than in court rooms across the land. That might take a minor miracle, but, much to the relief of a nation-in-waiting, there was one standing in the wings by the name of Babe Ruth.

With an Eye Toward the '20s

The new decade began with busy courtrooms and busier baseball board rooms peopled by lawyers and officials intent on charting a new era of stability. Two major forces were brought to play. One of these was the appointment of a baseball commissioner with Zeus-like power to oversee the conduct of the game. To see to it that the job got done without endless bickering, the game's czars appointed Judge Kenesaw Mountain Landis. Not even the most prescient among them had the remotest inkling as to the zeal and deadly dispatch Landis would bring to his two-fisted, imperious control of the national pastime. The appointment was announced after the conclusion of the 1920 season.

The other change was to be enforced at the beginning of the 1920 season. That was the banishment of foreign substances to the ball. The rule put the spitball out of bounds except for the pitchers who were "grandfathered," and thus permitted to use it until their careers were over. This change was not nearly as spectacular on the surface of things as was the appointment of the game's new chief executive, but the players knew immediately what that meant not only as far as their batting and pitching averages were concerned, but for the entire strategy of the game itself. It didn't take a rocket scientist to figure out that the days of one-run, station-to-station baseball were about over. That rule change, as much as anything else, brought on the "Age of Ruth," with its big-inning and bombast and high scoring, extra basehit extravaganzas.

How all this would sit with John McGraw remained to be seen. Could he make the shift from the "one-run-game" he felt was the way the game should be played to what he sensed immediately would be a slugfest featuring "big, stupid freeswingers"—like "The Babe," who for reasons both economic and artistic was no hero for a baseball purist like "Muggsy"?

Well sir, the important thing to remember is that McGraw was nobody's baseball fool. With a lineup stacked by the likes of hitters like Ross Youngs, Frank Frisch George Kelly, Dave Bancroft and Irish Meusel, he would find a way to come to grips with the new realities and use his talent whenever the situation called for it to beat the brains out of opposing ballclubs, especially those hated Yankees who were sitting right under his nose at the Polo Grounds, and who would menace the firm grip McGraw & Co. had on New York's fandom. It is worth noting that the Giants' transition from the deadball to the so-called lively ball era was made without a hitch at the Polo Grounds. After their disastrous 1915 eighth place finish, the Giants wound up in either first or second place each year between 1917 and 1926, a ten year stretch that bridged both eras.

Out there in the hub of the heartland, Chicago's Cubs were making adjustments of their own. William Wrigley, who bought into principal ownership of the Cubs, brought in Bill Veeck, Sr., who became the club's president, and the two of them presided over a wild and woolly ride through the roaring '20s that almost matched the town's frenzied, boozed-up denizens in a ragtime romp that swept the city with it. And they kept at it until, at last, they crashed through the pennant barrier with a winner of their own in 1929.

Perhaps the biggest contributor to whatever success the Cubs enjoyed in 1920 was Grover "Pete" Alexander, by this time a 33-year-old, wily practitioner of the pitcher's arts. Well on his way to Cooperstown, "Old Slow and Away," as he was often called, kept right on working his one-hour-plus magic through another seven shutouts, including a 1 to 0 gem over Burleigh Grimes and his Brooklyn pennant winners. His last, and record-setting 90th shutout on April 28, 1928, incidentally, also came against the ornery and embattled Grimes, then with Pittsburgh's Pirates.

The age of the baseball bombadier might have been dawning, but that was not a part of Pete Alexander's world. His 1.91 ERA led the league during a season when the league average ballooned to 3. 13. One of his better efforts of the 1920 season came on July 9, when he gave up only a single

The enigmatic yet loveable Pete Alexander, who won 27 for a 1920 Cubs team that could muster only 75 wins. His 1.91 ERA led the N.L., and his many other record-making feats put him in the Hall of Fame in 1938.

earned run in beating the Giants 3 to 2 in 13 frames. His overall log that year showed 27 wins and 14 losses, 11 of his wins coming in succession, for a fifth place ball club that was manhandled by the Giants 15 to 7 in the season series. Sly Pete went four and two against New York's second placers. Others of the Cub hurling corps were not quite so fortunate, nor could they match McGraw's threesome of Jesse Barnes (20 and 15), Fred Toney (21 and 11) and the little portsider, Artie Nehf (21 and 12). Only Hippo Vaughn, at 19 and 16, came close.

The 1920 Season Series

May 18	NY	8	Chi	6	Nehf, WP	Martin, LP
May 19	NY	17	Chi	2	Barnes, WP	Martin, LP
May 20	Chi	4	NY	2	Alexander, WP	Nehf, LP
May 21	NY	2	Chi	1	Toney, WP	Tyler, LP
June 22	Chi	10	NY	4	Carter, WP	Benton, LP
June 23	NY	2	Chi	1	Toney, WP	Alexander, LP
June 24	NY	3	Chi	1	Nehf, WP	Vaughn, LP
July 8	Chi	8	NY	5	Tyler, WP	Toney, LP
July 9	Chi	3	NY	2	Alexander, WP	Barnes, LP
July 10	NY	8	Chi	5	Nehf, WP	Martin, LP
July 11	NY	3	Chi	2	Benton, WP	Vaughn, LP
August 5	NY	2	Chi	1	Barnes, WP	Vaughn, LP
August 6	NY	5	Chi	2	Benton, WP	Alexander, LP
August 6	NY	6	Chi	2	Douglas, WP	Tyler, LP
August 7	Chi	5	NY	2	Hendrix, WP	Nehf, LP
August 8	NY	7	Chi	1	Toney, WP	Vaughn, LP
August 20	Chi	5	NY	1	Alexander, WP	Benton, LP
August 21	NY	8	Chi	3	Barnes, WP	Tyler, LP
August 22	NY	4	Chi	1	Toney, WP	Vaughn, LP
September 9	Chi	3	NY	2	Alexander, WP	Douglas, LP
September 11	NY	2	Chi	1	Barnes, WP	Tyler, LP
September 22	NY	7	Chi	2	Douglas, WP	Tyler, LP

VII

ROARIN' WITH
THE TWENTIES

Settling into peacetime with more disposable income in their pock-
etbooks than ever before, Americans welcomed the '20s with a *joie de vivre*
unparalleled in the nation's history. That mantra of the 1980s and '90s,
"Let the Good Times Roll," might well have been chanted during those
heady days of racoon coats, speakeasys, Duesenbergs and Ruthian fourbag-
gers. The same euphoria was also being celebrated in the national pastime
where many of the traditions, strategies and constraints of the deadball era
were being brushed aside as a new generation of sluggers began making
baseballs disappear ever more frequently over distant outfield barriers. And
baseball's fans? They clamored for more and more, especially if a fellow
named Ruth was hittin' 'em!

New York and Chicago, increasingly universes unto themselves, were
pivot points, where, on any given day, big news from the Polo Grounds,
Yankee Stadium, debuting in 1923, Ebbets Field, located in the New York
borough of Brooklyn, Comiskey Park or Cubs (later Wrigley) Field was
likely to break at any moment. Magnates, managers and players were literally *the* news in the sports world in both cities.

In 1921 the first great inter-league rivalry came full bloom when the
Giants squared off against the Yankees in baseball's first crosstown World
Series since 1906, when the Cubs and White Sox dueled for the world's
championship. There was no love lost between the Big Apple's two Goliaths,
personified in the McGraw versus Ruth confrontation, which pitted "Mr.
Giants," who, into the '20s, owned New York as far as baseball aficionados
were concerned, against the big fellow whose impish bombast—and popularity—was seriously threatening McGraw's grip on New York's fandom.
And so the attendance wars raged on (seasonal totals soared to the million

mark), even as the bitter feud picked up on the diamond between players and among all others involved in this new and fascinating clash between Giant and Yankee loyalists.

John McGraw neither gave himself, nor received any respite from the intensity of the New York scenario when the Giants pulled into Chicago to play the Cubs. Tight ballgames, narrow escapes, bitter brawls and not a few failures in hundreds of previous encounters turned on red lights long before he stepped into the visitor's dugout at Wrigley Field. No matter if the players wearing Cub uniforms were scrubs or future Hall of Famers. Chicago in block letters across the front of the uniform was all he needed to see—and the war was on once again. And what applied to McGraw applied to his players. They didn't have to be revved up. In the dugout across the diamond the story was the same. That's precisely what made the Chicago-New York rivalry what it was for the half-century preceeding the lively ball era, and that's precisely what would carry it through the next decades. For the fans, that only added to the allure of the roaring '20s, which brought with them a foursome of Giant pennants, 1921 through 1924, and the Chicago championship of 1929, rounding out one of the most interesting eras in the history of the game.

The Season Standings: 1921 to 1924

	Team	Pos	Won	Lost	Pct.
1921	New York	1	94	59	.614
	Pittsburgh	2	90	63	.588
	Chicago	7	64	89	.418
1922	New York	1	93	61	.604
	Cincinnati	2	86	68	.558
	Chicago	5	80	74	.519
1923	New York	1	95	58	.621
	Cincinnati	2	91	63	.591
	Chicago	4	83	71	.539
1924	New York	1	93	60	.608
	Brooklyn	2	92	62	.597
	Chicago	5	81	72	.529

Number One and Counting...

The day of the heavy hitters had arrived. On only two occasions were the final scores in the Giants-Cubs season series reminiscent of those fiercely fought battles during the early 1900s. On July 8, the Giants' slick little southpaw, Artie Nehf, subdued Pete Alexander on a three-hitter, 1 to 0. Two days later at the Polo Grounds Rosy Ryan set down the Cubs on five hits in a 2 to 1 squeaker. Much more typical of the summer's games, however, were the 10 to 6 and 9 to 7 outings. On August 29, for example, the shillelaghs were busy as the Cubs lost an 8 to 7, 23-hit affair. The box score (below) also reveals the extent to which John McGraw had gone to retool his pennant-winning lineup. The booming bats of the Kellys and Meusels had already replaced the "punch and judy" hitters of the recent past. The August 29 game follows:

Chicago	AB	R	H	PO	New York	AB	R	H	PO
Flack, rf	4	2	2	2	Burns, cf	1	1	0	2
Hollocher, ss	4	2	2	0	Shea, p	1	0	0	1
Terry, 2b	4	1	2	1	Bancroft, ss	4	1	1	4
Deal, 3b	3	1	1	0	Frisch, 3b	4	1	1	1
Barber, lf	3	1	2	4	Youngs, rf	3	1	1	1
Maisel, cf	4	0	2	5	Kelly, 1b	3	0	0	7
Grimes, 1b	2	0	1	6	Meusel, lf	4	2	3	1
Killefer, c	2	0	0	6	Rawlings, 2b	5	1	1	5
Twombly, ph	1	0	0	0	Smith, c	1	0	1	2
Freeman, p	1	0	0	0	Synder, c	1	1	0	2
Jones, p	2	0	0	0	Toney, p	1	0	1	0
York, p	0	0	0	0	Sallee, p	1	0	0	0
Marriott, ph	1	0	0	0	Cunningham, cf	2	0	2	1
Totals	31	7	12	24	Totals	31	8	11	27

Line Score	Chicago	203 001 001	7–12–0
	New York	300 002 21x	8–11–1

2BH—Meusel, Youngs, Rawlings
3BH—Meusel
HR—Hollocher
SH—Deal, Kelly 2, Grimes 2, Barber, Burns, Youngs, Meusel
LOB—Chicago 2, New York 11
DP—Bancroft, Rawlings, Kelly; Burns, Bancroft, Frisch; Snyder and Bancroft
BB—Freeman 3, Jones 2
K—Jones 5, Sallee 1, Shea 1
HPB—Burns (by Freeman)
WP—Shea
LP—Jones
Umpires—McCormick and Klem
Time—2:02

An interesting note: The victory, which evened the Giants in wins at 77 with the league-leading Pirates, still had the marks of former years: nine sacrifice hits (both cleanup hitters were signalled to lay the ball down) were ordered in the game, all but one involving the 3–4–5–6 hitters in the lineup. That's right out of the deadball era playbook.

One way of illustrating the differences between McGraw's deadball and lively ball champions is to compare their 1917 and 1921 team statistics. Here are some of the more telling numbers.

	Hitting (Offense)						Pitching (Defense)				
	Runs	Opp.R.	HR	BA	SA	SB	Hits/G	CG	SH	Op.BA	ERA
1917 Giants	635	457	39	.261	.343	162	7.7	92	18	.234	2.27
1921 Giants	840	637	75	.298	.421	137	9.8	71	9	.286	3.55

The 1921 pennant chase turned out to be a renewal of those age-old skirmishes between the Giants and the Pirates, the Cubs having fallen on hard times that dumped them unceremoniously into also-ran status, plaguing them for a number of seasons while the elder Wrigley and his right-hand bauer, Bill Veeck, Sr., were painstakingly rebuilding a lineup that would eventually assert itself with the potent sticks requisite to the task of claiming another championship. During the last week in August, then, the Pirates visited the Polo Grounds, hopeful of increasing their lead and putting the race out of the Giants' reach.

Bill Curran, in *Big Sticks*, his interesting history of the slugging '20s, explains what happened in the five-game set that put the Giants back into pennant contention:

> Having completed his deals,[18] McGraw quietly awaited the arrival on August 24 of Pittsburgh manager George Gibson and his laid-back Buccaneers... The grim, reinforced Giants descended on their cocky visitors like a starved cougar on a spring lamb. Pittsburgh blew all 5 games and staggered from the Polo Grounds leading by just 2½ games ... the Giants overtook the Pirates on September 13, and coasted home 4 games in front.

During the course of the two crucial months of the season, August and September, the Cubs took on the new champions nine times, winning but three, as the Giants beat the great Alexander twice and trumped whatever aces were left, copping the season series 14 games to nine. Johnny Evers, who returned as the Cubs' manager, soon found that his old enemy had too much firepower, dropped five straight to the McGrawmen in two mid-season series, and was replaced by catcher Bill Killefer. It was the Hall of Famer's last tour of duty for the Cubs.

In New York the good news got better. In the 1921 World Series they thrashed the Yankees five games to three in the last of the nine-game world's championship series. And they did it after losing the first two games of the series. The key? Showing "The Big Dummy," as McGraw once called George Herman Ruth, what the game was all about while saddling him with eight whiffs and one meaningless home run. Was a victory ever so sweet? McGraw and his Giants returned to the top of baseball's Everest, and as for New York, well, that, too, was the "Little Napoleon's," and, Mr. Ruth be damned—at least for now!

The 1921 Season Series

May 18	NY	3	Chi	2	Sallee, WP	Martin, LP
May 19	Chi	5	NY	3	York, WP	Nehf, LP
May 20	NY	10	Chi	6	Perritt, WP	Vaughn, LP
May 21	Chi	5	NY	2	Tyler, WP	Ryan, LP
June 15	NY	6	Chi	2	Sallee, WP	Vaughn, LP
June 16	Chi	5	NY	4	Alexander, WP	Nehf, LP
June 17	Chi	11	NY	10	Jones, WP	Ryan, LP
June 18	NY	10	Chi	3	Douglas, WP	York, LP
June 19	NY	9	Chi	1	Barnes, WP	Vaughn, LP
July 8	NY	1	Chi	0	Nehf, WP	Alexander, LP
July 9	NY	6	Chi	5	Benton, WP	Vaughn, LP
July 10	NY	2	Chi	1	Ryan, WP	Tyler, LP
July 11	Chi	7	NY	2	Cheeves, WP	Douglas, LP
August 6	Chi	7	NY	4	Cheeves, WP	Ryan, LP
August 7	NY	7	Chi	2	Barnes, WP	Alexander, LP
August 8	NY	6	Chi	3	Nehf, WP	Martin, LP
August 9	Chi	8	NY	7	Cheeves, WP	Douglas, LP
August 28	NY	4	Chi	2	Barnes, WP	Alexander, LP
August 29	NY	8	Chi	7	Shea, WP	Jones, LP
September 20	Chi	7	NY	6	Cheeves, WP	Nehf, LP
September 21	NY	9	Chi	7	Shea, WP	Jones, LP

Big Sticks at Work

The heavy howitzers were booming. In New York the Giants hit .304 as a team, featuring a roster studded with six future Hall of Famers, all position players, and eight .300 hitters. The Cubs' lineup, which, except for Pete Alexander, was devoid of HOF'ers, had four solid .300 hitters and a team BA of .293. That kind of smasheroo was necessary just to stay even in a league whose ERA had ballooned to 4.10. Two St. Louisans, Rogers Hornsby of the Cardinals, and George Sisler of the Mound City's Browns, led their respective leagues with BA's over the .400 mark. Hornsby, with 42, and another Browns swatsmith, Kenny Williams, with 39, led their leagues in the homer brigade. The deadball and the one-run game had given way to thunderous cannonading, free swingers who were taking their cuts from the heels up, and an offensive attack that changed, almost overnight, to scoring runs in bunches. There was no difference in the attack of the New York and Chicago clubs from any other team in either league. The game of August 5, a 38 hit orgy in which the Giants stomped the Cubs 19 to 7, and a day at Wrigley Field on which the Cubs and Phillies went absolutely berserk, pounding out 49 runs and 51 hits in a record-setting game won by the Cubs, 26 to 23 are cases in point.

New York vs. Chicago at the Polo Grounds, August 5, 1922

Chicago	AB	R	H	PO	New York	AB	R	H	PO
Heathcote, cf	4	0	3	4	Bancroft, ss	6	1	3	1
Hollocher, ss	4	1	1	5	Groh, 3b	4	1	3	0
Terry, 2b	5	0	0	2	Rawlings, 2b	2	1	2	1
Grimes, 1b	1	1	0	3	Frisch, 2b,3b	4	2	1	3
Callaghan, rf	2	1	1	0	Meusel, lf	6	4	4	2
Friberg, rf, 1b	5	0	1	4	Youngs, rf	2	0	2	0
Miller, lf	4	1	3	1	King, rf	3	2	1	1
Krug, 3b	3	1	0	2	Kelly, 1b	5	3	5	12
O'Farrell, c	2	1	0	2	Stengel, cf	2	0	1	0
Hartnett, c	2	0	0	1	Cunningham, cf	4	2	2	1
Cheeves, p (LP)	0	0	0	0	Smith, c	2	0	0	4
Stueland, p	1	1	1	0	Snyder, c	3	0	3	1
Jones, p	1	0	0	0	Gaston, c	1	0	0	1
Morris, p	2	0	1	0	J. Barnes, p	0	1	0	0
					Jonnard, p (WP)	4	2	0	0
					V. Barnes, p	0	0	0	0
Totals	36	7	11	24	Totals	48	19	27	27

Line Score Chicago   013 000 030   7–11–2
            New York   332 433 10x   19–27–1

2BH—Meusel, Frisch, Snyder, King, Kelly 2, Callaghan

DP—Groh, Frisch, Kelly; Kelly, un.; Terry, Hollocher, Friberg

3BH—Groh, Meusel, Kelly, Rawlings

BB—J. Barnes 2, Jonnard 2, Cheeves 1, Stueland 1, Jones 1, Morris 1

Right: **Bruin catcher Bob O'Farrell's 1922 season showcased a .324 BA. He was the N.L.'s 1926 MVP and managed a good 1927 Cardinals ballclub. (George Brace photograph)**

HR—Hollocher
SB—Frisch
K—J. Barnes 1, Jonnard 3, Morris 2, Chicago pitchers 0
SH—Heathcote
LOB—New York 10, Chicago 7
HBP—Kelly by Cheeves
PB—Smith 1, O'Farrell 1
Time—2.30

Chicago vs. Philadelphia at Wrigley Field, August 25, 1922

Philadelphia	AB	R	H	PO	Chicago	AB	R	H	PO
Wrightstone, 3b	7	3	4	0	Heathcote, cf	5	5	5	4
Parkinson, 2b	4	1	2	4	Hollocher, ss	5	2	3	5
C. Williams, cf	3	1	0	2	Kelleher, ss	0	0	0	0
Lebourveau, cf	4	2	3	0	Terry, 2b	5	2	2	2
Walker, rf	6	2	4	2	Friberg, 2b	1	0	1	0
Mokan, lf	4	2	3	1	Callaghan, rf	7	3	2	2
Fletcher, ss	3	1	0	0	Miller, lf	5	3	4	1
J. Smith, ss	4	2	1	1	Krug, 3b	5	4	4	1
Leslie, 1b	2	1	0	4	O'Farrell, c	3	3	2	1
Lee, 1b	4	4	3	6	Hartnett, c	0	0	0	4
Henline, c	2	1	2	4	Kaufmann, p (WP)	2	0	0	0
Withrow, c	4	1	2	0	Barber, ph	1	2	0	0
Ring, p (LP)	2	0	1	0	Stueland, p	1	0	0	0
Weinert, p	4	2	1	0	Maisel, ph	1	0	0	0
Rapp, ph	0	0	0	0	Eubanks, p	0	0	0	0
Morris, p	0	0	0	0	Osborne, p	0	0	0	0
Totals	53	23	26	24	Totals	46	26	25	27

Line score	Philadelphia	032 130 086	23–26–4
	Chicago	1[10]0 [14]01 00x	26–25–5

2BH—Terry, Krug 2, Mokan, Hollocher, Grimes, Withrow, Friberg, Parkinson, Walker
DP—Smith, Parkinson, Lee 2, Wrightstone, Parkinson, Lee
3BH—Walker, Wrightstone
BB—Kaufmann 3, Ring 5, Weinert 5, Eubanks 3, Morris 1, Osborne 2
HR—Miller 2, O'Farrell
SB—Hollocher, Weinert
K—Ring 2, Weinert 2, Stueland 1, Morris 1, Osborne 3
SH—Leslie, O'Farrell, Hollocher, Walker
HBP—Grimes by Weinert
Umpires—Hart and Rigler
LOB—Philadelphia 16, Chicago 9
Time—3:01

Though John McGraw might much have preferred the kind of tilt that took place on May 15, when his Giants, courtesy of Artie Nehf, shut down the Cubs and 16-game winner Vic Aldridge, 1 to 0, he had to be contented more often than not with those wild and wooly 15 and 20 hit games. Still, all that was simply prelude to The Big Event and an opportunity to show New York—and the baseball world—that the Giants' World Series win over the Yankees was not an illusory wraith that could be swept aside by The Babe with a swat or two into the far reaches of the Polo Grounds. And when the time came, McGraw's pitching staff picked up where it left off in 1921, shutting The Sultan down with a composite 7 for 33 for the two series. The Yankees went quietly: no title, and not even a place to call home after the Giants pulled the rug out from under their tenancy.

King of the Big Apple. The spoils of two successive world's championships. Better than the Babe. McGraw was atop his Everest. Nearing 50, stout, and beginning to show the wear of the many diamond battles and the many years stacking one on top of another, John Joseph McGraw surely must have felt that, for all the grinding and relentless pressure that he put on himself and paried from competitors incessantly after his scalp, it was worth it.

Significa from the 1922 Notebook

>> The Giants opened the season with a 20-game homestand that resulted in a 16 and 4 record. They left town leading the league.

>> On July 23 Ray Grimes, who hit .354 in 1922, drove home a run against the Braves, marking the 17th straight game in which he had garnered an RBI to set the ML record.

>> Bob O'Farrell, barrel-chested Cubs' catcher, hit for a robust .324. In 1926 he was the National League's MVP and in 1927 he piloted the second place Cardinals. Rookie Gabby Hartnett was his understudy.

>> The Giants' pitching staff was the first to win a world's championship without a 20-game winner.

>> Three future Hall of Famers hit *four* inside-the-park homers in spacious Braves Field on April 29: George Kelly (2), Dave "Beauty" Bancroft and Ross Youngs, who enjoyed a 5 for 5 day as the Giants won 15 to 4.

>> Righthander Jesse Barnes, a Giant mainstay (82 and 43 in five-plus seasons with the Giants), threw a no-hitter at the Phils on May 7. The only baserunner was Cy Williams, who walked and was erased in a double play.

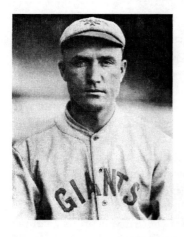

Left: David "Beauty" Bancroft came to New York for the 1920 season in a trade that sent Art Fletcher to the Phillies. He was a Giant sparkplug on two world championship teams in 1921 and 1922. (Dennis Colgin photograph)

The 1922 Season Results

May 13	Chi	3	NY	0	Cheeves, WP	Ryan, LP
May 14	NY	5	Chi	4	Douglas, WP	Alexander, LP
May 15	NY	1	Chi	0	Nehf, WP	Aldridge, LP
May 16	Chi	3	NY	2	Cheeves, WP	Toney, LP
June 7	NY	9	Chi	4	Ryan, WP	Cheeves, LP
June 8	NY	11	Chi	5	Causey, WP	Aldridge, LP
June 9	Chi	4	NY	3	Alexander, WP	Nehf, LP
July 11	NY	4	Chi	0	J. Barnes, WP	Cheeves, LP
July 12	NY	5	Chi	1	Toney, WP	Alexander, LP
July 13	Chi	5	NY	4	Aldridge, WP	Causey, LP
July 14	Chi	8	NY	4	Cheeves, WP	Nehf, LP
August 3	NY	5	Chi	0	Nehf, WP	Aldridge, LP
August 4	Chi	3	NY	2	Kaufmann, WP	McQuillan, LP
August 4	NY	2	Chi	1	Scott, WP	Alexander, LP
August 5	NY	19	Chi	7	Jonnard, WP	Cheeves, LP
August 6	Chi	10	NY	3	Osborne, WP	J. Barnes, LP
August 18	NY	17	Chi	11	Jonnard, WP	Cheeves, LP
August 19	Chi	2	NY	1	Alexander, WP	Nehf, LP
August 20	NY	5	Chi	4	Scott, WP	Kaufmann, LP
September 13	NY	8	Chi	3	Nehf, WP	Cheeves, LP
September 14	NY	7	Chi	6	Ryan, WP	Aldridge, LP
September 15	NY	7	Chi	6	Hill, WP	Osborne, LP

1923: A New Kind of Threepeat?

In order to win three consecutive World Series a team must first win three consecutive pennants. John McGraw's Giants had done the latter in the three-year, 1911–'13 stretch of pennant winning seasons. In 1923 his team was at the cusp of pulling off the former. They had won two Subway Series in 1921 and '22, and had won them decisively. They had every reason to believe that a third straight was doable, if not inevitable.

The refurbished Polo Grounds, with a beefed-up seating capacity of 54,000, and without those pestiferous Yankee tenants, was now the exclusive showcase of McGraw's wondrous baseball machine. It didn't matter that just a stone's throw away in the Bronx, the House That Ruth Built, with 62,000 brand new seats to be filled, was being readied for a third straight Yankee pennant. There was, so far, only one "House of Champions," and that was on the hallowed ground of Coogan's Bluff. Across the way they could have their Ruth. After all, he had his chance in 1921 and '22, had been judged, and had been found wanting.

The reckoning would come in due time. First there was a pennant to be won. And it all started with season openers. Beside 600 policemen assigned to the Yankee Stadium opener, Governor Al Smith, A.L. President Ban Johnson, various other franchise officials and the usual host of invited guests, there were 74,000 fans on hand to greet the American League champions. One of those invited guests was Christy Mathewson, now president of the Boston Braves. One can only wonder what must have been going on in his mind. His Giants heart, never far from his fond memories of those golden years of yore, must have skipped a beat as he might well have imagined how it would have been to throw a fadeaway or two at those American League heroes from the new Yankee Stadium mound.

The Yankees won their opener and yes, Ruth hit the Stadium's first home run. The Giants, too, got off to an explosive start, soon claiming first place by winning 10 of their first 15 games. The point having been made, the two champions ultimately went on to win their respective pennants, the Giants by a 4½ game margin that was actually every bit as secure as Team Huggins's whopping 16 game A.L. bulge. Before attending to the climax of the season, however, a note or two about the rest of the world, wherever, for New Yorkers, that might have been.

Chicago had not fallen off the end of the horizon. Though still preoccupied with rebuilding its faltering forces, the Cubs under Wrigley and Veeck were taking a step or two to bring about a serious challenge to New York's success. Two new faces, later instrumental in overtaking the Giants, were added to the Bruin roster. They were batterymates Leon "Gabby" Hartnett, who was used more regularly in 1923 than in his '22 rookie season, and Guy Bush, the swarthy righthander known as the "Mississippi Mudcat," up for his first major league cup 'o coffee with a mini-testing debut on September 17. By 1926 he would be ready to begin a span of nine double figure victory seasons for the Cubs and specialize in knocking off the Giants.

The Giants, too, would continue to add stars-in-the-making to a growing list of future Hall of Famers. One of these was "Memphis Bill" Terry, a young man who started his professional career in the Georgia-Alabama League, where, at 16, he threw a no-hitter on June 30, 1915. His ML debut was just five days before that of Lewis Robert Wilson, the one and only "Hack," on September 24. That swelled the ranks of the future Famers on McGraw's 1921 to '24 champs to eight, and the addition of Freddie Lindstrom in 1924 would raise the total to nine.

As for the October days of reckoning, the record book would show that John McGraw's world championship days were over. From the standpoint of The Big Title, the king was dead. The new king, with his court of overpowering home run hitters, wore the most famous number in baseball's history, number 3. In 1923 New York's new reigning monarch led his Yankees to a crushing four to two defeat of the Giants. Though there might be one more pennant for John McGraw to savor in 1924, it was followed by another World Series defeat, this time to Walter Johnson and his Washington Senators. The long trek toward the end of the trail for "Little Napoleon" had begun.

Noteworthy Items from the Giants-Cubs 1923 Scrapbook

>> In a rock'em-sock 'em game on April 30 the Cubs bombed Pittsburgh with six homers, including two each by Gabby Hartnett and Barney Friberg, to win their game in the ninth, 12 to 11.

>> On May 7, Giant center fielder Casey Stengel was suspended for ten days for retaliating to Phils' pitcher Philip "Lefty" Weinert's brushback pitches.

>> In a September 16 game at Wrigley Field the fans showered umpire Moran with bottles and debris over a call that went against the Cubs. Commissioner Landis, a spectator, shook his cane angrily at the crowd, but to no avail. After the game, which the Giants won 10 to 6, manager McGraw and several others were escorted by police to the clubhouse.

>> The next day, September 17, George Kelly set an ML record by hitting home runs in the third, fourth and fifth innings. The Giants won that game also, thereby winning the season series, 12 games to 10.

>> Pete Alexander finished the season at 22–12, his eighth 20-game season. He won 30 or more three straight times with Philadelphia.

>> Giant righthander Jack Bentley (13–8) hit .427 in 89 at-bats, including a scorching 10 for 20 as a pinch hitter. He would be charged with

the defeat in the seventh game of the 1924 World Series, the game made famous by the"pebble-hit" that bounced over Freddie Lindstrom's head to score Muddy Ruel with the winning run and gave Washington (and Walter Johnson) a World Series victory.

The 1923 Season Series

May 8	NY	4	Chi	1	Nehf, WP	Alexander, LP
May 9	Chi	9	NY	6	Aldridge, WP	Jonnard, LP
May 11	NY	7	Chi	4	Scott, WP	Dumovich, LP
June 5	NY	8	Chi	3	J. Barnes, WP	Cheeves, LP
June 6	Chi	6	NY	1	Aldridge, WP	Nehf, LP
June 7	Chi	9	NY	7	Alexander, WP	J. Barnes, LP
July 14	NY	6	Chi	5	McQuillan, WP	Cheeves, LP
July 15	Chi	9	NY	5	Alexander, WP	Jonnard, LP
July 16	Chi	7	NY	4	Kaufmann, WP	V. Barnes, LP
July 16	NY	3	Chi	1	Bentley, WP	Keen, LP
July 17	NY	7	Chi	3	Ryan, WP	Osborne, LP
July 26	Chi	11	NY	10	Fussell, WP	Ryan, LP
July 28	NY	6	Chi	1	Bentley, WP	Alexander, LP
July 28	Chi	7	NY	5	Aldridge, WP	Nehf, WP
July 29	NY	15	Chi	3	Ryan, WP	Kaufmann, LP
August 26	NY	4	Chi	3	Ryan, WP	Aldridge, LP
August 27	NY	8	Chi	4	Nehf, WP	Cheeves, LP
August, 28	Chi	4	NY	1	Alexander, WP	McQuillan, LP
September 14	Chi	7	NY	1	Keen, WP	McQuillan, LP
September 15	Chi	3	NY	2	Kaufmann, WP	Watson, LP
September 16	NY	10	Chi	6	Ryan, WP	Alexander, LP
September 17	NY	13	Chi	6	Bentley, WP	Aldridge, LP

One More for the Giants

This one was a white-knuckle special. With less than 10 games to play the Giants and Dodgers both had a solid crack at winning the 1924 pennant. But, while the Giants were saddling the third strong contender, Pittsburgh's Pirates, with a three-game sweep of their final series of the season, Wilbert Robinson's Brooklyn club was unable to make a dent in New York's precarious lead. Then, on September 27, while the Dodgers were losing to Boston, the Giants beat the Phillies 5 to 1 to clinch an unprecedented fourth straight N.L. crown.

And where were the Cubs? As late as mid–July Chicago's improving ballclub was right behind the pace-setting New Yorkers with a 44 and 33 record. But—always that *but* for the Cubs of the '20s—there wasn't enough pitching and there were more than enough lineup changes and playing lapses to cost the men of manager Bill Killefer dearly. Pete Alexander, who wound up with a 12 and 5 mark, didn't get in his usual number of innings because of a broken wrist in mid–August, and without an Alexander around the Cubs were just another team, fated to a fifth place finish, though nine games above the .500 mark, slightly less than their 1923 finish at 83 and 71, good for fourth place.

John McGraw's 10th and final National League champion was almost a carbon copy of his 1921–'23 winners, the two most outstanding ingredients being their consistency and team balance. There were, once again, no 20-game winners, but there was more than enough punch to win the slugfests. That, combined with their experience and savvy, carried the day. Their Hall of Fame infield, though missing Beauty Bancroft, who was shipped off to Boston with Casey Stengel in November of 1923, which on any given day might have fielded George Kelly at first, Frankie Frisch at second, Travis Jackson at short and Fred Lindstrom at third, also had Bill Terry waiting in the wings to be platooned with Kelly at first to give McGraw a right-left kayo punch in the middle of the lineup. Add to those stellar performers the likes of Hack Wilson, just beginning to make his heavy lumber felt around the league, and the versatile Ross Youngs, who could hit superbly anywhere in the batting order and field up a storm in right field, and the lineup began to take on awesome proportions.

As it finally turned out, however, John McGraw was to pilot his last World Series victory on October 8 at the Polo Grounds when his Giants went a game up on the American League champions, the Washington Senators. Pitcher Jack Bentley, (remember his 1923 hitting?) who solved one of Walter Johnson's pitches for a home run, aided by a lineup featuring a Hall of Famer at every position aside from New York's battery, brought the New Yorkers home a winner, 6 to 2. Here is that historically significant box score of Game 5 played at the Polo Grounds on October 8, 1924:

Washington	AB	R	H	PO		New York	AB	R	H	PO
McNeely, cf	4	0	1	1		Lindstrom, 3b	5	0	4	1
Harris, 2b	5	0	1	8		Frisch, 2b	5	0	1	1
Rice, rf	4	0	0	1		Youngs, rf	3	0	1	1
Goslin, lf	4	1	2	1		Kelly, cf	4	1	1	2
Judge, 1b	4	1	3	3		Terry, 1b	2	1	1	12
Bluege, ss	3	0	0	0		Wilson, lf	3	0	0	3
Ruel, c	2	0	0	6		Jackson, ss	3	1	1	1
Miller, 3b	3	0	1	3		Gowdy, c	4	2	1	6
Leibold, ph	1	0	0	0		Bentley, p	3	1	2	0

Washington	AB	R	H	PO		New York	AB	R	H	PO
Johnson, p	3	0	1	1		McQuillan, p	1	0	1	0
Tate, ph	0	0	0	0		Taylor, pr	0	0	0	0
Totals	32	2	9	24		Totals	33	6	13	27

Line Score				
Washington	000	100	010	2–9–1
New York	001	020	03x	6–13–0

2BH—Frisch
DP—Rice Johnson, Ruel; Bluege, Harris, Judge
3BH—Terry
K—Johnson 3, Bentley 4, McQuillan 1
HR—Bentley, Goslin
BB—Johnson 2, Bentley 3, McQuillan 1
SH—Wilson, Jackson, Bluege
Umpires—Connolly, Klem, Dineen, Quigley
HPB—Youngs (by Johnson)
Time—2:30
LOB—Washington 9, New York 8
Attendance—49, 211

Highlights from the 1924 Cubs-Giants Notebook

>> After recovering from a broken wrist, Grover Cleveland Alexander took the hill against the Giants on September 20 in search of his 300th major league victory. A 7 to 3 win in a 12 inning thriller at Wrigley Field did the trick.

>> Cub shortstop Charlie Hollocher's belated start was more than auspicious. In his first at-bat of the season he drilled a shot over first base that hit fair and then curved foul, directly into a hole along the right field grandstand. While rightfielder Ross Youngs was frantically digging for it, the Cubs' midfielder circled the bases for an inside-*and*-outside-the-park dinger. The Cubs lost their season series opener on May 14 with the Giants, however, 6 to 4.

>> During the July 12–15 series with the Cubs, Giants first baseman George Kelly set a record with seven homers in six straight games. Numbers 3–4–5–6 came at the expense of Cub pitching.

>> On a special "day" August 5, Giant catcher Hank Gowdy was honored by military officers, who joined in celebrating the angular catcher's big day. Gowdy was the first major leaguer to enlist in the service in World War I and saw action on the Marne, Argonne-Meuse, St. Mihiel and Alsne-Marne battle fronts. With Gowdy behind the

plate, the Giants beat the Cubs in ten innings, 2 to 1. Cub rookie Guy Bush, who went all the way, was the loser.

>>   "The Fordham Flash," Frankie Frisch, enjoyed a 6 for 7 day on September 7, as the Giants trashed the Braves 22 to 1 in the opening game of a twinbill.

>>   The Giants led the N.L. in BA, OB% and SA. Their relievers accounted for 21 saves, most, by far, in the N.L. Slender Giant curveballer Claude Jonnard led with five saves.

The 1924 Season Series

May 14	NY	6	Chi	4	McQuillan, WP	Kaufmann, LP
May 15	Chi	6	NY	4	Alexander, WP	Ryan, LP
May 16	NY	16	Chi	12	Jonnard, WP	Blake, LP
May 17	Chi	4	NY	2	Aldridge, WP	V. Barnes, LP
June 5	Chi	6	NY	4	Keen, WP	V. Barnes, LP
June 7	Chi	3	NY	1	Alexander, WP	Dean, LP
July 12	NY	14	Chi	3	McQuillan, WP	Keen, LP
July 13	NY	9	Chi	6	Bentley, WP	Kaufmann, LP
July 14	NY	7	Chi	0	V. Barnes, WP	Milstead, LP
July 15	NY	9	Chi	4	Nehf, WP	Kaufmann, LP
August 3	NY	10	Chi	2	Nehf, WP	Kaufmann, LP
August 4	NY	5	Chi	1	Bentley, WP	Keen, LP
August 4	Chi	5	NY	2	Blake, WP	Jonnard, LP
August 5	NY	2	Chi	1	Dean, WP	Bush, LP
August 6	NY	5	Chi	2	McQuillan, WP	Kaufmann, LP
August 7	NY	5	Chi	3	Nehf, WP	Jacobs, LP
August 24	Chi	2	NY	1	Aldridge, WP	McQuillan, LP
August 25	Chi	3	NY	2	Wheeler, WP	V. Barnes, LP
August 25	NY	11	Chi	7	Nehf, WP	Wheeler, LP
September 19	NY	10	Chi	4	Nehf, WP	Blake, LP
September 20	Chi	7	NY	3	Alexander, WP	Mann, LP
September 21	Chi	3	NY	0	Kaufmann, WP	Bentley, LP

The 1925 to 1929 Season Standings

Year	Team	Pos.	Won	Lost	Pct.
1925	Pittsburgh	1	95	58	.621
	New York	2	86	66	.586
	Chicago	8	68	86	.442
1926	St. Louis	1	89	65	.578
	Chicago	4	82	72	.532
	New York	5	74	77	.490

Year	Team	Pos.	Won	Lost	Pct.
1927	Pittsburgh	1	94	60	.610
	New York	3	92	62	.597
	Chicago	4	85	68	.556
1928	St. Louis	1	95	59	.617
	New York	2	93	61	.604
	Chicago	3	91	63	.591
1929	Chicago	1	98	54	.645
	Pittsburgh	2	88	65	.575
	New York	3	84	67	.556

The National League celebrated its 50th birthday in 1925 with special festivities in every N.L. city. Old timer games were played, celebrities attended the gala proceedings and each franchise had its own distinctive contribution to make to the grand jubilee. President John Heydler proclaimed May 8 as the day on which the "Jubilee Game" would be played in Boston. The Braves' foe that day would be the oldest team in the league, the Cubs, nee White Stockings. That game turned out to be about the only thing the Cubs celebrated in 1925, and they managed to make Beantown's fandom happy, losing 5 to 2. That was par for the course in a season that saw the Bruins deposited in the dank recesses of the N.L. basement, a first in the proud franchise's history.

1925 was also the midpoint of the "Roaring Twenties," a time when New York became the unquestioned hub of the nation's entertainment, sports, communications and financial circles. If it was big, or sensational, or trendy, it probably originated, and definitely was popularized in The Big Apple. The Giants and the Yankees had seen to it that the same was true in the world of baseball. Both were expected to recapture their league's titles once again, setting up yet another Subway Series.

Pittsburgh in the N.L., and the A.L.'s Washington Senators, however, had other ideas about that, and even though they were hard pressed to overcome the Gothamites, they took the World Series entirely out of New York. The Giants got off to their customary fast start and led the league in the early stages of the campaign but faltered in July, and a fine Pirates club moved into first place, won the pennant, and then took care of Walter Johnson & Co. in seven games to bring the world's championship back to the National League.

In Chicago, where three managers mismanaged an inferior Cub ballclub, there were few bright spots, but their eighth place finish was a bit deceiving. They wound up just a half game, at 68–86, behind the Phils and Dodgers, who tied for seventh at 68–85. Boston, in fifth, wasn't much better, finishing at 70 and 83. The final standings, thus, showed but a 2½ game difference between fifth and eighth. That put a chasm between the lot of them and the first division, where the McGrawmen finished off the season trailing the Pirates by 8½ games.

During the season the Giants took on the Cubs in the usual 11-home-game and 11-away-game arrangement, and the New Yorkers were undoubtedly happy that the mid-westerners appeared on the schedule as often as they did. Guy Bush was a Chicago winner twice in the season series, as was old Pete Alexander, who, despite his advancing years and increasingly disastrous bouts with John Barleycorn,[19] won 15 games in 1923, roughly 22% of Chicago's total. Beyond those two, "Sheriff" Blake and Tony Kaufmann each won a game from New York for a total of 6 out of 22 tries, the most dismal Cub record since 1874, when the Mutuals pulverized the White Stockings nine times in ten attempts.

There was a strong enough signal in that disastrous 1925 season for the two Bills, Wrigley and Veeck, Sr., to start revamping the stumbling Chicago lineup, infusing it with both a fresh managerial outlook, and ballplayers who knew how to win. An encouraging start was made with the hiring of a tough-minded Irishman who in his own subtle and quiet way was as much a martinet as John McGraw. That man was baseball-wise "Marse Joe" McCarthy. And there was one other addition to the Cubs ball-club by dint of an overlooked detail in the otherwise alert and on-top-of-things front office of the Giants. It seems Hack Wilson was assigned minor league status with a 1925 demotion, not recalled to the New York roster, and, consequently, left unprotected. By virtue of having finished last, the Cubs had first choice in the October draft, and they used it to snap Wilson out from under the noses of the astonished Giants. He promptly became one of the 1926 Cubs. Now McCarthy would have not only another powerful stick in the batting order. He would also have a fun-loving, late night rounder in the "best" tradition of the old White Stockings, who would be more than happy to keep "'Ole Alex" company at the local watering holes. The Wilson signing also meant *fini* for Rabbit Maranville, another of those small hours of the morning carousers. Three the likes of Alexander, Wilson and Maranville (the "unholy trinity" would find a final resting place at Cooperstown), would have been a wicked overload—even for a McCarthy!

The 1925 Season Series

May 17	NY	10	Chi	3	Scott, WP	Cooper, LP
May 18	NY	5	Chi	2	Greenfield, WP	Alexander, LP
May 19	Chi	8	NY	2	Bush, WP	Nehf, LP

May 20	NY	6	Chi	1	V. Barnes, WP	Blake, WP
June 8	Chi	10	NY	4	Alexander, WP	Bentley, LP
June 9	NY	9	Chi	7	Scott, WP	Bush, LP
June 10	NY	5	Chi	3	Dean, WP	Blake, LP
June 11	NY	7	Chi	4	Nehf, WP	Jones, LP
July 11	NY	10	Chi	3	V. Barnes, WP	Blake, LP
July 12	Chi	9	NY	8	Bush, WP	Scott, LP
July 13	NY	3	Chi	1	Greenfield, WP	Cooper, LP
July 14	NY	6	Chi	3	Bentley, WP	Blake, LP
July 28	NY	10	Chi	3	Bentley, WP	Cooper, LP
July 29	Chi	4	NY	2	Blake, WP	Greenfield, LP
July 30	NY	4	Chi	2	Scott, WP	Alexander, LP
July 31	NY	4	Chi	3	Nehf, WP	Kaufmann, LP
August 18	NY	7	Chi	1	Nehf, WP	Cooper, LP
August 19	NY	7	Chi	6	Huntzinger, WP	Bush, LP
September 18	NY	8	Chi	3	V. Barnes, WP	Cooper, LP
September 19	Chi	6	NY	2	Blake, WP	Scott, LP
September 20	NY	6	Chi	2	Fitzsimmons, WP	Bush, LP

1926: Under New Management

In his first tour around The Big Circuit in 1926 Joe McCarthy and his Cubs leapfrogged from the National League dungeon over the Giants into fourth place. They had turned a 68–86, 1925 pumpkin into a sturdy 82–72, 1926 chariot that was being primed for a serious run on the senior circuit's top spot. John McGraw recognized the McCarthy challenge immediately, pointing to the Chicago club early in the season as a challenger to be reckoned with.

Before Bill Wrigley's new field marshall could get his team into a "McCarthy Mode," however, there was a firestorm to pass through. The McCarthy machine was, by design, built on a minimum of mental gaffes to overcome a lack of talent here or there, as well as reliable pitching and superior offensive power, and, above all, discipline. The latter, literally translated, meant my-way-or-the-high way, not at all unlike John McGraw, though administered behind the scenes and with far less bombast.

That's what made the afore-mentioned firestorm inevitable. And it centered around Pete Alexander. The Cubs would either be a team managed by McCarthy in every sense of the term, or it would be a ballplayer's ball club, led more by a team leader, or leaders, than the manager. Old Alex, with a mind of his own, would more likely than not be that team leader. And, in the course of several early season weeks, the thing ran its course, with Alexander winding up in St. Louis and McCarthy in the driver's seat.

Joe McCarthy, who came to the Cubs in 1926 to set the Wrigley House in order—and did, winning the pennant in 1929 with a power-laden lineup that featured a punishing offense, mastery of the game's fundamentals, and steady, though unspectacular pitching. (George Brace photograph)

In the short term, pitching's most eminent ancient warrior won out, a World Series champion over the vaunted Yankees. The longer term, however, was another story. As the '20s roared on so did the men of McCarthy, and by 1927 they were ready to make the league sit up and take notice.

Back east in Manhattan that New York Hall of Fame infield, consisting of Terry, Kelly, Frisch, Jackson and Lindstrom, plus the Bright's Disease-stricken Ross Youngs and veteran Irish Meusel in the outfield, though capable of battering a team into submission on any given day, lacked those prototypical extra McGraw touches such as dominant pitching, preventing them from overtaking any of the first division ballclubs. But there was another and more ominous factor in the Giants' descent from their second place finish in 1925, and that was the friction of grating personalities and a new mindset that made for tension, grousing and contention inevitable between John McGraw and his players. This is the way the venerated baseball historian Donald Honig[20] characterized it:

> A more complicated man had emerged from the brutality of a triumpant world war, from the radical ideas of the intellectual marketplace, from the contempt for Prohibition, from the whirligig pace of the decade. The will of John McGraw was losing its capacity to break the spirits of men who were playing in front of larger, noisier, more adulatory crowds, and some of those spirits were as rock-hard as his own. First baseman Bill Terry, greatest of all McGraw's players, was openly contemptuous of his crotchety skipper, talked back to him, and then worse, refused to talk to him at all. Fred Lindstrom, McGraw's intense, intelligent young third baseman, was another example of the new breed... (But) It was Frisch who sent McGraw into his blackest rages ... because of the similarities in their personalities and not the differences

that the old generation and the new went at each other with the wrath of historical antagonists.

There was, of course, a price to pay, and it showed up in the won-loss column where the Giants registered a fifth place, 74–77 season, their worst since their eighth place finish in 1915. A dozen seasons later baseball had changed, players had changed, and the world had changed. Radically. John Joseph McGraw, into his mid–fifties and in the late autumn of his career, was hard put to adjust, and it is quite likely that, while his last several ball clubs contended for one last banner to fly atop the Polo Grounds mast, he was simply not minded to bend to the new realities, and in fact would not. Iron-willed to the end, he would take the consequences— on *his* terms.

Chicago native "Freddie" Lindstrom played his first game at the Polo Grounds before his 19th birthday and was Mc-Graw's third baseman in the 1924 world series. Outspoken, Lindstrom, along with Bill Terry, were the first of McGraw's players to mix it up verbally with the "Little Napoleon," who was at first aghast that they actually talked back to him. (Dennis Colgin photograph)

Highlights from the 1926 notebook

>> The Cubs bounced back from their dismal 1925 record of 6 and 16 in the season series with the Giants to a winning, 14 and 8 record in 1926. Before the Cubs sold Pete Alexander to the Cardinals on June 22, he won his last game against the Giants in a Chicago uniform on May 8, 6 to 4. On May 22 he was feted with a "Day," and received an automobile, among other gifts, from fans and players.

>> On May 23 Hack Wilson powered a laser shot that hit the facing of Wrigley Field's center field scoreboard, the first player to do so. His 1926 RBI total, 109, was the first of five straight 100-plus RBI seasons, a major factor in Chicago's rise to pennant contention.

>> Both the Giants and the Cubs averaged a high 4.4 runs per game during the season. Despite that, the losing team in their season series scored two runs or less in 14 of the season's 22 games.

>> Guy Bush beat the Giants five times without a loss, establishing a reputation as the new "Giant Killer."

>> Charlie Root, spotted by McCarthy while pitching for Minneapolis, beat the Giants twice, but absorbed five of Chicago's eight losses to New York in 1926. His losses included two 2 to 1 cliffhangers, a 5 to 4, and a 2 to 0 disappointment. He finished his rookie season at 18 and 17.

>> Frankie Frisch concluded the New York phase of his Hall of Fame career with a .322 BA and averaged 88 runs in eight seasons. He averaged 28 stolen bases and less than 20 strikeouts per season.

>> Ross Youngs finished his career in 1926 with a .322 lifetime BA. One of baseball's brightest stars during the '20s, he was felled by Bright's Disease in 1927. He was accompanied throughout his last season by a specially assigned medical assistant. He made his last appearance against the Cubs at the Polo Grounds on August 10 in a 2 to 0 victory, contributing a fine running catch to the Giants' win.

>> Mel Ott, 17, brought up at the end of the season, had a 3 for 3 day on September 3, as the Giants mauled the Braves 17 to 3.

The 1926 Season Series

May 6	NY	2	Chi	1	V. Barnes, WP	Root, LP
May 7	Chi	6	NY	0	Kaufmann, WP	Scott, LP
May 8	Chi	6	NY	4	Alexander, WP	McQuillan, LP
May 9	Chi	8	NY	7	Bush, WP	Scott, LP
June 6	NY	15	Chi	3	Fitzsimmons, WP	Piercy, LP
June 8	Chi	2	NY	1	Root, WP	Scott, LP
July 17	NY	8	Chi	3	Greenfield, WP	Blake, LP
July 18	Chi	2	NY	1	Root, WP	McQuillan, LP
July 19	Chi	9	NY	5	Huntzinger, WP	Scott, LP
July 20	Chi	16	NY	2	Jones, WP	Greenfield, LP
August 3	NY	5	Chi	4	Fitzsimmons, WP	Root, LP
August 3	Chi	5	NY	3	Bush, WP	Greenfield, LP
August 9	NY	4	Chi	3	Greenfield, WP	Kaufmann, LP
August 10	NY	2	Chi	0	V. Barnes, WP	Root, LP
August 11	Chi	11	NY	1	Bush, WP	Ring, LP
August 17	Chi	7	NY	0	Bush, WP	McQuillan, LP
August 18	NY	2	Chi	1	V. Barnes, WP	Root, LP

August 19	Chi	2	NY	1	Blake, WP	Greenfield, LP
September 20	Chi	4	NY	2	Kaufmann, WP	Scott, LP
September 20	Chi	2	NY	1	Bush, WP	V. Barnes, LP
September 21	NY	5	Chi	2	Fitzsimmons, WP	Root, LP
September 22	Chi	3	NY	2	Jones, WP	Poetz, LP

Back Among the Contenders

"The Rajah" was a piece of work, all right. "Mr. Blunt." Controversial. Ornery. Outspoken and often crude. But the man could play—and, oh my, how he could hit. And circumstances being what they were in the Giants' clubhouse, John McGraw decided that putting up with Rogers Hornsby couldn't be any worse than putting up with the "Fordham Flash," Frankie Frisch. Consequently, a trade with the Cardinals was consummated on December 20, 1926. Its immediate effect was seismic. Hot Stove League buffs everywhere had plenty to talk about all winter long. It would remain to be seen how the trade would play out in 1927, but the smart money was on an inevitible trade, ultimately moving the immovable from the presence of the irresistible—and sooner than later. Indeed, Hornsby was in a

Texan Ross "Pep" Youngs, Hall of Fame Giant outfielder-second baseman, who hit a career-high .356 in 1924. He led both leagues with 26 assists from the outfield in 1920. (Dennis Colgin photograph)

Braves uniform for the 1928 season. But first came 1927, "Mugsy" and "Rajah." The bottom line question begging for an answer was: could the trade bring with a pennant?

As it turned out neither Frisch nor Hornsby was around for a World Series engagement. In 1927 the Pirates overcame stiff challenges from the world's champions, the Frisch-led Cardinals, from New York, and from the resurgent Cubs. That the Giants didn't win the pennant somewhat assuaged Mr. William Wrigley, but not enough to prevent him from needling his associates to put Hornsby in a Chicago uniform no matter the price. That took a little time, but by 1929 the deed was done.

The conclusion of the 1927

pennant chase was a thriller involving four ball clubs. In his *Concise History of Major League Baseball*, Leonard Koppett[21] capsulates the run to the ribbon this way:

> On Labor Day, the Pirates, Cards, Cubs, and Giants were still closely bunched. Then the Pirates won 11 straight and the Cubs dropped out, but the Giants and Cards kept coming. In the next to the last week, the Pirates lost the last three of a four-game series to the Giants at Forbes Field, letting the Cards climb to within two games. But they won the next four at Chicago while the Cards lost two of three in Cincinnati, and Pittsburgh finished a game and a half ahead of St. Louis and two ahead of New York.

It's worth noting that as late as September 1, "Marse Joe" had his Cubs up there in the top slot with a 73 and 49 record. The days of shoddy play afield and losing close ball games were fast disappearing. The Cubs were once again a foe to be respected. The lineup that would soon bring the pennant to Wrigleyville was gradually being assembled.

On August 29, the Cubs took on the Giants at the Polo Grounds in a doubleheader that had all the earmarks of one of those old Giants-Cubs struggles with the leadership of the league on the line. Beyond the 1927 season a key figure or two was still to be added: Kiki Cuyler, from the Pirates, Hornsby from the Braves, righthander Pat Malone and reliever Mike Cvengros. But the lineup that opened the twin bill already bore the marks of a McCarthy ball club. The final touches would soon be put into place.

Chicago	AB	R	H	PO		New York	AB	R	H	PO
Adams, 2b, 3b	5	2	2	1		Reese, 3b	2	1	1	2
English, ss	4	1	2	3		Lindstrom, lf	3	0	1	0
Webb, rf	4	0	0	0		Fitzsimons, p (WP)	1	0	0	0
Wilson, cf	2	2	0	1		Roush, rf	5	1	0	1
Stephenson, lf	4	1	2	2		Hornsby, 2b	5	1	1	2
Grimm, 1b	4	0	1	10		Terry, 1b	1	1	0	15
Hartnett, c	3	0	0	6		Jackson, ss	4	2	1	3
Yoter, 3b	2	0	0	0		Harper, rf	3	1	1	1
Scott, ph	1	0	0	0		Cummings, c	4	0	1	3
Bush, p	0	0	0	0		V. Barnes, p	0	0	0	0
Carlson, p (LP)	1	0	0	0		Mueller, lf	3	1	2	0
Gonzalez, ph	1	0	1	0		Ott, ph	1	0	0	0
Beck, 2b	0	0	0	1		Henry, p	0	0	0	0
Tolson, ph	0	0	0	0		Grimes, p	0	0	0	0
Pick, pr	0	1	0	0						
Heathcote, ph	1	0	0	0						
Totals	34	7	8	24		Totals	32	8	8	27

Line Score   Chicago   301 011 010   7–8–2
              New York   007 000 10x   8–8–1

2BH—Stephenson 2, English,Lindstrom
3BH—Adams
HR—Mueller
SH—English, Mueller
LOB—New York 12, Chicago 8
DP—Blake, Hartnett, Grimm
BB—Barnes 2, Fitzsimmons 2, Grimes 1, Carlson 3, Blake 5, Bush 2
K—Blake 3, Bush 1, Fitzsimmons, Grimes 1
HPB—Wilson, Stephenson (by Barnes) Reese (by Blake)
Umpires—Klem and McLaughlin
Time—2:10
Attendance—30,110

The Giants swept the August 29 doubleheader, narrowing the Cubs' lead at that point to 2½ games over the Pirates and Cardinals, and 3½ ahead of the Giants. The McGrawmen went on to finish the season in third place, relegating the Cubs to a fourth place finish. Did you notice that Burleigh Grimes, the spitballing Hall of Famer, appeared in a relief role? His one season under McGraw showcased a 13-game winning streak that was finally shut off by the Phillies on September 26. His 1927 record was a sparkling 19 and 8. And that other fellow who served a one year term under McGraw, Hornsby, wound up the season leading the league in runs scored (133) and games played (155) while hitting .361, second to Paul Waner for the batting crown, and driving home 125, to place third behind Hack Wilson and leader Waner.

Significa from the 1927 Scrapbook

>> On July 19 John McGraw Day was celebrated at the Polo Grounds, honoring him during his 25th anniversary year with the Giants. The foe that

Travis Jackson's entire Hall of Fame career was spent in a New York Giants uniform (1922–1936), covering two championship eras. (Dennis Colgin photograph)

day? Of course—the Cubs, who beat the Giants, 8 to 5, putting the McCarthymen in first place by percentage points.

>> Between June 5 and 16 the Cubs piled up 12 consecutive victories. During the season they also managed to win 15 extra inning games, establishing a club record.

>> Bill Terry opened the season with a grand slam against the Phillies at the Polo Grounds in a 15 to 7 win.

>> Mel Ott's first ML tater came on June 27, an inside-the-parker, the only one of his career. It was hit off Charlie Root, helping Freddie Fitzsimmons beat the Cubs 6 to 4.

>> On May 14 Guy Bush hurled 18 innings before finally beating the Braves and Charlie Robertson, who also went all the way.

>> Charley Root led both leagues with 26 wins. Ted Lyons of Chicagos' Pale Hose won 22 to lead the junior circuit. The Cubs' burly righthander also turned in a one-hitter against the Pirates on July 8.

>> Travis Jackson and Rogers Hornsby each had four, 4-hit games.

>> During his 25-game hitting streak Hack Wilson hit a sizzling .387 (36 for 93). On the season he hit .318, led the league in homers with 30, and in putouts, with an even 400.

>> The Giants tied for the league lead with 817 runs scored, but permitted 69 more runs to score than the Pirates. New York's 109 homers (the Yankees smashed 158) and .427 SA led the league, as did their 16 pitching staff saves.

>> One of John McGraw's all time favorites, Ross Youngs, finally succumbed to Bright's Disease on October 22 after having been bedridden for most of 1927.

The 1927 Season Series

May 7	Chi	6	NY	4	Root, WP	Fitzsimmons, LP
May 8	NY	5	Chi	4	V. Barnes, WP	Roy, LP
June 11	Chi	2	NY	1	Root, WP	Grimes, LP
June 12	Chi	7	NY	6	Root, WP	McQuillan, LP
June 13	Chi	6	NY	2	Blake, WP	Fitzsimmons, LP
June 14	Chi	4	NY	2	Osborne, WP	Clarkson, LP
July 16	NY	6	Chi	5	Benton, WP	Bush, LP
July 16	NY	4	Chi	3	Henry, WP	Blake, LP
July 18	Chi	6	NY	4	Carlson, WP	Songer, LP
July 18	NY	3	Chi	2	V. Barnes, WP	Root, LP
July 19	Chi	8	NY	5	Osborne, WP	Clarkson, LP

July 20	NY	5	Chi	4	Songer, WP	Blake, LP
July 27	NY	6	Chi	4	Fitzsimmons, WP	Root, LP
July 28	NY	6	Chi	5	Grimes, WP	Bush, LP
July 29	Chi	5	NY	4	Root, WP	V. Barnes, LP
August 29	NY	8	Chi	7	Fitzsimmons, WP	Carlson, LP
August 29	NY	4	Chi	1	Benton, WP	Root, LP
August 30	NY	7	Chi	3	Grimes, WP	Jones, LP
September 9	NY	7	Chi	2	Grimes, WP	Weinert, LP
September 10	Chi	2	NY	1	Bush, WP	Benton, LP
September 11	Chi	7	NY	5	Carlson, WP	V. Barnes, LP
September 12	NY	7	Chi	5	Fitzsimmons, WP	Root, LP

In the Thick of It

Both Rogers Hornsby and Burleigh Grimes, John McGraw's 1927 ace, wound up in different uniforms as the 1928 season got underway. One cannot help but wonder whether, despite the problems each was capable of causing, the Giants might not have captured the N.L. flag had they been in McGraw's lineup. Grimes led the league with 25 wins and Hornsby won the batting title, amassed almost 100 ribbies, and, as usual, wore out his welcome. But even though they weren't around, the Giants appeared to have been poised to win it all without them. They stormed through September, winning 20 games, but the eventual champions, St. Louis, and Chicago's Cubs beat them in crucial late–September games to seal their second place fate. In fact, it was Chicago that threw enough sand into the New York machinery during the course of the 1928 campaign to prevent the Giants from playing in another Subway Series. The Cubs, with a 14 to 8 bulge in the season series, seemed to show up at just the wrong times all year long as far as McGraw & Co. were concerned.

One of those "wrong times" was on September 27 at the Polo Grounds when

They called him "Fat Freddie," but the wily and determined Fred Fitzsimmons was a 20-game winner just the same. He won 170 games in a 13-season career with the Giants before moving over to Brooklyn, where his 16 and 2, 1940 record helped the Dodgers to a second place finish.

Cub standouts Kiki Cuyler, Gabby Hartnett, Riggs Stephenson and "Jolly Cholly" Grimm, who paced the Bruins during the late '20s and '30s. (Dennis Colgin photograph)

former Giant hurler Artie Nehf beat New York's brilliant rookie, Carl Hubbell in the first of two. The game turned on a controversial play near home plate involving Randy Reese, caught in a run-down between third and home, and Cub catcher, sturdy Gabby Hartnett, accused of illegally blocking the plate. John McGraw protested the game and Umpire in Chief, Bill Klem, filed a report to N.L. president John Heydler. Heydler responded to McGraw's protest by upholding Klem's decision on the play, which ruled that Hartnett had not illegally blocked home plate. It was a decision that rocketed McGraw into orbit, a decision that he never forgave either Klem or Heydler. But the Cub victory stood. That victory, combined with two others the last two games of the series, along with St. Louis victories, cost the Giants the pennant, having been administered a blow from which there was no recovery.

Although they wound up in third place, the Cubs made almost as strong a bid to win the pennant as the Giants did. Getting off to a slow start, McCarthy's charges found themselves in fifth place after the opening round

Bill Klem, nattily attired in umpiring cap and bowtie, generally regarded as the greatest umpire in the game's history, was on hand for many Cubs-Giants battles. (Dennis Colgin photograph)

of games in April. But by mid–June the three top teams in the league had taken a firm grip on the pennant chase with St. Louis on top, New York in second and Chicago third. And that is the way the race ended, although the Cubs had moved into second place by Labor Day, only to be bumped, finally, by the Giants' furious September rush that netted 20 victories. Although there was to be one more second place finish for the Giants under McGraw, in 1931, "Little Napoleon's" days as the National League's pace-setter had, to all intents and purposes, gone down in flames with the failure of his ballclub to bring home a winner during September's last week finale.

From the Giants-Cubs 1928 Notebook

>> The Cubs opened on April 18 before a packed house of 46,000 at Wrigley Field, sending the throng home disappointed as they lost to Cincinnati's Reds, 9 to 6, in a combined 28-hit orgy.

>> Edd Roush, who had been bundled off to Cincinnati with Christy Mathewson in 1916, was brought back to New York in 1927 in a trade that sent future Hall of Famer George Kelly to the Reds. In 1928 Roush was joined in the outfield by another future HOF-er, Frank "Lefty" O'Doul. O'Doul became the third Famer to be moved on by McGraw within the space of two seasons, and each of them, Hornsby, Grimes and O'Doul lasted but a single season at the Polo Grounds. The constant shuffling irked particularly two more Famers, Bill Terry and Fred Lindstrom.

>> An early season winning streak extended to 13 games when the men of McCarthy beat Boston on May 19 by a 3 to 2 count.

>> Larry Benton enjoyed a career year, winning a league-leading 25 games for the Giants. The big righthander was traded to the Giants

by the Boston Braves during the 1927 season, finishing at 17 and 7 (13 and 5 with New York). 1928 was his only 20-game season.

>> On July 12 the Giants purchased Carl Hubbell from Beaumont of the Texas League. The famed "Meal Ticket" wound up the season with a 10 and 6 record, along with a strong 2.83 ERA. His first victory over the Cubs came on July 31, an 8 to 7 squeaker.

The 1928 Season Series

May 12	Chi	4	NY	2	Malone, WP	Benton, LP
May 13	Chi	5	NY	4	Blake, WP	Faulkner, LP
May 14	Chi	8	NY	2	Root, WP	Fitzsimmons, LP
May 15	Chi	10	NY	7	Jones, WP	V. Barnes, LP
June 3	NY	10	Chi	5	Fitzsimmons, WP	Nehf, LP
July 20	NY	4	Chi	3	Faulkner, WP	Malone, LP
July 21	Chi	2	NY	1	Nehf, WP	Fitzsimmons, LP
July 21	Chi	5	NY	1	Bush, WP	Faulkner, LP
July 22	Chi	4	NY	2	Root, WP	Aldridge. LP
July 28	NY	3	Chi	2	Genewich, WP	Nehf, LP
July 29	NY	4	Chi	3	Benton, WP	Jones, LP
July 29	Chi	3	NY	1	Bush, WP	Aldridge, LP
July 30	NY	4	Chi	1	Faulkner, WP	Malone, WP
July 31	NY	8	Chi	7	Hubbell, WP	Blake, LP
July 31	Chi	10	NY	4	Root, WP	Walker, LP
August 14	NY	10	Chi	2	Benton, WP	Root, LP
August 15	Chi	6	NY	5	Blake, WP	Genewich, LP
August 16	Chi	6	NY	2	Nehf, WP	Aldridge, LP
September 27	Chi	3	NY	2	Nehf, WP	Hubbell, LP
September 27	NY	2	Chi	0	Genewich, WP	Root, LP
September 28	Chi	7	NY	5	Bush, WP	Benton, LP
September 29	Chi	6	NY	2	Blake, WP	Fitzsimmons, LP

Finally

Decades are eons in baseball. The Wrigley-Veeck team, movers, shakers and helmsmen of the Cubs' fortunes since 1919, had done their best to put their team into a position to make the leap from the ranks of the also-rans to the senior circuit's elite contenders once again. That mission was accomplished. Almost. During a decade of maneuvering, trading, acquiring ball players, releasing them, bad seasons and good—some of them very good, indeed—they hadn't yet presided over a champion. Would 1929 be the year? Would it finally bring that long awaited championship?

The pitching staff, assembled over the course of the previous three

1929 Cubs pitching staff, paced by "Pat" Malone (22–10), Charley Root (19–6) and Guy Bush (18–7 with a league-leading eight saves), led National League pitching staffs with 14 shutouts and league-lows in hits per game (9.9) and opponents' BA (.284). (Grover Land, pictured to the left of "Pat" Malone was the bullpen and staff practice catcher.) (George Brace photograph)

seasons, had depth and adequate relief pitching. Pat Malone, who had lost eight of his first nine decisions in 1928 and then proceeded to win 17 of his next 22, was back for his second full season, joined by Charlie Root, the durable breaking ball artist who had won 17 games on average the past three seasons, and Guy Bush, 15 and 6 in 1928. It was a solid unit. "Jolly Cholly" Grimm, banjo-playing first sacker, and Woody English, a line-drive hitting shortstop, combined with Norm McMillan or Clyde Beck at third to provide the Cubs with a steady infield. Around the outfield Kiki Cuyler, acquired after the 1927 season from the Pirates, Riggs Stephenson and the inimitable Hack Wilson formed an outer garden trio that was second to none in the league, especially in the power and speed department. It was a McCarthy ballclub, capable of blasting just about anyone to kingdom come. But, somehow, there seemed to be a missing piece. Second base? That had been manned by Freddie Maguire, a dextrous magician with a glove, who, in 1928, had fashioned an unbelievably enormous defensive season for the Cubs, piling up 51 Fielding Runs[22] as he led the league in assists (524), putouts (410), and double plays (126). Now, as far as Joe McCarthy was concerned, there was nothing wrong with Freddie that another 30 or 40 points on his batting average wouldn't cure. The trouble was that they just weren't there. Beside, there was this Hornsby fellow in Boston. Was he available?

Well, yes, he was. A simple matter of several ballplayers, including Freddie Maguire among them, and $200,000 would pry "The Rajah" loose from Boston's Braves. Bill Wrigley, over Bill Veeck's misgivings, complied, and on November 7, 1928, Hornsby became a Cub. McCarthy, who knew exactly what all this meant, for better and for worse, made his peace with the deal in a hurry. Better to have the big stick and beef up the middle of the order still more, than to wonder if his men might come up short in one of the many slugfests going on around the league. Now his lineup was set. It only remained to get his ball club through the season without a disabling injury or some other unforeseen complication.

There were complications. They came in the form of the Cubs' ancient enemies, the Pirates, and, of course, the Giants. Each had designs on the flag and each put up a solid fight, especially Donie Bush's Pirates, who seemed to have the right answers in 13 out of 22 games with the Cubs. The season series count against McGraw's Giants was a bit better, at 12 to 10 in favor of the Cubs, but the total against the two top contenders was a subpar 21 and 23.

And there were injuries, the most striking of which was Gabby Hartnett's strange "dead arm" problem that kept him out of the lineup except for pinchhitting and one game behind the plate the entire season. A battery of five catchers, headed by Zack Taylor and ancient Mike Gonzalez were hustled in and out of McCarthy's lineups, but none filled the shoes of Chicago's popular receiver. That was not an insignificant problem—either offensively or defensively.

Nonetheless, through it all the thunderous Cub attack, led by Wilson, league leader in RBIs, and Hornsby with his gaudy .380 BA, plus league leadership in runs scored, a career-high 156, and assists (547), Cuyler's league-leading 43 stolen bases to go along with a smart .360 average and 111 runs scored, and Riggs Stephenson's .362, scored runs by the baleful to make up for any fielding lapses or other inadequacies. As for the pitching, the Cubs' staff subdued their rivals enough to produce a 22-game winner in Pat Malone, a winning streak of 11 in a sterling 18 and 7 season for Guy Bush, 19 wins for Charlie Root, and an additional 33 victories contributed by Sheriff Blake and the veterans Art Nehf and Hal Carlson. The pitching, though not sensational, got the job done and Joe McCarthy asked no more—as usual.

In late July the pennant was still up for grabs. The Cubs had moved into a tissue thin lead over Pittsburgh and New York, facing a three game set with the Giants at Wrigley Field. They opened with a Charlie Root shutout over Carl Hubbell, 2 to 0 on July 23, followed that with an 8 to 7 nail-biter the next day and finished off the Giants 8 to 5, to sweep the McGrawmen while setting a series attendance mark in excess of 100,000. By season's end the home attendance figures had soared well over the million mark, and their grip on the league's top spot kept pace, finally producing a 10½ game margin over the second place Pirates and 13½ over the Giants. An additional bottom line or two at season's end: Roger Hornsby, the league's MVP, and Hack Wilson had been placed on *The Sporting News'* ML All Star Team; the team had opened up a gaping 224 Run Differential, having scored 982 times (a club record) against their opponents' 758; their pitching staff had permitted a league low 9.9 hits per game

Guy Bush, a Giant-killer in the Jack Pfiester (1906–11) tradition. A Cub winner for a dozen seasons, Bush won 18 and saved another eight in the Cubs' pennant-winning, 1929 season. (George Brace photograph)

and it had led the league in shutouts. Further, the Cubs led the league in Fielding Average and had committed the fewest errors.

Finally. Bill Wrigley, Bill Veeck, Joe McCarthy, millions of Cubs fans, and the Cub players had done it. The old era had come to a close with a record-setting winner. Not even their loss to Connie Mack's Athletics in a painful World Series against a powerhouse much like their own could take away the luster of their decisive N.L. pennant win. Perhaps a new era, though it would come in those disastrous post-stock market crash years, would bring a new dynasty to the Windy City.

The 1929 Season Series

May 10	Chi	5	NY	4	Root, WP	Scott, LP
May 11	NY	6	Chi	0	Benton, WP	Blake, LP
June 1	NY	7	Chi	4	Scott, WP	Bush, LP
June 2	NY	4	Chi	1	Benton, WP	Blake, LP

Serious Lumber: Rogers Hornsby and "Hack" Wilson with Philadelphia A's Al Simmons and Jimmie Foxx in 1929 pre–World Series pleasantries. These four Hall of Fame sluggers propelled 1,368 homers into and out of major league grandstands. (Dennis Colgin photograph)

June 3	NY	4	Chi	1	Hubbell, WP	Malone, LP
June 4	Chi	10	NY	9	Nehf, WP	Fitzsimmons, LP
July 10	Chi	6	NY	2	Bush, WP	Hubbell, LP
July 11	Chi	8	NY	3	Malone, WP	Fitzsimmons, LP
July 11	NY	16	Chi	12	Walker, WP	Blake, LP
July 12	NY	4	Chi	3	Benton, WP	Malone, LP
July 13	Chi	4	NY	0	Carlson, WP	Henry, LP
July 23	Chi	2	NY	0	Root, WP	Hubbell, LP
July 24	Chi	8	NY	7	Cvengros, WP	Fitzsimmons, LP
July 25	Chi	8	NY	5	Cvengros, WP	Benton, LP
August 18	Chi	1	NY	0	Malone, WP	Benton, LP
August 20	NY	4	Chi	1	Fitzsimmons, WP	Bush, LP
August 20	Chi	1	NY	0	Carlson, WP	Hubbell, LP
August 21	Chi	9	NY	2	Root, WP	Benton, LP
September 18	NY	7	Chi	3	Hubbell, WP	Blake, LP
September 19	Chi	5	NY	0	Malone, WP	Benton, LP
September 21	NY	4	Chi	1	Walker, WP	Root, LP
September 22	NY	5	Chi	4	Fitzsimmons, WP	Bush, LP

VIII

REPRISE AND FINI

The Giants and Cubs had been at each other's throats for better than a half century as the 1930s dawned. Behind them was a long-standing and well established tradition of grinding, no-quarter-given rivalry, more often than not tumultuous and querulous. The Ansons, Ewings, Mathewsons, Browns, Alexanders and Bancrofts had all had their day, storied and bigger-than-life heroes who added zest, sparkle and surpassing artistry to the continuing struggle for supremacy. Beginning with the latter years of the 1870s, each decade of baseball had added its share of new stars, brilliant field leaders and front office moguls.

As 1930 approached, the Chicago and New York franchises girded for another round of pitched battles in the Wrigley Field and Polo Grounds trenches. Not much thought was given to the years ahead. At San Antonio, Texas, where the Giants trained, and at Bill Wrigley's Catalina Island, out west off the California coast, where his defending N.L. champs were training, both clubs were primarily preoccupied with their opening day lineups. That they were entering a decade that would reprise former championships and then, almost unbelievably and quite suddenly, write fini to their days of domination and glory, would have been the last thing on their minds. Nor would it have been believed had some sere forecast such a future impossibility. But that is exactly what the 1930s had in store. How those years were played out is the concern of this last era of the New York–Chicago saga, an era that might well be remembered as one of reprise and fini.

Up, Up and Away

During the 1930s, that stark and dismal era of The Depression, there was that startling paradox of baseball's soaring popularity, with its new heroes and nationwide adulation, and a country sinking deeply into the financial and psychological depths of an economy gone wildly awry. Strangely, the full effect of the American free-fall hardly made a dent during the 1930 season. The game's profits, in fact, rose by half a million dollars over the 1929 take. But leaner days, as we now know, were ahead. It wasn't only profits that soared, however. So did the more tightly woven and lower seamed baseball. What had begun as an upward trend in base hits, circuit smashes and double digit scoring in the late '20s, reached a dizzying summit as the 1930s began. And the 'ole horsehide was hit with no more authority in the American League than it was in the National League, especially in New York and Chicago. It was simply a murderous year that finally disgorged outlandish offensive figures, a swollen listing of .300 hitters, and huge bites out of the record books. Check the numbers below for a comparison of the 1930 season with the others listed, and—you might pause just long enough to note the difference between the Giants and Cubs heyday era of the early 1900's with that of the explosive late '20s and early '30s:

Year	N.L.BA	N.L.Runs	N.L.Hits/Gm	N.L.HR
1908	.239	4139	7.7	151
1928	.281	5796	9.7	610
1929	.294	6609	10.7	754
1930	.303	7025	10.9	892
1931	.277	5537	9.8	493
1960*	.255	5250	8.7	1042

* Last season with an 8-team N.L, showing differences, especially in HR's hit.

The Cubs and Giants, finishing second and third in 1930 behind the scrappy St. Louis Cardinals, were huge contributors to the senior circuit's hitting spree. Here are some of the key 1930 New York and Chicago numbers:

Player	RBI	HR	R	BA	SA	OB%
Hack Wilson, Chi	190	56	146	.356	.723	.454
Kiki Cuyler, Chi	134	13	155	.355	.547	.428
Bill Terry, NY	129	23	139	.401	.619	.452
Gabby Hartnett, Chi	122	37	84	.339	.630	.404
Mel Ott, NY	119	25	122	.349	.578	.458
Fred Lindstrom, NY	106	22	127	.379	.575	.425
Travis Jackson, NY	82	13	70	.339	.529	.386
James Hogan, NY	75	13	60	.339	.517	.378
Fred Leach, NY	71	13	90	.327	.482	.361

Left: Bill Terry (Hall of Fame, 1954), superstar first baseman, who broke in with the 1923 N.L. champion Giants. He will be remembered as the last 20th century, N.L. .400 hitter, but he was actually more valuable to the Giants as a solid, astute team leader who won pennants in three of his first six years as the New York skipper. *Right:* Size 6 spikes, size 18 collar, and 200 pounds of solid muscle on a 5'6" frame, Hack Wilson terrorized N.L. pitchers with his oversized shillelagh. His 190 RBI's in 1930 still stand as the mark to beat—in either league! (Dennis Colgin photographs)

Player	RBI	HR	R	BA	SA	OB%
Riggs Stephenson, Chi	68	5	56	.367	.476	.421
Charlie Grimm, Chi	66	6	58	.289	.403	.359
Woody English, Chi	59	14	152	.335	.511	.430
Chicago (team stats)	940	171	998	.309	.481	.369
New York (team stats)	880	143	959	.319	.473	.378
National League Ave/tm	705	112	878	.303	.448	.360

The 1930 race wound up with the Cubs trailing by two games and the Giants by five and the Cardinals winning the pennant. How, with such overpowering hitting up and down the batting order of the Giants and Cubs, could St. Louis pull it off? They had *even more* hitting than their pursuers! *Every* starter hit .300, plus another four players who filled in, and their busy bats produced a boisterous .314 team BA. There was no one to match Hack Wilson's still-standing record of 190 RBIs or Bill Terry's .401 BA, the last .400 registered in N.L. history, but John McGraw's former second sacker, Frankie Frisch, now riding herd on the Cards (he hit .346 and scored 121 runs himself), led an attack that never let up, enabling them to overcome pitching and any other weaknesses that might have cropped up, to literally outrace two arguably stronger ball clubs. This is the way the final standings looked:

Team	Won	Lost	Pct.
St. Louis	92	62	.597
Chicago	90	64	.584
New York	87	67	.565

As always, injuries played a part, but in 1930 it was more than an injury that saddened Cub followers. Veteran hurler Hal Carlson, into his fourth Cubs season and 14th overall, died quite unexpectedly of complications stemming from a stomach hemorrhage on May 30. Prior to his untimely death he had won four games, and was sorely missed the remainder of the season. Just two days later Rogers Hornsby broke his ankle sliding and wound up playing in only 42 games in 1930, most of them before the injury. Beyond those twin disasters, the Cub fortunes took a nose dive over the loss of Joe McCarthy, who was replaced by Hornsby, who, in turn, wound up managing the team the last four games of the seasson because "Marse Joe" left the club after having heard that the front office was getting ready to replace him for the 1931 season. Getting rid of McCarthy was, in the estimation of Peter Golenbock, "as bad a judgement about baseball talent as Will Wrigley would ever make."[23]

New York, once again just a few wins away from a World Series that would have given John McGraw another chance to match wits with Connie Mack, did not sustain any seriously damaging injuries, but there was a specter hanging over Coogan's Bluff. That was the growing realization that the once mighty McGraw was no longer the dreaded battler who would find a way, within or outside the rules if it had to be, to beat you. Age, health, the burdens he had carried for so many years, the new breed of younger players, and the utter upside-down character of the game he once loved beyond reason, had all caught up with him. The sands of time were hurrying on to the end of his career. And he knew it. His 1930 club was characterized this way by Bill Curran:

> The enigma of 1930 was the New York Giants... To begin, there was their record team batting average and their 143 home runs... The Giants also

boasted the league's best defensive lineup ... plus at least three quality starters... Yet, *the malaise that had afflicted the club for three years* (ital., ed.) endured. John McGraw's interminable petulance and wrong-headedness must have been more than young ball-players could handle.[24]

Even so, the Giants took the Cubs to task in 13 of the season series games. Of the five games that the winning team scored in double figures, the Giants nailed down four. Further, Carl Hubbell shut the Cubs out on September 16, and if the Giants needed runs by the bushel, they had that, too, bludgeoning the Cubs 14 to 12 on May 12. All things considered, what was needed to capture the flag was there but the most all of that TNT could produce was a third place finish. The real race taking place instead, however, was just how long it would take before the old master would call it a day.

The 1930 Season Series

May 9	Chi	6	NY	5	Carlson, WP	Pruett, LP
May 10	NY	9	Chi	4	Genewich,LP	Malone, LP
May 11	NY	9	Chi	7	Hubbell, WP	Root, LP
May 12	NY	14	Chi	12	Benton, WP	Blake, LP
June 14	Chi	8	NY	5	Malone, WP	Genewich, LP
June 15	Chi	7	NY	4	Donohue, WP	Blake, LP
June 16	Chi	8	NY	5	Root, WP	Hubbell, LP
June 30	NY	10	Chi	3	Blake, WP	Genewich, LP
July 1	NY	7	Chi	5	Fitzsimmons, WP	Bush, LP
July 2	NY	9	Chi	8	Pruett, WP	Nelson, LP
July 20	NY	13	Chi	5	Mitchell, WP	Bush, LP
July 21	Chi	6	NY	0	Malone, WP	Chaplin, LP
July 22	Chi	5	NY	4	Root, WP	Donohue, LP
July 22	NY	6	Chi	1	Walker, WP	Teachout, LP
July 23	NY	8	Chi	6	Fitzsimmons, WP	Blake, LP
August 21	NY	13	Chi	6	Walker, WP	Blake, LP
August 22	Chi	12	NY	4	Root, WP	Donohue, LP
August 23	NY	4	Chi	2	Malone, WP	Hubbell, LP
August 24	Chi	3	NY	2	Bush, WP	Heving, LP
September 16	NY	7	Chi	0	Hubbell, WP	Petty, LP
September 17	Chi	5	NY	2	Malone, WP	Chaplin, LP
September 18	NY	6	Chi	2	Fitzsimmons, WP	Bush, LP

The Winds of Change

The end of one of the most spectacular rivalries the game has known, and of the domination of the National League, both as championship teams, and as powerful influences in the conduct of the national pastime, was not yet in sight. Three scores of years had gone by since the New York and Chicago ballclubs had first crossed swords, and, moving into the 1930s, they were still powerful forces to be reckoned with.

But the storm clouds began to gather. As the Cubs and Giants prepared for the 1931 campaign, Chicago braced for its first full season without Joe McCarthy. In New York, John McGraw was still the manager. Or was he? He was not, in fact, the same manager who not only had filled out the lineup card, managed the team right on down to the last call on every pitch delivered or taken, and had a decisive say in almost every phase of the franchises operation, as in days of yore. As his own end approached, John McGraw was, at best, a shadow of his former driving and dominating persona. The 1931 season would be left largely in the hands of Bill Terry, Carl Hubbell, Mel Ott, Travis Jackson, and Freddie Lindstrom, all future Hall of Famers, who would, by personal example and sheer force of team leadership, pick up the slack left by the increasingly disinterested McGraw. And who ever might have imagined that it would come down to that!

In Chicago Bill Wrigley had bet his Juicy Fruit profits on Rogers Hornsby. Unless you were a ballplayer who played under both McCarthy and Hornsby you couldn't have begun to understand what such a change would bring. A perfectionist who didn't drink or smoke (most insisted that the only thing he ever read was the racing form), Hornsby turned the clubhouse into a sweatshop in a hurry. He was especially hard on Hack Wilson, benched from time to time, and constantly pestered by the take sign on orders from his new boss. At least McCarthy had cut him some slack for his bouts with the bubbly, but that, of course, was out-of-bounds with the tee-totaling Hornsby. Save for an exception

By now the elder Giants statesman, John McGraw, his last championship behind him, still scheming and plotting trouble for his N.L. foes. His managerial record: 2,763 wins, 1,948 losses in regular season play (.586 W%). He played on, or managed 14 National League champions.

or two, the others weren't much better off. It was, by all counts, a charged and threatening situation. That signed, sealed and delivered Wilson's ticket to oblivion.

That the Giants and Bruins finished 2–3 behind the St. Louis Cardinals in 1931 was something of a major achievement, all things considered. The standings:

Team	Pos.	Won	Lost	Pct.
St. Louis	1	101	53	.656
New York	2	87	65	.572
Chicago	3	84	70	.545

The pennant chase, just a tad short of a romp for the Cardinals, featured the same three teams in the three top spots throughout the summer. St. Louis' commanding spread came shortly after mid-season, leaving the rest of the league to their own devices and whatever individual honors they could salvage after the the Cards' field boss, Frankie Frisch, had picked up MVP laurels. One of those individual honors, the batting title, came down to the last at bat of the season, giving Chick Hafey a .3488 BA, to Bill Terry's .3486. Some 52 points lower than his league-leading .401 in 1930, the Giant captain suffered with the rest of the league, putting up with a ball somewhat drained of its 1930 zip. Here is Woody English's comment on the 1931 ball:

> The balls that used to carry into the stands were just long fly balls... We knew that the ball was a lot deader. You could tell when the ball was hit to you on the ground. The balls that used to be hit real sharp, now they came down on two or three big bounces to you [From Golenbock, (op. cit.)—page 227].

So much for 1930's 7,025 runs, 13,260 hits, 54, .300 hitters and New York's .319 team BA, all enduring records, among many more.

By season's end things had sorted themselves out both in Chicago and New York at least to this extent: Hornsby's and McGraw's days were numbered. It would be highly unlikely that either would make it through another season, though for different reasons. The bottom line for both, however, would appear to be inevitable. For the first time in the history of the great rivalry the season series between the two N.L. titans almost seemed inconsequential, but let the record show that Chicago eked out an 11 to 10 margin over the Giants.

From the 1931 Cubs-Giants Notebook

>> On April 24 Rogers Hornsby stung three of those slightly more than mushy N.L. hardballs, sending them into the seats, as the Cubs dispatched the Pirates 10 to 6. His eight ribbies were enough to win it. Later in the season, on September 13, the "Rajah" delivered a pinch-hit grand slam in the bottom of the 11th that unraveled the Braves, 11 to 7. In the second game of that day, Guy Bush set down Boston with a one-hitter, 8 to 1.

>> A Cardinal-Cub twinbill on July 12 before 45,715, results in 23 two-baggers, a record, because of the altered ground rules. The Cubs won the first game 7 to 5, the Cards, the second, 17 to 13. On the same day Mel Ott became the youngest player, at 22, to hit the century mark in homers, in his sixth ML campaign.

>> What turned out to be John McGraw's last triumph over the Cubs came in a double header on August 25 at the Polo Grounds, as his Giants won two, by scores of 5 to 3, a Hubbell victory over Charlie Root, and 7 to 1, as righthander, Jim "Tiny" Chaplin, beat Jakie May.

>> A 51,556 throng of Cub fans, the largest ever assembled at Wrigley Field, cheered in wild glee as a Kiki Cuyler four-bagger beat Brooklyn, 7 to 5, in the bottom of the tenth inning.

>> Although his record dipped a bit to 14 and 12, Carl Hubbell led N.L. pitchers in Ratio (hits plus walks allowed per nine innings), at 10.23, the lowest opponents' BA, .227, and he lowest opponents' on base percentage, .282.

>> Mel Ott and Bill Terry tied for the N.L. lead in Total Player Rating, each logging a 3.6. Ott's 80 BB led the league, as did Bill Terry's 20 triples.

The 1931 Season Series

May 9	NY	5	Chi	4	Heving, WP	Root, LP
May 10	NY	5	Chi	0	Fitzsimmons, WP	Malone, LP
June 6	Chi	5	NY	1	Smith, WP	Berly, LP
June 7	Chi	8	NY	3	Bush, WP	Fitzsimmons, LP
June 8	NY	6	Chi	1	Mitchell, WP	Malone, LP
June 9	NY	10	Chi	2	Morrell, WP	Sweetland, LP
June 22	Chi	11	NY	4	Bush, WP	Berly, LP
June 24	NY	2	Chi	0	Hubbell, WP	Smith, LP
June 24	Chi	14	NY	4	Teachout, WP	Heving, LP
July 14	Chi	8	NY	4	Bush, WP	Morrell, LP

July 15	Chi	5	NY	4	May, WP	Heving, LP
July 16	Chi	5	NY	2	Root, WP	Mitchell, LP
July 17	NY	7	Chi	6	Chaplin, WP	Smith, LP
August 24	Chi	8	NY	4	Smith, WP	Mitchell, LP
August 24	NY	2	Chi	1	Fitzsimmons, WP	Blake, LP
August 25	NY	5	Chi	3	Hubbell, WP	Root, LP
August 25	NY	7	Chi	1	Chaplin, WP	May, LP
August 26	Chi	4	NY	3	Malone, WP	Walker, LP
August 26	Chi	7	NY	4	Bush, WP	Fitzsimmons, LP
September 20	Chi	16	NY	6	Malone, WP	Hubbell, LP
September 20	Chi	7	NY	6	Warneke, WP	Parmalee, LP

1932: Reprising a Chicago Championship

In 1932 the Cubs won their 13th N.L. championship. And they did it at a time when it seemed least likely. Before the season even began William K. Wrigley, the popular and hard-working gum magnate who so dearly loved his Cubs, passed on. Before the season ended, the abrasive Rogers Hornsby would also be history, and one of Wrigleyville's all time favorites, Charley Grimm, would be brought in to oversee Cub fortunes. But there was really no indication at the start of the season, given the continuing downward trend of the Cubs, that 1932 would bring anything better than another third or fourth place finish.

However, the new Cub CEO, Bill Wrigley's son Phil, came on in his father's stead to wind up in the right place at the right time as the Bruins pulled it all together down the stretch to reprise their former championships with a determined ballclub that won the pennant by four games over the hard-charging Pirates. Note that the championship race involved the Cubs, Pirates, Dodgers and Phillies, *not* the Giants and the Cards, both of whom fell all the way into the second division, St. Louis tumbling to seventh from its top-of-the-world spot after having beaten the Philadelphia A's for the 1931 World's Championship. That was characteristic of the 1930s. One team after another came on to win a pennant, lose its traction and then regain its touch, Chicago capturing the bunting in 1932, '35, and '38, St. Louis coming back in 1934, and New York bouncing back under Bill Terry in 1933, '36, and '37. Between them, then, the three teams won nine of the ten N.L. titles in the decade, three apiece.

On September 20, 1931, in the second game of a double header, Lon Warneke, who came to be known as the "Arkansas Hummingbird," beat the Giants 7 to 6 in the last meeting of the season between the two clubs. When the bell rang for the first New York-Chicago encounter of the 1932 season, once again Warneke was chosen. This time the lean righthander beat the McGrawmen 9 to 2 in what proved to be a historic game, for it was on this very occasion that the Giants met the Cubs for the last time under John McGraw's direction. At the time no one could, of course, know that, and Hornsby's Cubs, busily engaged in surprising baseball insiders with their first place perch, were primarily concerned with winning another ballgame. Lon Warneke went on to beat the Giants five times in 1932 while turning in a sterling 22 and 6 mark for the pennant winners. He was the big difference not only in the 14 to 8 bulge Chicago enjoyed in the season series, but in their season's success, as well. The lineups for that historic tussle reveal the changes both clubs had undergone. Gone from the Cubs' batting order was Wilson, and Hornsby, while with the club, played in fewer than 20 games.

Lonnie Warneke, "The Arkansas Humming Birad," who paced the Cubs' pitching staff of the 1930s.

The Giants were clearly in transition with a new infield except for Bill Terry and with new pitchers moving into the Polo Grounds.

Those changes, however, paled in significance, at least in terms of the history being made, to the announcement John McGraw made to his wife on returning home after the Giants had lost to the Phillies on June 1. Terse, and directly to the point he said, "It's over." What followed through the course of the next several days captured the interest of the baseball world—and beyond—and was splashed across the Americas in the media. The most immediate adjustment was made at the Polo Grounds where the managerial reins were turned over to Bill Terry. But the big story revolved around the "Little Napoleon" who had so forcefully driven the Giants ever since July 2, 1902, when he first signed a contract to manage the New Yorkers. Now, within a month of 30 years later, it was all over, though no one anywhere expected it to end the way it did.

Experienced and able New York sportswriters like John Drebinger of the *Times* gave no hint of what was coming because they had none. Drebinger's writeup of McGraw's last game presented the usual routine, albeit clever coverage. A partial sample follows:

Not even the inspiring presence of John McGraw proved of sufficient influence to shake the Giants out of the doldrums and prevent them from slipping back into the National League cellar yesterday (June 1) as they opened a five-game series with the Phillies at the Polo Grounds by losing, 4 to 2... McGraw, who is still far from recovered from the sinus attack which kept him home ever since his team returned from the West, paid only a brief visit to the Park... He gave his men a heart-to-heart talk, selected Willie Walker to do the pitching and remained only long enough to see Bill Terry hammer Edgar Holley for his seventh homer of the season in the third, a shot that was immediately followed by Mel Ott's sixth circuit clout of the year. He then left for home, hopeful that things would remain that way [June 2, 1932, *New York Times*].

As it turned out, the Giants lost. But despite that, it might still be observed that at least McGraw left while he was ahead. And, as if especially decreed by the baseball gods, he had lasted just long enough to see the man he appointed to follow him, Bill Terry, put his ball club a run up on the Phillies. Incidentally, the next hitter, Mel Ott, who followed Terry as the Giants' manager, also homered, hiking the lead to 2 to 0. And that was the last John Joseph McGraw saw of a team that was his. On Saturday, June 4, Bill Terry walked to the plate to a thunderous, standing ovation as New York welcomed the Giants' new pilot. The king named McGraw was dead, and the Gotham faithful were, with their tumultuous welcome, acclaiming the new king. The world was ready to move on.

A week or so after the appointment of Bill Terry as manager of the Giants, the Cubs pulled into town for a four game set with the Giants who were on a six game tear, having annexed their sixth straight at the expense of Pat Malone, 6 to 3. Terry chose "King Carl" Hubbell to pitch the next game. His opponent was Burleigh Grimes, who seemed to pop up just about everywhere as his career progessed. This time, in a Cubs outfit, his sixth uniform change in six years (you will recall that he was a Giant in 1927), he threw his spitter well enough to put the Giant winning streak on the shoals by a 3 to 1 count. His next conquest of the Manhattanites came on August 27, when the Cubs were in the midst of stampeding the Giants, winning eight of their last 10 with Terry's charges.

While the Cubs were winging their way to the N.L. championship, the Giants and Cardinals were waging a battle for dubious honors involving the sixth slot in the league. Neither won, the two teams ending up in a 72–82 tie. The Cardinals made the trip from the penthouse to the N.L.'s lower level in less than a year, and Bill Terry, who knew long beforehand, also knew that an about-face was in order. And he knew exactly where he would start: in spring training at Los Angeles in 1933 there would be a concerted effort to stiffen the backbone of his ballclub with a renewed emphasis on all the "little things" that make for a complete team effort. Shades of John J!

The Cubs, meanwhile, had survived Rogers Hornsby, who gave way to Charlie Grimm, and a near tragic shooting of Billy Jurges, the shortstop who completed the Cubs' revamped infield, a fine unit featuring manager Grimm at first, rising star Billy Herman at second, and Woody English, who had moved from short to third. Jurges, floored by a pistol shot fired by Violet Valli, recovered, but it was necessary in the wake of the shooting to bring Mark Koenig, a Yankee infielder, to man the shortstop slot. Cuyler, Stephenson and Johnny Moore, though not as colorful or potent with a stick in his hands as the departed Hack Wilson, were a formidable outfield trio. And with the N.L.'s best catcher, Gabby Hartnett, behind the plate shepherding a fine pitching staff composed of Guy Bush (19–11), Charlie Root (15–10), Pat Malone (15–17) and 22-game winner Lon Warneke, the Cubs peeled off 14 straight wins between August 20 and September 1 to take a commanding eight game lead, finally to win the pennant by four over a game, but outclassed Pittsburgh club.

The 1932 World Series? Again—red faces in Chicago. Not only did the Yankees beat them four straight, but the Cubs suffered additional humiliations stemming from the hotly berated Mark Koenig's World Series share, and—what else?— the Babe and another of his prodigious baseball feats, real or fancied: The Called Shot.

William Jennings Bryan Herman, better known as "Billy," came along to light up the Cub infield with a league leading 527 assists and a .314 BA for the 1932 champs. The Cub Hall of Famer was a mainstay through the '30s, and was also one of the game's premier hit-and-run men. (Dennis Colgin photograph)

The 1932 Season Series

May 10	Chi	9	NY	2	Warneke, WP	Gibson, LP
June 15	NY	6	Chi	3	Fitzsimmons, WP	Malone, LP
June 16	Chi	2	NY	1	Grimes, WP	Hubbell, LP
June 18	NY	4	Chi	2	Bell, WP	Bush, LP
June 18	Chi	3	NY	0	Warneke, WP	Fitzsimmons, LP
July 17	Chi	3	NY	1	Malone, WP	Hoyt, LP
July 17	Chi	8	NY	2	Root, WP	Gibson, LP
July 18	NY	13	Chi	3	Bell, WP	Bush, LP
July 19	Chi	5	NY	4	Warneke, WP	Gibson, LP
July 20	NY	9	Chi	1	Hubbell, WP	Grimes, LP
August 7	Chi	8	NY	2	Warneke, WP	Bell, LP
August 7	NY	8	Chi	1	Hoyt, WP	Malone, LP
August 9	Chi	4	NY	3	Tinning, WP	Hubbell, LP
August 27	Chi	6	NY	1	Grimes, WP	Fitzsimmons, LP
August 27	Chi	5	NY	0	B. Smith, WP	Hoyt, LP
August 28	Chi	5	NY	4	Malone, WP	Luque, LP
August 30	Chi	4	NY	3	Bush, WP	Hoyt, LP
August 31	Chi	10	NY	9	Herrmann, WP	Gibson, LP
September 13	Chi	3	NY	1	Root, WP	Bell, LP
September 13	NY	3	Chi	2	Schumacher, WP	Warneke, LP
September 14	NY	4	Chi	3	Hubbell, WP	Malone, LP
September 15	Chi	8	NY	7	Warneke, WP	Gibson, LP

The 1932 National League Standings

Team	Won	Lost	Pct.
Chicago	90	64	.584
Pittsburgh	86	68	.558
Brooklyn	81	73	.526
Philadelphia	78	76	.506
Boston	77	77	.500
New York	72	82	.468
St. Louis	72	82	.468
Cincinnati	60	94	.390

1933–1935: One for Each

THE 1933 TO 1935 STANDINGS

Year	Team	Pos.	Won	Lost	Pct.
1933	New York	1	91	61	.599
	Pittsburgh	2	87	67	.565
	Chicago	3	86	68	.558

Year	Team	Pos.	Won	Lost	Pct.
1934	St. Louis	1	95	58	.621
	New York	2	93	60	.608
	Chicago	3	86	65	.570
1935	Chicago	1	100	54	.649
	St. Louis	2	96	58	.623
	New York	3	91	62	.595

In 1933 three ancient antagonists renewed a rivalry that dated back to the turn of the 20th century. In the year of Chicago's Century of Progress, after all had been said and done, there wasn't much progress or change in the National League's final outcome over those historic early days. Nor was there any change whatsover in the final scores of the games played in 1933. As a matter of plain fact, the entire season series between the Giants and the Cubs read like a chapter out of 1905 or '06. Observe: in seven of the contests the losing team was shut out (New York took 4, Chicago 3); in four games there were 2 to 1 scores (each won two); and in seven games that summer New York won by one run, three times, and Chicago took four. Finally, in the 22 games, the losing team scored no more than four runs (twice), and on average scored a paltry 1.32 runs per game. Are we looking at 1903 or 1933 here?

Bill Terry, for one, was looking at 1933 when he took his players out west for his first spring training as the Giants' helmsman. Fixing his steely eyes on the task ahead, he ordered a complete review of baseball's fundamentals, something that one would have thought unnecessary for a team inherited from John McGraw. But because Terry was a "ballplayer's" manager, his charges took it, and in the long run, judging by the steady play of the team all summer long, "Memphis Bill's" springtime emphasis paid off. In spades. By mid-season they were rather comfortably situated in first place, winning game after game on timely hits, game-saving putouts and one run scores. A late season rush put the blue ribbon out of sight for the Cubs, Braves and Cards. And the Pirates, who lacked the kind of pitching that put the Giants over the top by five full games, simply weren't up to overtaking Terry and Co. in the season's dog days.

Having taken his lumps with the last McGraw ballclub in 1932, Bill Terry had been determined to take his own team into the 1933 season. Win or lose, it was going to be done with *his* kind of team. Consequently, there were many lineup changes. So many, in fact, that there was a 50 percent personnel turnover.

	1932 McGraw/Terry	*1933 Terry*
1b	Terry	Terry

The 1933 Giant Powerhouse: Bill Terry, Lefty O'Doul and "Master Melvin" Ott. They lifted the New Yorkers to a world's championship over Joe Cronin's AL champions, the Washington Senators. (Dennis Colgin photograph)

	1932 McGraw/Terry	1933 Terry
2b	Critz	Critz
ss	Marshall	B. Ryan/Jackson
3b	Vergez	Vergez
lf	Joe Moore	Joe Moore
cf	Lindstrom	K. Davis
rf	Ott	Ott
c	Hogan/O'Farrell	Mancuso/Richards
p	Hubbell, Fitzsimmons, Walker, Mooney, Luque (RP)	Hubbell, Schumacher, Fitzsimmons, Parmalee, Luque (RP)
sub	Jackson, Koenecke, Fullis	O'Doul, Leslie, Dressen

The changes, along with the renewed emphasis on team fundamentals turned out to be enough to produce a championship ball club. And there were additional pluses: Terry's "Big Three," a bellweather pitching

Prince Hal Schumacher, Bill Terry's right-handed ace, who helped Carl Hubbell pitch the Giants to pennants in 1933, 1936 and 1937. (Dennis Colgin photograph)

staff that included the N.L.'s 1933 MVP Carl Hubbell, "Prince Hal" Schumacher and Freddie Fitzsimmons to accompany the biggest plus of all, the 1933 World's Championship, a decisive victory over Joe Cronin's Washington Senators. That brought the World Series trophy back to the Giants for the first time since 1922.

Runnerup Pittsburgh fell five games short of the persistent and steady Giants, but Chicago's Cubs, who like the Giants, entered their first full season under a new manager, Charlie Grimm, finished only a game out of the Pirates' runnerup spot. Grimm didn't trade or shift players around, preferring instead to go with the same 1932 pennant-winning roster, except for the addition of outfielder Floyd "Babe" Herman, the storied "hero" of many innovative base-running exploits, and whose 93 RBIs led the Cubs in 1933.

While the Cubs would finish in the same third place spot in 1934, "Jolly Cholly" was in command of a sound, pennant-contending team that reclaimed the N.L. championship just two seasons later. His seasoned pitching staff, with Guy Bush registering 20 wins, and the Warneke, Tinning, Root and Malone combination with another 56 W's, kept the Cubs in ballgames all summer long. Had there been an adequate reliever, the outcome might easily have tilted in the Cubs' favor.

Jottings from the 1933 Giants-Cubs Notebook

>> On July 2 Carl Hubbell pitched a "two-for-one" as he went 18 innings to beat the Cardinals in posting a record-making 1 to 0 win, and on August 1, he broke the Cubs' Ed Reulbach's legendary record for pitching consecutive scoreless innings, racking up 45⅓ before being scored on by the Braves in a losing, 5 to 1 effort.

>> The one and only Babe Herman, as tall and lean as Hack Wilson was squat and short, became the Cubs' Slugger of the Year on July 20,

when he plated eight runs with three four baggers and a single, beating the Phillies 10 to 1. Later, on September 30, Herman hit for the cycle as the Cubs beat Dizzy Dean, to help pin down Guy Bush's 20th victory, 12 to 2.

>> The first major league All Star Game was played in Chicago's Comiskey Park on July 6 with 49,200 on hand to see the stars of both leagues. Woody English, Gabby Hartnett and Lon Warneke were chosen to represent the Cubs, while Bill Terry, Carl Hubbell Lefty O'Doul and Hal Schumacher represented the Giants. John McGraw, making his last appearance as a manager, led the National League team. Connie Mack's American Leaguers won the game, 4 to 2.

"The Meal Ticket," Carl Hubbell, reflecting on his 2 to 1 win over the Cubs on September 16, one of his 23, 1933 victories. The N.L.'s 1933 MVP (he repeated in 1936) paced a strong staff with a 1.66 ERA. He was named to the Hall of Fame in 1947. (Dennis Colgin photograph)

The 1933 Season Series

May 2	Chi	11	NY	0	Warneke, WP	Schumacher, LP
May 4	NY	2	Chi	1	Fitzsimmons, WP	Tinning, LP
May 4	NY	5	Chi	4	Parmalee, WP	Bush, LP
May 16	NY	4	Chi	1	Hubbell, WP	Malone, LP
May 18	NY	3	Chi	0	Schumacher, WP	Grimes, LP
May 18	Chi	10	NY	1	Bush, WP	Fitzsimmons, LP
June 18	NY	2	Chi	0	Parmalee, WP	Warneke, LP
June 19	NY	3	Chi	0	Schumacher, WP	Root, LP
June 20	Chi	5	NY	3	Tinning, WP	Bell, LP
June 21	NY	3	Chi	1	Fitzsimmons, WP	Malone, LP
July 7	Chi	4	NY	3	Root, WP	Clark, LP
July 8	Chi	2	NY	1	Bush, WP	Schumacher, LP

Bill Terry's 1933 Giants. Back row: Watty Clark, Homer Peel, John Salveson, Bill Shores, Adolfo Luque, Frank Lefty O'Doul, Herman Bell, "Harry the Horse" Danning, Joe Moore. Standing, 2nd row: Gus Mancuso, Johnny Vergez, Freddie Fitzsimmons, George "Kiddo" Davis, Carl Hubbell, Blondy Ryan, "Prince Hal" Schumacher, Joe Malay, Mel Ott, Leroy Parmalee. Seated: Hughie Critz, Travis Jackson, Frank Snyder, Manager Bill Terry, Tom Clarke, Charley Dressen, Byrnie James. Seated in front: Mr. Schaeffer (trainer), Phil Weintraub, Al Smith, Joe Troy (mascot), Glenn Spencer, Paul Richards. Missing when picture was taken: Sam Leslie. (George Brace photograph)

July 9	Chi	4	NY	0	Warneke, WP	Hubbell, LP
July 9	Chi	2	NY	1	Tinning, WP	Fitzsimmons, LP
August 19	NY	8	Chi	4	Hubbell, WP	Warneke, LP
August 20	NY	6	Chi	1	Schumacher, WP	Malone, LP
September 13	Chi	2	NY	0	Bush, WP	Hubbell, LP
September 14	Chi	4	NY	3	Malone, WP	Fitzsimmons, LP
September 15	NY	5	Chi	1	Schumacher, WP	Tinning, LP
September 15	NY	4	Chi	0	Bell, WP	Warneke, LP
September 16	NY	2	Chi	1	Hubbell, WP	Nelson, LP
September 16	NY	6	Chi	3	Shores, WP	Bush, LP

1930's Interlude

The rush of Giant and Cub pennant-winning teams in the 1930s, six all told, was temporarily halted by Frankie Frisch's Gashouse Gang in 1934, one of gamiest, rowdy, and above all, determined of St. Louis' many champions. The Cardinals rode a 33 and 12 stretch down to the wire to finally beat out Terry's New Yorkers, finishing the season with a pair of wins over Cincinnati while Casey Stengel's Dodgers were busy answering Bill Terry's pre-season query as to whether the Dodgers were still in the league by smacking them twice in succession at the Polo Grounds. That put an end to the Giants' hopes of repeating their 1933 World Series victory.

In the meantime the Cubs could do no better than 86 wins, the same number that had relegated them to a third place finish in 1933. That kind of treadmill exercise kept them in the same old third place finish in 1934. Once again Charlie Grimm went with virtually the same ballclub as his 1933 team. This time there was, as in the previous season, once essential change, again in the outfield, with the famed Phillies slugger, Chuck Klein, moving into left field. When it was all over in September, however, the bottom line was: no cigar. One thing they did manage, however, and that was to turn around the New York-Chicago season series by winning 11 of the 21 games played (a September 8 rainout was cancelled from the schedule), as compared to their 9 and 13 showing of 1933.

But while neither Chicago nor New York was able to sustain pennant continuity, there was indeed significant news eminating from Coogan's Bluff. The first piece of news had to do with the death of John McGraw, which took place on February 25 at his New Rochelle, New York, home. His passing was marked with all the solemnity and respect commensurate with his special standing in the world of baseball, and in particular with New Yorkers. What he had done, and what he had meant to baseball is voluminously documented. Among the many, many tributes extended him, one, well known among baseball buffs everywhere, seems to have summed them all, Connie Mack's "There has been only one manager and his name is John McGraw."

One other rather special event took place at the Polo Grounds, where the Giants played host to the 1934 All Star Game on July 10. On that auspicious occasion "King Carl" Hubbell managed to upstage the American League's second straight win over the senior circuit by crushing the A.L. attack during his three-inning stint with six whiffs, five of them in succession. With his screwball, a pitch that that breaks in the opposite direction a curveball does, working to perfection, he struck out the heart of the American League lineup, Babe Ruth, Lou Gehrig, Jimmie Foxx, Al Simmons, and Joe Cronin. It was a legendary feat, one, unfortunately, that has dwarfed "The Meal Ticket's" many other exceptional achievements, such as his no-hit masterpiece against the Pirates on May 8, 1929, and his 24-game winning streak from July 17, 1936 to May 27, 1937.

The box score of the 1934 All Star Game follows:

American League	AB	R	H	PO		National League	AB	R	H	PO
Gehringer, Det, 2b	3	0	2	2		Frisch, StL, 2b	3	3	2	0
Manush, Wash, lf	2	0	0	0		Herman, Chi, 2b	2	0	1	0
Ruffing, NYY, p	1	0	1	0		Traynor, Pit, 3b	5	2	2	1
Harder, Clv, p (WP)	2	0	0	1		Medwick, StL, lf	2	1	1	0
Ruth, NYY, lf	2	1	0	0		Klein, Chi, lf	3	0	1	1
Chapman, NYY, rf	2	0	1	0		Cuyler, Chi, rf	2	0	0	2
Gehrig, NYY, 1b	4	1	0	11		Ott, NYG, rf	2	0	0	0
Foxx, Phl, 3b	5	1	2	1		Berger, Bos, cf	2	0	0	0
Simmons, Chi, cf, rf	5	3	3	3		Waner, Pit, cf	2	0	0	1
Cronin, Wash, ss	5	1	2	2		Terry, NYG, 1b	3	0	1	4
Dickey, NYY, c	2	1	1	4		Jackson, NYG, ss	2	0	0	0
Cochrane, Det, c	1	0	0	1		Vaughan, Pit, ss	2	0	0	4
Gomez, NYY, p	1	0	0	0		Hartnett, Chi, c	2	0	0	9
Averill, Clv, ph, cf	4	1	2	1		Lopez, Brk, c	2	0	0	5
West, StL, cf	0	0	0	1		Hubbell, NYG, p	0	0	0	0
						Warneke, Chi, p	0	0	0	0
						Mungo, Brk, p (LP)	0	0	0	0
						Martin, StL,	0	1	0	0
						Dean, StL, p	1	0	0	0
						Frankhouse, Bos, p	1	0	0	0
Totals	39	9	14	27		Totals	36	7	8	27

Line Score   American League   000 261 000   9–14–1
                  National League   103 030 000   7–8–1

2BH—Foxx, Simmons 2, Cronin, Averill, Herman
3BH—Chapman, Averill
HR—Frisch, Medwick
SB—Gehringer, Manush, Traynor, Ott
LOB—American 12; National 5
DP—Lopez and Vaughan
K—Gomez 3, Hubbell 6, Warneke 1, Mungo 1, Dean 4
BB—Gomez 1, Ruffing 1, Hubbell 2, Warneke 3, Mungo 2, Dean 1, Frankhouse 1
Umpires—Pfirman and Stark (N.L.) and Owens and Moriarity (A.L.)
Managers—Cronin (A.L.), and Terry (N.L.)
Time—2:44
Attendance—48,363

The 1934 Season Series

May 13	Chi	7	NY	3	Bush, WP	Bell, LP
May 14	Chi	3	NY	2	Warneke, WP	Schumacher, LP

May 15	NY	10	Chi	3	Hubbell, WP	Root, LP
May 23	NY	5	Chi	2	Schumacher, WP	Bush, LP
May 24	NY	7	Chi	1	Hubbell, WP	Tinning, LP
June 20	NY	12	Chi	7	Fitzsimmons, WP	Root, LP
June 21	Chi	4	NY	0	Warneke, WP	Hubbell, LP
June 22	Chi	15	NY	2	Lee, WP	Clark, LP
June 23	Chi	5	NY	4	Warneke, WP	A. Smith, LP
July 14	Chi	11	NY	4	Weaver, WP	Bell, LP
July 15	NY	5	Chi	3	Schumacher, WP	Malone, LP
July 17	NY	5	Chi	3	Parmalee, WP	Warneke, LP
July 17	Chi	2	NY	1	Lee, WP	Hubbell, LP
July 18	NY	8	Chi	6	Fitzsimmons, WP	Bush, LP
August 26	Chi	7	NY	1	Warneke, WP	Fitzsimmons, LP
August 27	Chi	1	NY	0	Lee, WP	Schumacher, LP
August 28	NY	3	Chi	1	Parmalee, WP	Weaver, LP
August 29	Chi	1	NY	0	Warneke, WP	Gumbert, LP
September 5	NY	5	Chi	1	Schumacher, WP	Bush, LP
September 6	NY	2	Chi	1	Parmalee, WP	Lee, LP
September 7	Chi	4	NY	2	Warneke, WP	Hubbell, LP

1935 and the September Streak

For Giant fans the 1935 season would have been an unqualified success if the pennant race had ended after 120 games. In late August, Team Terry was in first place. Detroit, over in the A.L., looked as if it might sidetrack the Yankees, and if they were to succeed, would hand the Big Apple's bragging rights to the Giants on a silver platter. St. Louis' defending world champions and the Cubs were in hot pursuit of the Giants, but as the three frontrunners approached September, New York's heroes still looked as though they could win it all.

Then came The Streak. Between September 4, when the Cubs were down 2½ games in the standings, and September 27, they reeled off 21 straight wins, absolutely astounding the baseball world, while knocking the Giants and Cardinals out of contention. Cubs boss Charlie Grimm used only seven different pitchers during the run to pennant gold. Southpaw Larry French, acquired from the Pirates in a blockbuster deal in November of 1934, moving Guy Bush, Babe Herman and Jim Weaver to Pittsburgh (the Pirates also gave up Freddie Lindstrom in the swap) and "Big Bill" Lee each won five times during the streak, Lon Warneke and Charlie Root added four apiece, and the young portsider Roy Henshaw added two more. The streak's 21st win came from Tex Carleton.

In beating the Cardinals on September 27 the Cubs clinched the pennant. By season's end, two days later, they had won their 100th game, sporting a four game lead over the Cards and an 8½ game bulge over the 3rd place Giants.

This is the box score of the 21st straight win that clinched the 1935 pennant for the Cubs:

St. Louis	AB	R	H	PO	Chicago	AB	R	H	PO
Martin, rf	4	1	1	4	Galan, lf	5	2	3	2
King, cf	3	0	1	4	Herman, 2b	4	2	2	3
Frisch, 2b	4	1	2	4	Lindstrom, cf	5	0	4	0
Medwick, lf	4	0	0	0	Hartnett, c	5	0	1	3
J. Collins, 1b	4	0	0	5	Demaree, rf	5	0	0	0
DeLancey, c	3	0	1	5	Cavarretta, 1b	4	0	1	13
Durocher, ss	4	0	0	3	Hack, 3b	4	1	3	0
Gelbert, 3b	4	0	1	1	Jurges, ss	4	0	0	5
J. Dean, p (LP)	3	0	0	1	Lee, p (WP)	4	0	1	1
Totals	33	2	6	27	Totals	40	5	15	27

Line Score	Chicago	002 100 101	5–15–2
	St. Louis	200 000 000	2–6–1

2BH—Galan, Hack, Lindstrom
HR—Hack
SB—Martin
DP—Gelbert, Frisch, J. Collins; Herman, Jurges, Cavarretta; Frisch, Durocher, J. Collins
BB—Lee 2, J. Dean 0
K—Lee 1, J. Dean 3
Umpires—Klem, Rigler, Reardon and Pinelli

Sparked by MVP winner Gabby Hartnett, a young and tightly knit infield consisting of 19-year-old Phil Cavarretta, who replaced bossman Grimm, Billy Herman, who led the N.L. in hits with 227, Billy Jurges and "Smilin' Stan" Hack, and an outfield of Augie Galan, Frank Demaree and Chuck Klein, the Cubs had enough punch, better than average speed and outstanding pitching to stack up their 100 wins. Reserves Fred Lindstrom, Woody English, catcher Ken O'Dea and Kiki Cuyler chipped in as needed to lend versatility to the Chicago attack.

During the course of the season New York's number one nemesis turned out to be their arch rivals, the Cubs, who beat them 14 times. The first clash of the season came in a May 8 doubleheader the Giants won by scores of 3 to 1 and 6 to 2. After a 6 to 4 defeat at the hands of Charlie Root, the Giants ran off another three straight, to win five of the first six encounters. But beginning on July 19 the Cubs won 11 of the last 12 games in the season series to run up a 14 to 8 edge, four of which came during their September streak when the big four of the staff, Warneke, French, Root and Lee, each won, and in that order.

In their fourth try since the world's championship year of 1908, the Cubs once again brought no joy to Wrigleyville, losing the World Series to Detroit's Tigers in six games. Though Lon Warneke pitched well, winning two games, Detroit prevailed despite losing Hank Greenberg to an injury in the second game, find enough wherewithal to scratch out the four games they needed to win. In Chicago the age-old chant went up: Wait till next year! Hadn't they said that before, a time or two?

1935 Significa

>> Augie Galan, diminutive Cub speedster, hit into a triple play on the last day of the season. Strangely, his speed had enabled him to escape *any twinkillings* during regular season play. He was victimized only 72 times in a 16 year career amounting to almost 6,000 times at bat!

>> Babe Ruth, in a cameo N.L. appearance at the start of the 1935 season with the Braves, added six home runs to his record-setting total of 714. He hit one on opening day against Carl Hubbell, and he hit for the distance against the Cubs' Tex Carleton on May 21. Number 714 was dished up by former Cub hurler Guy Bush, an orbital clout travelling in the neighborhood of 600 feet at Pittsburgh's spacious Forbes Field on May 25.

>> On May 30, 63,943 New York diehards were wedged into the Polo Grounds for a Memorial Day twinbill with the Dodgers. That set the all time attendance record. The Giants took two from the Dodgers, adding to their N.L. lead over the Cardinals and Pirates.

The 1935 Season Series

May 8	NY	3	Chi	1	Parmalee, WP	Warneke, LP
May 8	NY	6	Chi	2	Castleman, WP	Lee, LP
May 23	Chi	6	NY	4	Root, WP	Chagnon, LP
May 25	NY	13	Chi	0	Schumacher, WP	Henshaw, LP
May 26	NY	3	Chi	2	Hubbell, WP	Warneke, LP
June 23	NY	8	Chi	0	Fitzsimmons, WP	Warneke, LP
June 24	Chi	10	NY	9	Henshaw, WP	A. Smith, LP

June 25	NY	3	Chi	2	Castleman, WP	Warneke, LP
June 25	Chi	10	NY	5	Kowalik, WP	A. Smith, LP
June 26	NY	5	Chi	2	Schumacher, WP	Root, LP
July 19	Chi	9	NY	3	Warneke, WP	Schumacher, LP
July 20	Chi	7	NY	2	French, WP	Parmalee, LP
July 21	Chi	5	NY	4	Root, WP	Hubbell, LP
July 21	Chi	11	NY	5	Warneke, WP	Stout, LP
August 22	Chi	4	NY	3	Warneke, WP	Stout, LP
August 23	Chi	7	NY	4	French, WP	Castleman, LP
August 24	NY	9	Chi	4	Hubbell, WP	Carleton, LP
August 25	Chi	5	NY	4	Lee, WP	Schumacher, LP
September 16	Chi	8	NY	3	Warneke, WP	Gumbert, LP
September 17	Chi	5	NY	3	French, WP	Stout, LP
September 18	Chi	15	NY	3	Root, WP	Castleman, LP
September 19	Chi	6	NY	1	Lee, WP	Hubbell, LP

Finishing at the Top

The long, distinguished era of the grand old Chicago-New York rivalry, which began before the White Stockings' 1876 pennant, captured during the National League's inaugural year, was about to come to an end—and with still more pennant flags waving. Although the rivalry would continue beyond the 1930s, it would do so without pennant fever, and that would inevitably relegate the bitter struggles to a lesser competitive edge. Further, with the last putout at the Polo Grounds on September 29, 1957, the final New York chapter of the Giants' franchise history had been written, closing out any hope of renewing the spice and dash of a heated pennant chase between the two arch enemies a la "the old days." And as a matter of plain fact, there was another rivalry brewing in the heartland that would come to replace, nearly as significant and intense, the New York-Chicago rivalry had that captured the baseball's undivided attention for such a long time. This one would involve the Cubs with another ancient adversary, the St. Louis Cardinals. As for the Giants, they would move on to San Francisco to make a fresh start with new rivalries, ballparks, fans, style, and finally, a totally new baseball identity.

That was unforeseen as the 1936 season commenced. During the 1930s the Giants and Cubs fought one another for every run, as usual, resulting in three pennants for each team. The final threesome, then, which resulted in 1936 and '37 championships for Bill Terry's Giants, and one last Cub trophy in 1938, represents a rousing *denouement* to the absorbing saga of the nation's two metropolitan centers competing for the national pastime's highest honors.

The 1936 to 1938 Season Standings

Year	Team	Pos.	Won	Lost	Pct.
1936	New York	1	92	62	.597
	Chicago	2(t)	87	67	.565
	St. Louis	2(t)	87	67	.565
1937	New York	1	95	57	.625
	Chicago	2	93	61	.604
	Pittsburgh	3	86	68	.558
1938	Chicago	1	89	63	.586
	Pittsburgh	2	86	64	.573
	New York	3	83	67	.563

The steady, grinding impact of 13 previous seasons caught up with Hall of Famer Bill Terry, the Giants' brilliant warrior. Bum knees, broken fingers and aging legs convinced him that his playing days were about over. And, as was usually the case with playing managers, the strain of managing the ballclub extracted its own additional toll. Consequently, Terry envisioned a limited role for himself in the 1936 scheme of things. But when the time came to bring the Giants home a winner there he was, pain, bruises, injuries and all, to take command from his familiar first base battle station. Forsaking his part time playing role, he led the Giants through a 15 game winning streak in August that brought them from a 4½ game deficit to the league's top spot, three games up on their principal rivals, the Cubs and Cardinals.

The streak came to an end on August 28. Two days later the Giants moved into Chicago to meet Grimm's Cubs for a twinbill. Bill Terry assigned his aces, Carl Hubbell and Hal Schumacher, to meet "Big Bill" Lee and Larry French. Chicago's chance to level the Giants' precarious hold on first place lay directly ahead. Unfortunately for the Wrigleyville faithful, Terry and Company dashed their hopes with a sweep by scores of 6 to 1 behind Hubbell, and 8 to 6, as Dick Coffman won in relief of Hal Schumacher. Behind 6 to 5 going into the ninth of the nightcap, the Giants came up with three tallies, the big blow coming off the bat of Mel Ott, who homered after both bossman Terry and Hank Lieber singled. The two victories, though dulled a bit by Lon Warneke's 1 to 0 win the next day, put the Giants in command of the race. They never looked back, finally clinching the pennant on September 24, beating Boston as 11-game winner Schumacher singled home the game's winning run. The Game Two box score, August 30, 1936:

New York	AB	R	H	PO	Chicago	AB	R	H	PO
Joe Moore, lf	5	1	4	0	Allen, lf	5	2	0	2

New York	AB	R	H	PO	Chicago	AB	R	H	PO
Whitehead, 2b	4	0	0	4	Cavarretta, 1b	5	2	3	8
Terry, 1b	5	2	2	14	Herman, 2b	5	0	1	4
Lieber, cf	4	2	2	3	Demaree, rf	4	0	0	2
Ott, rf	5	3	4	0	Hack, 3b	3	1	2	1
Jackson, 3b	5	0	1	1	Galan, cf	5	0	2	4
Mancuso, c	5	0	0	2	Hartnett, c	4	1	1	3
Bartell, ss	4	0	1	3	Jurges, ss	3	0	1	3
Schumacher, p	1	0	0	0	French, p	3	0	1	0
G. Davis, ph	1	0	0	0					
Gumbert, p	0	0	0	0					
Danning, ph	1	0	1	0					
Coffman, p	0	0	0	0					
Totals	40	8	15	27	Totals	37	6	11	27

Line Score	New York	020 010 203	8–15–2
	Chicago	201 111 000	6–11–1

2BH—Terry, Danning
HR—Lieber, Ott, Cavarretta 2
SB—Ott, Hack
SH—Whitehead, French
LOB—New York 8, Chicago 10
DP—Bartell, Whitehead, Terry; Herman, Cavarretta, Jurges
BB—Schumacher 2, Gumbert 3, French 1
K—Schumacher 1, Gumbert 1, French 3
PB—Hartnett
WP—Schumacher
Umpires—Pinelli, Magerkurth, Quigley and Moran
Time—2:05

Earlier in the season the Cubs, who led most of the way through July, were aided no little by a 15-game winning streak of their own that extended from June 4 to June 21. The streak enabled them to jump from a fourth place, eight game deficit to a half game behind the front running Cardinals.

Right: "Rowdy Richard" Bartell, a McGraw type ballplayer who starred at shortstop for the championship Giant teams of 1936 and 1937. (George Brace photograph)

A third streak, this one by Carl Hubbell, was the monster streak of the season, however. And it was to continue in 1937. Beginning on July 17 and ending, at least for 1936, with a 5 to 4 conquest of the Phillies on September 23, the N.L.'s 1936 MVP dealt screwballs, changing speeds and edge-of-the-strike zone misery to every team in the league. The final record for "King Carl" read 26 wins, an .813 winning percentage, but 7.85 hits allowed per game, a 9.68 Ratio, a 2.31 ERA and a .276 opponents' on base percentage. *Each* was a league-leading figure.

The 1936 Gehrig and DiMaggio-led Yankees, meanwhile, swept to the first of four consecutive A.L. pennants with one of the franchise's premier ballclubs. That set up another subway series, the first since 1923, when they finally crashed the McGraw barrier to win their first world's championship. They apparently were not about to lose another, especially to the arch, inter-league rival Giants, shoving them aside in six games while running up a 20-run differential, 43 to 23. Perhaps Bill Terry's men would fare better in 1937 when Terry would devote all his time and energies to piloting the ball club, his active career having ended with a single in four at-bats in the final game of the 1936 World Series.

The 1936 Season Series

May 2	Chi	5	NY	4	Root, WP	Coffman, LP
May 12	NY	5	Chi	4	A. Smith, WP	Henshaw, LP
May 14	NY	5	Chi	0	Hubbell, WP	Warneke, LP
June 3	NY	3	Chi	0	Schumacher, WP	C. Davis, LP
June 4	Chi	8	NY	5	Warneke, WP	Castleman, LP
June 26	Chi	3	NY	1	C. Davis, WP	Schumacher, LP
June 27	NY	11	Chi	2	Gumbert, WP	Warneke, LP
June 28	Chi	3	NY	0	French, WP	Hubbell.LP
June 28	Chi	6	NY	0	Lee, WP	Coffman, LP
July 12	NY	8	Chi	6	Gumbert, WP	Warneke, LP
July 13	Chi	1	NY	0	Lee, WP	Hubbell, LP
July 14	Chi	6	NY	1	C. Davis, WP	Schumacher, LP
July 29	NY	7	Chi	2	Gabler, WP	Lee, LP
July 30	NY	3	Chi	1	Hubbell, WP	C. Davis, LP
July 31	Chi	3	NY	1	French, WP	Gumbert, LP
August 30	NY	6	Chi	1	Hubbell, WP	Lee, LP
August 30	NY	8	Chi	6	Coffman, WP	French, LP
August 31	Chi	1	NY	0	Warneke, WP	Gabler, LP
September 1	NY	7	Chi	4	Gumbert, WP	Lee, LP
September 11	NY	5	Chi	1	Hubbell, WP	C. Davis, LP
September 12	Chi	6	NY	0	Warneke, W P	Schumacher, LP

Team Terry Repeats

As was the case so many times before, the Cubs and Giants, scrapping gamely throughout the season to gain an edge in the pennant chase, came down to *the* most crucial series of the N.L. season, booked for a three game set that began with Chicago only 2½ games behind the league-leading Gothamites. That kind of scenario had been a throbbing part of many an N.L. season in years past, and in late September of 1937, it was to be reenacted once again. The boys from Wrigleyville invaded the Polo Grounds on September 21 with an 11 to 8 lead in the season series and needed a sweep of the impending three game set to retake the league lead. That they might pull it off was not beyond the realm of possibility, and seemed quite likely after they vanquished the Giants 7 to 5, upping their season series lead to 12 and 8 while reducing New York's lead to a game and a half behind Gabby Hartnett's potent bludgeon and the combined pitching efforts of Larry French, Charlie Root, who got the win, and "Big Bill" Lee, who mopped up, aided considerably by a timely twin-killing in the Giants' ninth.

But that's where the Giants drew a line in the Polo Grounds dirt. Calling on Cliff Melton, a rookie southpaw they called "Mountain Man," or, on some occasions "Mickey Mouse," because of his oversized ears, the Terrymen squelched the Cubs 6 to 0 on a Melton six-hitter that hoisted the Giants lead back to 2½ games as the North Carolinian upped his season record to 18 and 9. It proved to be the pivotal game of the season for both clubs. The final standings a week later read New York, 95 and 57, and Chicago, 93 and 61, the Cubs still behind by three games. Terry's charges had hung on to garner New York's 15th N.L. pennant since its first trip to the championship circle in 1888.

"The Mountain Man," Cliff Melton, whose rookie year (20 and 9) with the Giants helped win a 1937 pennant. (George Brace photograph)

Earlier in the season Carl Hubbell had picked up just where he left off at the end of the 1936 season with 16 successive victories it tow. He started off the year with a three-hitter that dampened Boston's season opener for number 17.

On May 27 he relieved Hal Schumacher in Cincinnati, picking up his 24th straight. The two-season record of 24 in a row ended on Memorial Day in Brooklyn, where the Giants bowed to the Dodgers, their ace routed in the fourth stanza. The win skein had rivited the baseball world's attention on each outing, and the record went down not only as another of Hubbell's many Hall of Fame credentials, but as one of the game's sterling accomplishments.

"King Carl" was also involved in another of those matchups that drew sustained interest and attention over a number of seasons, much like the Mathewson and Brown encounters during the early 1900's. The attraction during the '30s was any game with the Cardinals that pitted Dizzy Dean against the master of the screwball, Hubbell.

A 7 and 3 log favored Hubbell before their last meeting on June 27. On that day Mel Ott's two homers provided all the punch the legdary Giant needed to beat Dean, upping his record to 8 and 3 against the Cardinal great.

Clinching the pennant on September 30 against Philadelphia, the Giants, undaunted by the prospect of another World Series with "that team" in the Bronx, finished the 1937 season with "Memphis Bill's" third blue ribbon in six tries. He had proven to be just as good a manager as he was a first baseman, a rather extraordinary accomplishment.

Although they might have been undaunted, it made little difference to the men of Joe McCarthy, who once again whipped the Giants, this time in one game less than it took in 1936. The margin was four games to one as the Yankees blunted the Giant attack, holding them to but 12 runs in the five games. Lefty Gomez, Red Ruffing, Tony Lazzeri, who would wind up in a Cub uniform for the 1938 season, and George Selkirk, who drove in several of the Yankees' game-busters, proved to be a bit too much for a game but out-classed Giants ball club.

Terry remained with the Giants through the 1941 season, thus ending a brilliant career spanning a score of years, all with the Giants. His successor, the very last of the McGraw men to pilot the Giants, was Mel Ott, who managed the club from 1942 on into the 1947 season. The tie between the old and the new was finally severed, covering nearly all of the lengthy and distinguished stretch of championship baseball that was "New York."

The 1937 Season Series

May 9	NY	4	Chi	3	Hubbell, WP	Lee, LP
May 10	Chi	4	NY	3	Shoun, WP	Schumacher, LP
May 11	NY	10	Chi	1	Castleman, WP	Parmalee, LP
May 21	Chi	8	NY	5	Shoun, WP	Schumacher, LP
May 22	NY	3	Chi	2	Castleman, WP	French, LP
June 3	Chi	2	NY	1	Shoun, WP	Gumbert, LP
June 4	Chi	6	NY	5	Bryant, WP	Melton, LP
June 4	NY	4	Chi	2	Castleman, WP	Lee, LP
June 22	Chi	5	NY	0	Lee, WP	Gumbert, LP
June 23	NY	8	Chi	4	Hubbell, WP	Shoun, LP
June 24	Chi	10	NY	5	Bryant, WP	Gumbert, LP
July 23	Chi	11	NY	3	Root, WP	Hubbell, LP
July 24	Chi	10	NY	5	French, WP	Schumacher, LP
July 25	NY	5	Chi	0	Gumbert, WP	Lee, LP
July 30	Chi	5	NY	3	Lee, WP	Gumbert, LP
July 31	Chi	7	NY	1	Carleton, WP	Hubbell, LP
August 1	Chi	5	NY	4	French, WP	Melton, LP
August 25	NY	8	Chi	7	Brennan, WP	C. Davis, LP
August 25	NY	4	Chi	2	Gumbert, WP	French, LP
September 21	Chi	7	NY	5	Root, WP	Coffman, LP
September 22	NY	6	Chi	0	Melton, WP	Carleton, LP
September 23	NY	8	Chi	7	Hubbell, WP	C. Davis, LP

The Final Hurrah

On Wednesday, October 14, 1908, Orval Overall tossed a three hit shutout that whipped the Detroit Tigers, 2 to 0, and won the world's championship. That turned out to be a date to mark for all time, for it was the last such championship in the venerable franchises history to date. 1910, 1918, 1929, 1932 and 1935 had all come and gone, and in each of those seasons Cub pennant winners failed in their quest for World Series gold. But that didn't deter those game Wrigleyville warriors from trying again.

What didn't work in 1936 or '37, was bound to work next year. So there was no reason to believe, especially in the environs of Chicago's famed intersection of North Clark and Addison Streets, where the town's beloved Cubbies held forth, that their heroes wouldn't get the job done in 1938. And lo and behold, the Cubs emerged from a furious summerlong fray with the Pirates and Giants, victors once again. The difference between this ballclub and all the others in between that somehow fell just short of the World Series spoils, so the prevailing wisdom held, was that fate would confer a special measure of invincibility on this gang of irrepressible

Opening day of the 1938 championship season at Wrigley Field. Note the extra rows of fans surrounding the outfield. The ivy, which was planted a year earlier, began taking on its Wrigley trademark growth during the late '30s. (George Brace photograph)

gladiators. It would seem the wise sages in Wrigleyville were right. At least, that is, on September 28, another of those red letter days in Bruin history, because that was the day, or would it be better to say evening, that Cub manager Gabby Hartnett shot down the onrushing Pirates with one of baseball's most famous home runs, a bullet into the Wrigley Field bleachers that most of Chicago's million or so who claimed to have been there didn't even see because of the darkness descending on the playing field. The loquacious and very popular field general had this to say about his most memorable moment in The Bigs:

> A lot of people have told me they didn't know the ball was in the bleachers. Well, I did—maybe I was the only one in the park who did. I knew the minute I hit it. When I got to second base I couldn't see third for the players and fans there. I don't think I walked a step to the plate—I was carried in. But when I got there I saw George Barr (ed: home plate umpire) taking a good look—he was going to make sure I touched that platter. That was the shot that did it. We went into first place... And we clinched the pennant down in St. Louis the next Saturday when we won and Pittsburgh lost to Cincinnati.

Left: Burly Gabby Hartnett, whose powerful bat and equally powerful catcher's arm were big factors in Chicago's return to prominence during the 1920s and '30s, restoring the Cubs to championship status in 1929, 1932, 1935 and 1938. *Right:* "Big Bill" Lee, aka "The General," a strong-armed Louisianian, who anchored the Cubs pitching corps during the '30s. His 1938 log: 22 wins, a .710 winning percentage and a 2.66 ERA. (George Brace photographs)

Carmichael, John P., and Others, *My Greatest Day In Baseball*, Grosset and Dunlap Pub., NY., 1945, p. 97.

From the standpoint of this review of the Cubs-Giants rivalry over almost three quarters of a century, it is fitting that the last of these many spine-tingling pennant races once again featured the same three ball clubs, the Pirates, Giants and Cubs, that had given baseball buffs so much to cheer about as they so often and so valiantly battled one another for National League supremacy. The 1938 pennant chase was no exception. No more than five, and at most six games separated the three clubs all summer long. First the Cardinals and then the Giants dropped out of contention as September wore on, and that left Hartnett's Cubs and the Pirates of Pie Traynor to duel to the very end, winding up with one of the more thrilling games of the century on what must have literally been one of Pittsburgh's blackest days, and conversely, Chicago's most joyous.

And so Chicago won the right to do something about what had grown into a haunting, 30-year-old lapse in world championship laurels. Alas, the New Yorkers in the Bronx lay in wait, ready, willing, and once again able to break the hearts of National Leaguers everywhere. "Marse Joe" McCarthy, erstwhile Cub major domo, had his troops ready, led by "The Captain," Lou Gehrig, now in his last full season with the Yankees. In a repeat of the 1932 Series, which saw McCarthy on the other end of success, the Yanks disposed of the Cubs in four straight, outscoring them 22 to 9.

Another pennant in 1945 gave the Chicagoans one last shot at a world's championship, but that, too, foundered on the shoals of Detroit's determined, seventh game victory in a match that some wag had proclaimed, before it began, that neither team could win. Well, Detroit did, and that put the Cubs' hopes for The Ultimate Prize to bed for the rest of the century. Their fans, faithful as ever, are *still* waiting.

A Final Jotting from the 1938 Notebook

>> On September 22 "Big Bill" Lee posted his fourth consecutive shutout, beating the Phillies, 4 to 0. His 22 and 9 record led the Cubs in 1938.

>> Carl Hubbell, plagued by arm troubles, finished his season with a 13 and 10 mark. A loose piece of bone floating around in his elbow, the result of many, many "left-handed fadeaways," popularly known as a screwball. An operation was ordered in August, and though Hubbell came back for another five seasons, the old snap was gone. "The Meal Ticket" still had enough left to lead the league in Strikeouts/game, Ratio, and Opponents' On-Base %.

>> The Cubs won 21 of their last 24 games to wrap up the pennant.

>> The Phillies entertained the Cubs for their last game at Baker Bowl on June 30, after which they moved to Shibe Park, where both the Athletics (before moving to Kansas City in 1955) and Phils played their home games until 1971. The Cubs were poor guests, walloping the Philles 14 to 1.

>> Mel Ott's 36 home runs led the N.L. for the third consecutive season, his fifth league-leading total. He led the league once more, in 1942, his first year as the Giants' manager.

>> Chicago's pitching staff led the league in ERA (3.37) and strikeouts (583), and shared the league lead with the Giants in saves (18).

The 1938 Cubs, last of a long line of National League champions during the 1870-1940 era of prominence. Standing: Andy Lotshaw (trainer), Ken O'Dea, Jerome "Dizzy" Dean, Vance Page, Manager Leon "Gabby" Hartnett, Mr. Bob Lewis, Clay Bryant, Tony Lazzeri, Billy Jurges, Jack Russell, Roy "Hardrock" Johnson. Kneeling: Joe Marty, Carl Reynolds, Tex Carleton, Phil Cavaretta, Bob "Mike" Garbark, Charley Root, Frank Demaree, Stan Hack, Newell Kimball. Seated: Al Epperly, Billy Herman, Steve Mesner, Bill Lee, Jim Collins, Veto Laporte and Vince Garrity (bat boys), Larry French, John Corriden. Missing when the picture was taken: Jim Asbell, Kirby Higbe and Bob Logan. (George Brace photograph)

The 1938 Season Series

May 8	NY	4	Chi	2	Hubbell, WP	French, LP
May 10	NY	5	Chi	1	Gumbert, WP	Lee, LP
May 17	NY	6	Chi	5	Coffman, WP	Bryant, LP
May 18	Chi	4	NY	2	Root, WP	Hubbell, LP
May 19	Chi	1	NY	0	Lee, WP	Gumbert, LP
June 7	Chi	4	NY	2	Lee, WP	Melton, LP
June 8	NY	4	Chi	2	Gumbert, WP	French, LP
June 8	NY	4	Chi	1	Hubbell, WP	Bryant, LP
June 9	NY	8	Chi	5	W. Brown, WP	Carleton, LP
June 24	NY	5	Chi	3	Coffman, WP	Carleton, LP
June 25	Chi	5	NY	0	Bryant, WP	Gumbert, LP
June 26	NY	5	Chi	1	Hubbell, WP	French, LP
July 23	Chi	7	NY	4	Lee, WP	Gumbert, LP

July 23	Chi	3	NY	1	Dean, WP	Schumacher, LP
July 24	Chi	5	NY	4	Lee, WP	Hubbell, LP
August 2	Chi	7	NY	0	Bryant, WP	Hubbell, LP
August 3	NY	8	Chi	3	Gumbert, WP	Lee, LP
August 4	Chi	6	NY	0	French, WP	Lohrman, LP
August 23	NY	6	Chi	2	Gumbert, WP	French, LP
August 24	Chi	6	NY	1	Page, WP	Lohrman, LP
September 17	Chi	4	NY	0	Lee, WP	Wittig, LP
September 17	Chi	4	NY	2	Bryant, WP	Lohrman, LP

Fini

On July 7, 1870, the Chicago White Stockings played the New York Mutuals at Brooklyn's Union Grounds. That day the Mutuals emerged victorious 13 to 4 in the first game between the two cities staged by professional baseball players. From that time forward, through the second game of a September 17, 1938, doubleheader which was won by the Cubs, 4 to 2, the teams met each other 1,176 times, the Cubs victorious in 573 (.487%) of the games played, and the Giants, winners 603 times (.513%). The tally, which hovers so close to the .500 mark, takes us to the close of the New York-Chicago era of National League domination forged by the two venerable franchises. Remarkably, during that time they won a total of 29 pennants, 15 for New York and 14 for Chicago.

After the 1938 season each team garnered pennants, Chicago in 1945, and New York in 1951 and 1954, before the Giants heeded Horace Greeley's advice, given long before during the days of baseball's infancy, and moved west for their first San Francisco season in 1958. That brought an end to the Cubs and Giants rivalry with a stunning finality. No longer would there be that extra excitement in going to the Polo Grounds, especially when the Cubs were in town. It would prove to be something the older generations never quite got over.

In 1939 and '40 both the Giants and Cubs slipped into also-ran seasons as their teams began to show the signs of age. They had reached the end of the line, and with it the heated, oft-times bitterly contested competition that had marked their rivalry for the better part of fourscore seasons.

Most endings have a touch of poignancy and sadness, and for many so does this one. But the old box scores, pictures, and above all, the many, many memories conjured by the stories of yesterday's heroes, champions, goats, ne'er-do-wells, the dugout jockeys, the sluggers, the fireballing hurlers, the boys who kept the watering holes open way past the team's curfew, the winners, and the loveable losers—all these stand guard over "those good old days" when the Cubs were *really* Cubs and the Giants were *really* Giants.

APPENDIX A:
THE TWENTY BEST SEASONS,
1870 TO 1940

This listing of the 20 best seasons recorded by Giants and Cubs players between 1870 and 1940 is ranked sabermetrically,[25] featuring TPR ratings for Position Players and TPI ratings for Pitchers. Ties are arranged chronologically.

Position Players

Legend:
OB%   On Base Percentage
EXBH   Extra Base Hits
BR   Batting Runs (Runs contributed beyond league-average player)
FR   Fielding Runs (Runs saved beyond league-ave. pl.)
TPR   Total Player Rating (Sum of the player's offensive and defensive sabermetric measurements.)

Rank	Player/Tm/Yr	BA	OB%	R	RBI	EXBH	SB	BR	FA	FR	TPR
1)	R. Hornsby/Chi/1929	.380	.459	156	149	94	22	74	.973	1	7.2
2)	R. Hornsby/NY/1927	.361	.448	133	125	67	9	63	.972	3	6.9
3)	A. Devlin/NY/1906	.299	.396	76	65	33	54	27	.944	28	6.5
4)	G. Davis/NY/1899	.337	.393	68	57	27	34	16	.945	46	6.2
5t)	F. Pfeffer/Chi/1884	.289	.325	105	101	45	-	22	.903	46	6.1
5t)	R. Bartell/NY/1937	.306	.367	91	62	54	5	17	.958	38	6.1
5t)	M. Ott/NY/1938	.311	.442	116	116	68	2	61	.957	1	6.1
8)	D. Bancroft/NY[26]/1920	.299	.346	102	36	45	8	7	.955	38	5.7
9)	R. Bartell/NY/1936	.298	.355	71	42	42	6	6	.956	45	5.7
10t)	R. Dahlen/Chi/1896	.352	.438	137	74	58	51	37	.915	25	5.4
10t)	F. Frisch/NY/1924	.328	.387	121	69	55	22	27	.972	25	5.4
10t)	T. Jackson/NY/1927	.318	.363	67	98	57	8	16	.952	28	5.4

Rank	Player/Tm/Yr	BA	OB%	R	RBI	EXBH	SB	BR	FA	FR	TPR
10t)	W. Herman/Chi/1935	.341	.383	113	83	70	6	26	.964	19	5.4
14)	M. Ott/NY/1932	.318	.424	119	123	76	6	63	.984	2	5.3
15t)	M. Ott/NY/1929	.328	.449	138	151	81	6	59	.973	9	5.2
15t)	W. Herman/Chi/1937	.335	.396	106	65	54	2	25	.954	19	5.2
17)	H. Zimmerman/Chi/1912	.372	.418	95	99	69	23	50	.916	2	5.1
18t)	W. Terry/NY/1930	.401	.452	139	129	78	8	61	.990	13	5.0
18t)	W. Herman/Chi/1936	.334	.392	101	93	69	5	25	.975	15	5.0
20t)	J. Glasscock/NY/1890	.336	.395	91	66	42	54	27	.910	22	4.9
20t)	G. Davis/NY/1901	.301	.356	69	65	40	27	19	.939	23	4.9
20t)	W. Terry/NY/1932	.350	.382	124	117	81	4	49	.991	14	4.9
20t)	M. Ott/NY/1935	.322	.407	113	114	70	7	50	.990	6	4.9

Pitchers

Legend: RA   Ratio: Hits plus walks per nine innings pitched.

PH   Pitcher as Batter rating, expressed in Pitcher's Batting Runs.

PR   Pitching Runs: A measure of runs saved beyond what a league-average pitcher might save his team.

DF   Pitcher's Defensive rating, expressed in Fielding Runs for pitchers.

TPI   Total Pitcher Index, a rating on an equal numerical plane with TPR. The sum of Pitcher's Fielding, Batting and Pitching Runs.

Rank	Player/Team/Yr	W-L	Pct.	ERA	IP	CG	SH	K	RA	PH	PR	DF	TPI
1)	A. Rusie/NY/1894	36–13	.735	2.78	444.0	45	3	195	12.8	3	126	8	11.0
2)	C. Mathewson/NY/1905	31–9	.775	1.28	338.2	32	8	206	8.4	10	65	6	9.7
3)	J. Clarkson/Chi/1885	53–16	.768	1.85	623.0	68	10	308	8.6	2	67	8	8.7
4)	J. Clarkson/Chi/1887	38–21	.644	3.08	523.0	56	2	237	10.5	2	58	9	8.3
5)	C. Hubbell/NY/1933	23–12	.657	1.66	308.2	22	10	156	8.9	1	58	7	7.5
6)	C. Mathewson/NY/1908	37–11	.771	1.43	390.2	34	11	259	7.6	1	41	10	7.3
7)	A. Rusie/NY/1893	33–21	.611	3.23	482.0	50	4	208	12.8	3	77	3	7.2
8)	G. Alexander/Chi/1920	27–14	.659	1.91	363.1	33	7	173	10.0	4	50	2	7.1
9)	C. Mathewson/NY/1909	25–6	.806	1.14	275.1	26	8	149	7.5	7	44	6	7.0
10)	A. Rusie/NY/1890	29–34	.460	2.56	548.2	56	4	341	12.3	10	62	6	6.9
11)	M. Brown/Chi/1906	26–6	.813	1.04	277.1	27	9	144	8.5	1	49	2	6.8
12)	C. Mathewson/NY/1911	26–13	.667	1.99	307.0	29	5	141	10.0	0	48	7	6.7
13)	J. Clarkson/Chi/1886	36–17	.679	2.41	466.2	50	3	313	9.7	1	47	4	6.4
14)	J. Taylor/Chi/1902	23–11	.676	1.33	324.2	33	7	83	9.0	3	52	4	6.3
15)	L. Warneke/Chi/1933	18–13	.581	2.00	287.1	26	4	133	10.6	10	43	3	6.2
16)	A. Rusie/NY/1897	28–10	.737	2.54	322.1	35	2	135	11.5	3	64	2	6.1
17)	W. Hutchison/Chi/1890	42–25	.627	2.70	603.0	65	5	289	10.7	-4	58	5	5.9
18)	C. Griffith/Chi/1898	24–10	.706	1.88	325.2	36	4	97	10.8	-2	63	1	5.8
19)	J. McGinnity/NY/1904	35–8	.814	1.61	408.0	38	9	144	9.0	-1	51	3	5.6
20)	J. Meekin/NY/1894	33–9	.786	3.70	409.0	40	1	123	12.9	7	74	-3	5.5

APPENDIX B:
THEY WORE BOTH UNIFORMS

This roster of the better known players who wore both New York and Chicago uniforms includes nine Hall of Famers, indicated by an asterisk, and six other luminaries (~), each of whom made substantial contributions to both clubs during the 1871–1940 span of New York/Chicago transcendency.

Player	New York Years	Chicago Years
*Dick Bartell, SS	1935–38; 1941–43; 1946	1939
Al Bridwell, SS	1908–11	1913
Virgil Cheeves, RHP	1927	1920–23
*Bill Dahlen, SS	1904–07	1891–98
Frank Demaree, OF	1939–41	1932–38
~Larry Doyle, 2B	1907–16; 1918–20	1916–17
[27]Frankie Frisch, 2B/MGR	1919–26	1949–51
Miguel "Mike" Gonzalez, C	1919–21	1925–29
~George Gore, OF	1887–89; 1891–92	1879–86
*Burleigh Grimes, RHP	1927	1932–33
*Leon "Gabby" Hartnett, C	1941	1922–40
~Charles "Buck" Herzog, INF	1908–09; 1911–13; 1916–17	1919–20
*Rogers Hornsby, 2B	1927	1929–32
Billy Jurges	1939–45	1931–38; 1946–47
*George Kelly, UT	1915–17; 1919–26	1930
Hank Leiber, OF	1933–38	1939–41
*Fred Lindstrom, 3B–OF	1924–32	1935
Gus Mancuso, C	1933–38; 1942–44	1939
~Artie Nehf, LHP	1919–26	1927–29
Bob O'Farrell, C	1928–32	1915–25; 1934
Lee Parmelee, RHP	1937	1929–35
Joe Start, 1B	1871–76	1878
~Rip Van Haltren, LHP–OF	1894–1903	1887–89
Walt Wilmot, OF	1897–98	1890–95
*Hack Wilson, OF	1923–25	1926–31
~Heinie Zimmerman, INF	1916–17	1907–1916

APPENDIX C:
THE BEST BY DECADE

Each of the seven decades reviewed in this book is represented by a listing of the best New York and Chicago players starting with the 1870s. The players have been chosen on the basis of their Total Baseball Ranking.[28] With one exception—Ross Barnes, whose totals and average are based on three seasons of play—statistics for the five best players are figured on at least *four* seasons during the decade (for example: 1870 to 1879). Because of frequently changing franchises and player signings, the 1870s are represented by only four players. The other decades are represented by the top five players along with selected statistics from the best of their seasons during the decade they qualified.

The Legend:	TBR/Ave	Four season Total Baseball Ranking Sum with four season average.
	BR/A	Batting Runs/Adjusted: the number of runs contributed beyond what a league-average hitter contributed.
	PR/A	Pitching Runs/Adjusted: Runs saved beyond number saved by a league-average pitcher.

1870 to 1879

1) Adrian Anson, Chi, 3b, 1b
4.8/1.20 TBR/AV; 66GP; .356 BA; 59 RBI; 63 R; 2 HR; .450 SA; 16 BR/A (1876)

2) Ross Barnes, 1876 Chi, 2b
3.5/1.17 TBR/AV; 66 GP; .429 BA; 59 RBI; 126 R; 1 HR; .590 SA; 39 BR/A (1876)

3) Paul Hines, 1875 Chi, OF
2.3/0.58 TBR/AV; 69 GP; .328 BA; 36 RBI; 45 R; 0 HR; .399 SA; -4 BR/A (1875)

4) Joe Start, 1874 NY, 1b
1.7/0.43 TBR/AV; 63 GP; .314 BA; 46 RBI; 67 R; 2 HR; .395 SA; 7 BR/A (1874)

1880 to 1889

1) John Clarkson,
   Chi, RHP

   25.2/6.30 TBR/AV; W 53, L 16;
   .768 W%; 623 IP; 10 SH; 308 K;
   .239 Opp. BA; 80 PR/A; 1.85 ERA 1885)

2) Tim Keefe,
   NY, RHP

   16.4/4.10 TBR/AV; W 32, L 13;
   .711 W%; 400 IP; 7 SH; 227 K;
   .203 Opp. BA; 49 PR/A; 1.58 ERA (1885)

3) Fred Pfeffer,
   Chi, 2b

   14.2/3.55 TBR/AV; 112 GP; .289 BA; 101 RBI
   105 R; 25 HR; .514 SA; 22 BR/A (1884)

4) Larry Corcoran,
   Chi, RHP

   14.1/3.53 TBR/AV; W 35, L 23;
   .603 W%; 516.2 IP; 7 SH; 272 K;
   .229 Opp. BA; 42 PR/A; 2.40 ERA (1884)

5) Mickey Welch,
   NY, RHP

   14.0/3.50 TBR/AV; W 44, L 11;
   .800 W%; 492 IP; 7 SH; 258 K;
   .203 Opp. BA; 55 PR/A; !.86 ERA (1885)

1890 to 1899

1) Amos Rusie,
   NY, RHP

   31.2/7.80 TBR/AV; W 36, L 13;
   .735 W%; 444 IP; 3 SH; 195 K;
   .250 Opp. BA; 122 PR/A; 2.78 ERA (1894)

2) Bill Dahlen,
   Chi, ss

   19.4/4.85 TBR/AV; 121 GP; .357 BA;
   107 RBI; 15 HR; .586 SA; 28 BR/A (1894)

3) George Davis,
   NY, ss

   18.8/4.70 TBR/AV; 108 GP; .337 BA;
   57 RBI; 1 HR; .418 SA; 16 BR/A (1899)

4) Clark Griffith,
   Chi, RHP

   18.1/4.53 TBR/AV; W 24, L 10;
   .706 W%; 325.2 IP; 4 SH; 97 K;
   .246 Opp. BA; 62 PR/A; 1.88 ERA (1898)

5) Bill Hutchison,
   Chi, RHP

   13.6/3.40 TBR/AV; W 42, L 25;
   .627 W%; 603 IP; 5 SH; 289 K;
   .220 Opp. BA; 64 PR/A; 2.70 ERA (1890)

1900 to 1909

1) Christy Mathewson,
   NY, RHP

   30.0/7.50 TBR/AV; W 31, L 9;
   .775 W%; 338.2 IP; 8 SH; 206 K;
   .205 Opp. BA; 62 PR/A; 1.28 ERA (1905)

2) Mordecai C. Brown,
   Chi, RHP

   20.3/5.08 TBR/AV; W 20, L 6;
   .813 W%; .277.1 IP; 9 SH; 144 K;
   .202 Opp. BA; 49 PR/A; 1.04 ERA (1906)

3) Artie Devlin,
   NY, 3b

   15.5/3.88 TBR/AV; 148 GP; .299 BA
   61 RBI; 2 HR; .390 SA; 27 BR/A (1906)

4) Jack Taylor,
   Chi, RHP

   14.5/3.63 TBR/AV; W 23, L 11;
   .676 W%; .324.2 IP; 7 SH; 83 K;
   .227 Opp. BA; 49 PR/A; 1.33 ERA (1902)

5) Frank Chance,
   Chi, 1b

   13.2/3.30 TBR/AV; 124 GP; .310 BA
   49 RBI; 6 HR; .430 SA; 27 BR/A (1904)

1910 to 1919

1) Christy Mathewson,   25.5/5.63 TBR/AV; W 27, L 9;
   NY, RHP   .750 W%; 318.1 IP; 2 SH; 184 K;
                            .248 Opp. BA; 38 PR/A; 1.89 ERA (1910)

2) Jim Vaughn,   15.4/3.85 TBR/AV; W 22, L 10;
   Chi, LHP   .668 W%; 290.1 IP; 8 SH; 148 K;
                            .208 Opp. BA; 34 PR/A; 1.74 ERA (1918)

3) Art Fletcher,   14.6/3.65 TBR/AV; 133 GP; .286 BA
   NY, ss   66 RBI; 3 HR; .382 SA; 11 BR/A (1916)

4) George Burns,   12.1/3.03 TBR/AV; 154 GP; .303 BA
   NY, OF   60 RBI; 3 HR; .417 SA; 38 BR/A (1914)

5) Heinie Zimmerman,   11.5/2.88 TBR/AV; 145 GP; .372 BA
   Chi, 3b   99 RBI; 14 HR; .571 SA; 50 BR/A (1912)

1920 to 1929

1) Dave Bancroft,   17.1/4.43 TBR/AV; 153 GP; .318 BA
   NY, ss   67 RBI; 6 HR; .441 SA; 18 BR/A (1921)

2) Travis Jackson,   16.4/4.1 TBR/AV; 127 GP; .318 BA
   NY, ss, 3b   98 RBI; 14 HR; .486 SA; 16 BR/A (1927)

3) Frank Frisch,   14.8/3.70 TBR/AV; 145 GP; .328 BA
   NY, 2b, ss   69 RBI; 7 HR; .468 SA; 27 BR/A (1924)

4) Pete Alexander,   14.4/3.60 TBR/AV; W 27, L 14;
   Chi, RHP   .659 W%; 363.1 IP; 7 SH; 173 K;
                            .248 Opp. BA; 52 PR/A; 1.91 ERA (1920)

5) Gabby Hartnett,   11.3/2.83 TBR/AV; 120 GP; .302 BA
   Chi, C   65 RBI; 14 HR; .523 SA; 25 BR/A (1928)

1930 to 1939

1) Carl Hubbell,   22.1/5.53 TBR/AV; W 23, L 12;
   NY, LHP   .657 W%; 308.2 IP; 10 SH; 156 K;
                            .227 Opp. BA; 53 PR/A; 1.66 ERA (1933)

2) Mel Ott,   21.5/5.38 TBR/AV; 150 GP; .311 BA
   NY, 3b, OF   116 RBI; 36 HR; .583 SA; 61 BR/A (1938)

3) Billy Herman,   19.1/4.78 TBR/AV; 154 GP; .341 BA
   Chi, 2b   83 RBI; 5 HR; .476 SA; 26 BR/A (1935)

4) Dick Bartell,   16.2/4.05 TBR/AV; 145 GP; .298 BA
   NY, ss   42 RBI; 8 HR; .418 SA; 6 BR/A (1936)

NOTES

1. Throughout the book the standings for each season are presented. New York and Chicago are represented in each three-some of teams. In a season in which either New York or Chicago finished first or second, or first *and* second, a third team's record appears. When neither Chicago nor New York finished in first place, the third team appears as the pennant winner.

During the seasons of 1872 and 1873, Chicago did not play, and between 1877 and 1882 New York was not a member of the National League. During those seasons the record of *two* other teams in the league is presented.

2. Anson declared out for batting out of order. No PO charged to an individual Mets player.

3. Game called after seven innings because of darkness.

4. Jocko Flynn came out of nowhere to become a 20-game winner in his freshman season, one of the greatest rookie seasons in the game's history. He faded and disappeared after one major league season, never to be heard from again.

5. From "The Baseball Archive," *Letters in the Dirt*, No. 87, March 11, 2000, by Tim Wiles.

6. Op. cit.

7. Hopper, DeWolf, *Once a Clown Always a Clown*, Boston: Little, Brown and Co., 1927.

8. So pervasive was Cap Anson's effect on the Chicago franchise, that after he left, the original White Stockings team name, already metamorphosed to the Colts, changed to Orphans (for obvious reasons), then to Spuds, and still others, until finally, in 1907, Cubs was officially adopted as Chicago's team name.

9. Countless reviews of John McGraw's 1899 to 1902 negotiations with several teams and the league offices, as well, may be consulted to flesh out his remarkable story. Among the more concise are Leonard Koppett's history of *Major League Baseball* (Temple Univ. Press, Phila., 1998), *The Ball Clubs*, by Dewey and Acocella, Harper Perennial, NY, 1996, and *The New York Giants Baseball Club: 1870 to 1900*, McFarland, Jefferson, NC, 1996, by Marshall Wright.

10. Game called on account of darkness.

11. New York protested the May 7 and 8 games, the protest was upheld, and the games disallowed.

12. *Total Baseball*, John Thorn, Pete Palmer, Michael Gershman and David Pietrusza, eds., Total Sports, NY, 1999, sixth edition. p. 2018.

13. Taken from Nemec, David, *Baseball Chronology*, Publications International, Lincolnwood, IL, 2000. p. 33.

14. Bill Deane's complete listing of Cy Young and Rookie of the Year award winners that fills in the gap between 1900 and the initiation of both awards (Cy Young, 1956, and Rookie of the Year, 1947), may be found in *Total Baseball*, 1999 edition, pp. 262–63.

15. See Dewey and Acocella, *Biographical History of Baseball*, Carroll and Graf, NY, 1995, and *Ball Clubs*, by the same authors, published by Harpers, NY, 1993.

16. An interesting summary, as well as Vaughn's reaction to this game, may be found in Peter Golenbock's *Wrigleyville*, St. Martin's Pub., NY, 1999 ed., pp. 168–70.

17. Op. cit., p. 91.

18. Curran's *Big Sticks* (Harper Perennial, NY, 1991, pp. 135–36.) pointed out that McGraw filled in the spots he felt needed strengthening with a series of mid-season trades between 1919 and 1921, bringing Irish Meusel, Casey Stengel, and Johnny Rawlings to New York in exchange for cash and lesser rank ball players that make one wonder to this very day what was going on in the minds of his principal "patsies" in Philadelphia and Boston. Other trades in the '20s brought Hornsby, Grimes and Groh to the Polo Grounds, though each of the latter cost him bundles of cash and, in the most sensational deal of all, Frank Frisch.

19. There was a great deal of conjecture on just how much better Alexander might have been had he not been an alcoholic. Joe McCarthy, Alexander's last Chicago manager, had an answer for that. "Who knows? Maybe he might not have been so good. Maybe that was one of the things that helped make him as good as he is. In the final analysis, how much better *could* he have been?" (*Wrigleyville*, by Peter Golenbock, St. Martin's Press, NY, 1999 ed., p. 190.)

20. Honig, Donald, *Baseball America*, Galahad Books, NY, 1985, p. 147.

21. Koppett, Leonard, *Concise History of Major League Baseball*, Temple University Press, Philadelphia, 1998, p. 168.

22. Fielding Runs (FR), a linear measure used by sabermetricians, calculates the number of runs a players saves his team beyond that of a league-average player as a result of his defensive statistics in a given season. The all time, single season record for second basemen was set by Glenn Hubbard of Atlanta in 1985, with 62 FR. He is followed by Danny Richardson (1892, 58), Bill Mazeroski (1963, 57), Walter "Rabbit" Maranville (1914, 52, and then, in fifth place, Freddie Maguire (1928, 51).

23. Golenbock, Peter, *Wrigleyville*, St. Martin's, NY. 1999 ed., p. 224.

24. Curran, William, *Big Sticks*, Harper Perennial, NY. 1991, p. 261.

25. Sabermetric statistics and ratings are taken from the 1999 edition of *Total Baseball*. An explanation of the various linear measurements for Position Players and Pitchers may be found in the encyclopedia's glossary, beginning on page 2528.

26. In 1920 Bancroft played 42 games with Philadelphia before being traded to New York, where he played 108 games. TPR, Phl: 0.9; TPR, NY: 4.8. Season total: 5.7.

27. Frankie Frisch was manager of the Chicago Cubs, 1949–51. He was involved in one of the all time great blockbuster trades when the Giants and St. Louis Cardinals swapped Frisch and Rogers Hornsby.

28. The Total Baseball Ranking is a sabermetric measurement which ranks pitchers and position players by their total wins, contributed in all phases of play, presenting the sum of their Total Batter Rating and Total Pitcher Index. For a more detailed explanation see *The Official Encyclopedia of Major League Baseball: Total Baseball*, edited by John Thorn, Pete Palmer, Michael Gershman and David Pietrusza with Matthew Silverman and Sean Lahman. The sixth edition was published by Total Sports, Inc., NY, 1999.

SELECTED BIBLIOGRAPHY

Acocella, Nick, and Donald Dewey. *The Ball Clubs*. New York: Harper Collins, 1996.
____. *The Biographical History of Baseball*. New York: Carroll and Graf Publishers, 1995.
Admites, Paul, and Saul Wisnia. *The Best of Baseball*. Lincolnwood, IL: Publications International, 1997.
Alexander, Charles. *Our Game*. New York: Henry Holt and Company, 1991.
____. *John McGraw*. New York: Viking, 1988.
Allen, Lee. *The National League*. New York: Hill and Wang, 1961.
Anderson, David. *More Than Merkle*. Lincoln, NE: University of Nebraska Press, 2000.
Anson, Adrian Constantine. *A Ball Player's Career*. Chicago: Era Publishing Company, 1900.
Aylesworth, Thomas. *Baseball's Great Dynasties: The Chicago Cubs*. New York: Gallery Books, 1990.
____, with Benton Minks, John Bowman, ed. *The Encyclopedia of Baseball Managers: 1901 to the Present Day*. New York: Brompton Books Corporation, 1990.
Bartlett, Arthur. *Baseball and Mr. Spalding: The History and Romance of Baseball*. New York: Farrar, Straus and Young, 1951.
Blake, Mike. *Baseball Chronicles*. Cincinnati: Betterway Books, 1994.
Brown, Warren. *The Chicago Cubs*. New York: Putnam's Sons, 1946.
Carmichael, John P., et al. *My Greatest Day in Baseball*. New York: Grosset and Dunlap, 1945.
Chadwick, Bruce. *The Chicago Cubs*. New York: Abbeville Press, 1994.
Charlton, James, ed. *The Baseball Chronology*. New York: Macmillan, 1991.
Curran, William. *Big Sticks*. New York: Harper-Collins, 1990.
Danzig, Allison, and Joe Reichler. *The History of Baseball: Its Greatest Players, Teams and Managers*. Englewood Cliffs, NJ: Prentice-Hall, 1959.
Durso, Joseph. *Baseball and the American Dream*. St. Louis: The Sporting News, 1986.
Frommer, Harvey. *Primitive Baseball: The First Quarter Century of the National Pastime*. New York: Atheneum Press, 1988.

_____. *Shoeless Joe and Ragtime Baseball*. Dallas, TX: Taylor Publishing Company, 1992.

Goldstein, Warren. *Playing for Keeps: A History of Early Baseball*. Ithaca, NY: Cornell University Press, 1989.

Golenbock, Peter. *Wrigleyville*. New York: St. Martin's, 1999.

Graham, Frank. *The New York Giants*. New York: Putnam's Sons, 1952.

Guschov, Stephen. *The Red Stockings of Cincinnati*. Jefferson, NC: McFarland, 1998.

Hardy, James D. *The New York Giants Baseball Club: 1870 to 1900*. Jefferson, NC: McFarland, 1996.

Honig, Donald. *The Man in the Dugout*. Lincoln, NE: University of Nebraska Press, 1977.

_____. *A Donald Honig Reader*. New York: Simon and Schuster, 1988.

_____. *Baseball America*. New York: Galahad Books, 1985.

Hopper, De Wolff. *Once a Clown Always a Clown*. Boston: Little, Brown and Co., 1927.

Hynd, Noel. *The Giants of the Polo Grounds*. New York: Doubleday, 1988.

Kennedy, MacLean. *The Great Teams of Baseball*. St. Louis: The Sporting News, 1988 reprint by Horton Publishing Company.

Koppett, Leonard. *The Concise History of Major League Baseball*. Philadelphia: Temple University Press, 1998.

Lanigan, Ernest J. *The Baseball Cyclopedia*. New York: The Baseball Magazine Co., 1922.

Levine, Peter. A. G. *Spalding and the Rise of Baseball*. New York: Oxford University Press, 1985.

Lieb, Frederick G. *Baseball as I Have Known It*. New York: Tempo Publishing Co., 1977.

Mead, William B., and Paul Dickson. *Baseball: The President's Game*. Washington D.C.: Farragut, 1993.

McCullough, Ron. *Baseball Roots*. Toronto: Warwick, 2000.

Names, Larry D. *Bury My Heart at Wrigley Field: The History of the Cubs*. Neshkoro, WI: Sportsbooks Publishing Co., 1989.

Neft, David S., Richard Cohen and Michael L. Neft. *The Sports Encyclopedia: Baseball*. New York: St. Martin's Griffin, 1999 (19th edition).

Nemec, David. *The Great Encyclopedia of 19th Century Major League Baseball*. New York: Donald Fine Books, 1997.

Neyer, Rob, and Eddie Epstein. *Baseball Dynasties*. New York: W. W. Norton and Company, 2000.

Obojski, Robert. *All Star Baseball*. New York: Stein and Day Publishers, 1980.

Okrent, Daniel, and Harris Lewine. *The Ultimate Baseball Book*. Boston: Houghton Mifflin Company, 2000 edition.

Pfeffer, Fred. *Scientific Ball*. Chicago: N. Fred Pfeffer Publishers, 1889.

Rankin, June. *The New York and Brooklyn Baseball Clubs*. New York: Richard Fox Printer, 1888.

Reidenbaugh, Lowell. *Baseball's 25 Greatest Teams*. St. Louis: The Sporting News, 1988.

Rice, Grantland. *The Tumult and the Shouting.* New York: A. S. Barnes Pub., 1954.

Richter, Francis C. *Francis Richter's History and Records of Baseball.* Philadelphia: self-published, 1914.

Ritter, Lawrence. *The Glory of Their Times.* New York: Vintage Books, 1966.

Ryczek, William J. *Blackguards and Red Stockings.* Jefferson, NC: McFarland, 1992.

Segar, Charles, Ed. *The Official National League 75th Anniversary History.* New York, Jay Publishing Company, Inc., 1951.

Seymour, Harold. *Baseball: The Early Years.* New York: Oxford University Press, 1960.

Spalding, Albert Goodwill. *America's National Game.* New York, American Sports, 1911.

Sullivan, Dean A., editor. *Early Innings: A Documentary History of Baseball.* Lincoln, NE: University of Nebraska Press, 1995.

Thorn, John, Pete Palmer, Michael Gershman and Divid Pietrusza, editors. *The Official Encyclopedia of Major League Baseball: Total Baseball.* New York: Total Sports, 1999, sixth edition.

Voigt, David Q. *American Baseball, Volume I.* University Park, PA: The Pennsylvania University Press, 1983.

Wilbert, Warren N., and William Hageman. *Chicago Cubs: Seasons at the Summit.* Champaign, IL: Sagamore Publishing, 1997.

Wiles, Tim. "The Baseball Archive," *Letters in the Dirt.* March 11, 2000.

Williams, Peter. *When the Giants Were Giants.* Chapel Hill, NC: Algonquin Books of Chapel Hill, 1994.

Wright, Marshall D. *Nineteenth Century Baseball.* Jefferson, NC: McFarland, 1996.

_____. *The National Association of Professional Baseball Players: 1857–1870.* Jefferson, NC: McFarland, 2000.

Files Consulted

The Sporting News
Sporting Life
New York Sun
Chicago Tribune
St. Louis Democrat
New York Times
Chicago Post
New York World
USA Today Baseball Weekly

Journals, Guides, Magazines Consulted

Baseball Magazine
Baseball Digest

The Spalding Guide
The Reach Guide
SABR: Nineteenth Century Stars
SABR: Baseball's First Stars
SABR: Baseball Research Journal
SABR: The National Pastime
Beadles Dime Baseball
National Hall of Fame and Museum Yearbooks

INDEX